JUDAISM AND WORLD RELIGION

Judaism and World Religion

NORMAN SOLOMON

*Director of the Centre for the Study of Judaism and
Jewish–Christian Relations, Selly Oak Colleges, Birmingham*

St. Martin's Press   New York

First published in the United States of America in 1991

Printed in Great Britain

ISBN 0–312–06863–8

Library of Congress Cataloging-in-Publication Data
Solomon, Norman, 1933–
Judaism and world religion / Norman Solomon.
p. cm.
Includes index.
ISBN 0-312–06863–8
1. Judaism. I. Title.
BM561.S64 1991
296—dc20   91–23516
                                                         CIP

Contents

Chapter Contents

6 Messiah

8 Language and Dialogue

9 The Plurality of Faiths

1

What I Want to Prove

I was at first going to call this chapter 'Theses and Presuppositions of the Book'. Since the title was so pretentious that it inhibited me from writing, I decided that it might put you off too, gentle reader, which would be a pity, as there is plenty to come that you should enjoy (though some of it is undeniably tough). So I decided to be as straightforward as I possibly could, and to tell you just what I am setting out to do in the coming pages, sparing neither the revealed nor the hidden agendas.

The book ranges widely, I hope not too widely to retain focus, but I fear too widely for me to be confident that I have covered all the topics with equal competence. But I have to take the risk, for I must address, on the basis of traditional Jewish and other sources, several issues of concern in the contemporary world, ranging from conservation of the environment, through the ethical problems of economic life, to matters of state and religion. Besides social and political issues, there are philosophical ones: what is the ultimate hope for people ('Messiah'), how do we reconcile suffering and radical evil with traditional forms of belief in God, and why does God 'allow' such confusion and disagreement about fundamentals to prevail amongst religious believers?

At one level, the book may be regarded quite simply as a resource guide for the treatment of such topics within Judaism, though it does not claim to be comprehensive. Its deeper purpose – the 'hidden agenda' I want now to reveal – is to ask a question that *affects all religions equally*. It is this. The sources of our religions (Bible, Talmud, Church fathers, Quran, and the like) were all set down in writing in a world very different from ours. How can we extrapolate from them to our present circumstances? Even if we were people of perfect faith within our respective communities, ready and eager and obedient and wanting nothing better than to decide about conservation, or the welfare state, or the politics of the Near East, or the Third World debt problem, on the basis of our traditions, how is it possible to do so? To take some examples we shall meet in the coming pages, can we say (with 'liberation theologians') what is the Christan way to solve the problem of the poor in Brazil, the Islamic way to reform the world economy, or the Jewish way to ensure that biodiversity is maintained? (Of course, Jews, Christians and Muslims each have something to say on all these problems.) Obviously, some people think it is possible to formulate answers on the basis of their traditions. I shall aim to make explicit the processes of reasoning involved in this, and to show whether and how such extrapolation can be justified. Even in those instances where it is not logically justified, we shall have to ask whether there is some other justification for such a procedure: perhaps the fact that constant reference to a traditional source (for instance the Bible) and vocabulary (words of a creed, religious laws) helps social bonding within the faith community, gives a sense of continuity in an insecure world.

Around these two agendas, the hidden and the revealed, are a number of questions and assumptions which recur throughout the book, some explicitly, some without showing themselves openly. I shall list these as well as I can, saying a little about each, but in what order? Ah, I shall take a leaf from the Quran – actually, the Mishnah, order by order, does the same – and set the sections in order of length, longest first.

1.1   Ethics Stands Independent of Theology

Religious people often unthinkingly assume that ethics must be grounded in religious belief. Yet many who are not in any sense religious have strong ethical convictions which lead them to similar types of action to those which the religious ground in their theology; ethics can indeed be autonomous, and there is no philosophical justification for insisting that ethics should be grounded in anything outside themselves.

It was David Hume who first formulated the problem clearly:

In every system of morality which I have hitherto met with, I have always remarked, that the author proceeds for some time in the ordinary way of reasoning, and establishes the being of a God, or makes observations concerning human affairs; when of a sudden I am surprised to find, that instead of the usual copulations of propositions, *is*, and *is not*, I meet with no proposition that is not connected with an *ought*, or *ought not*. This

change is imperceptible; but is, however, of the last consequence. For as this *ought*, or *ought not*, expresses some new
relation or affirmation, it is necessary that it should be observed
and explained; and at the same time that a reason should be
given, for what seems altogether inconceivable, how this new
relation can be a deduction from others, which are entirely
different from it.[1]

Philosophers have tried numerous ways to 'reduce' ethics to something else, even to feelings and emotions; the one bridge it no
longer seems possible to cross is that between 'is' and 'ought',
which would actually *prove* ethics out of something or other. We
have tried heteronomous, autonomous and even theonomous
ethics, but the problem remains; even if God commanded something, does that *make* it intrinsically right, or is it right only contin-
gently, *because* God commanded it?

Kant, far from grounding ethics in theology, was frightened by
Hume into reversing the process; he grounded his belief in a deity
on his ethical certainty, leaving ethics as an autonomous realm.
Fortunately, we do not need to enter into the philosophical problems here, merely to be aware of them. The major consequence in
our context is that we shall have to notice the sly way in which
theologians try to make inferences from some premise or other to a
moral duty, forgetting Hume's stricture. We shall catch them, for
instance, arguing that, because God 'identifies with the poor', we
ought to adopt such and such a specific policy which is geared
towards welfare. The 'ought' does not follow, as one can soon see
if one tries to argue that because God punishes the wicked (for
example, he brought the flood, he destroyed Jerusalem) we ought
to punish the wicked; how does one know which aspects of God's
behaviour ought to be imitated? (There are of course other fallacies
involved in this type of argument.) In the end, one can only argue
on the basis of the general principle that one ought to help the
poor, that one ought to help in such and such an instance; one
does not 'prove' the duty out of God. And then the next set of
fallacies becomes evident, for it does not follow from the general
moral principle that one ought to help the poor, that one ought to
adopt such and such a welfare policy; perhaps another policy
would be more efficient, and that is something one can only work
out along economic and political lines.

Religions do, of course, call upon the faithful to perform good acts as commanded by God. This is acceptable, provided the acts really are good. It does not contradict the autonomy of ethics, though, as we learn from the fact that even in the Middle Ages there were discussions as to whether certain actions are good because God commanded them, or whether God commanded them because they are good.

1.2   Theology is Limited by the Special Disciplines

When I attend the Synagogue on Saturday afternoons in the summer and read the *Ethics of the Fathers* I am intrigued by the pairing of the names Ben Bag Bag and Ben He He, who were possibly disciples of Hillel early in the first century CE. They were thoughtful, pious men. Ben Bag Bag said,

> Turn it [the Torah] and turn it over again, for everything is in it, and contemplate it, and wax grey and old over it, and stir not from it, for thou canst have no better rule than this.[2]

But what exactly *is* contained in the Torah? The Torah as we know it consists of books – the Hebrew scriptures, the Talmud, and so on – and to that we may add the examples of the lives of pious people and the experience of the community of the faithful.

Martin Luther, in 1539, cited Joshua's stopping the sun rather than the earth as a decisive refutation of the 'error' of Copernicus in claiming that the sun was stationary and the earth moving.[3] Evidently, he thought that the Bible contained authoritative information on astronomy. Many Jewish writers have entertained even more embarrassing views on a variety of topics, but I prefer not to illustrate. Now, either they were wrong in their interpretation of scripture, or scripture was wrong. In Luther's case, the former might just be true, but very often there is no reasonable way to defend the scriptural or other source from a charge of simple error. Some people refuse to accept that scripture can be in error about anything, but my view (which I shall not argue here) is that scripture, and religious texts generally, are not reliable sources of scientific information.

But is 'scientific information' confined to astronomy, or physics, or even biology, including the theory of organic evolution? I think not. It includes also history, geography, economics, and in general all those subjects that are open to empirical confirmation or discon-firmation.

This is why, as I show in section 3.4, Adam Smith poses just as much of challenge to traditional religious thinking as did Coperni-cus – in a way even more, for, whereas it could be argued that the 'authentic' sources of religion were not in conflict with Copernicus, no such excuse is available in regard to the ethics of wealth creation. Likewise, the changing role of credit as societies have moved through feudalism to mercantilism has posed a challenge within the very heartland of religion to the traditional religious ban on usury, shared by Jews, Christians and Muslims; we devote section 4.4 to this topic.

The hard question we have to face again and again throughout the book is just where matters of legitimate theological concern end and where scientific or technical problems take over. It is certainly not possible to draw a sharp line between the two, and any line which is drawn will shift from time to time as new discoveries are made; but it is still clear that at any given time some matters are on one side of the fuzzy line and some on the other, and that along the fuzzy line itself one has to exercise special caution.

1.3 Theology Inputs Values

Though the connection between theology and ethics is not strictly logical, the faith communities all relate their ethics to the meta-physical assumptions of their faith – that is, to their concept of God and his revelation.

Sometimes this is enlightening. For instance, we shall note in 3.2.2 how Isadore Twersky shows that the halakhic rules of charity anchor a principle of faith into a detailed ethical code, combining 'the thesis of free, spontaneous giving with the antithesis of soul-less, obligatory contribution [to] produce a composite act which is subjective though quantified, inspired yet regular, intimate yet formal'.

Sometimes the potential input from theology is strange and disconcerting. In section 3.8, for instance, where I discuss econ-omic principles about the optimal allocation of resources, I note that those religious-minded people who think we would all be better off if we had fewer material goods rather than more differ from standard economists only in placing a higher premium on, for instance, facilities for meditation than on improved diet, housing, medical care, travel and entertainment. I have not actually read the work of any modern religious economist who integrates into the evaluation of goods the traditional concept that this world is but a preparation for the next; but, if an economist were consistently to work out the optimal allocation of resources bearing in mind the needs of the next world (according to his/her chosen metaphysics), that person would make some very startling recommendations indeed.

1.4 Christian, Jewish and Muslim Approaches

There is considerable danger in making broad comparisons between religions, in saying 'Christianity does this', 'Islam says that', and the like. First of all, the abstraction ('Christianity', 'Judaism') does nothing; actual Jews or actual Christian do things. Secondly, within each of the three faiths there has been, over the centuries, such a wide range of expression that not only is it impossible to define any one faith precisely, but there is considerable overlap between the faiths in most aspects.

Nevertheless, there is at least one significant and systematic difference of approach between Jews and Christians which is relevant to many of the topics discussed here. Modern Christianity tends to limit itself to broad ethical principles which it seeks to apply in the contemporary situation; this is in harmony with the Christian tradition, clearly expressed by Thomas Aquinas, within which 'natural law' is justified *in broad principle* by moral theology, but law is not derived directly from scripture. Within Judaism and Islam, however, with moral theology built on the foundation of specific laws (*halakhah, sharia*); therefore, the traditional Jewish approach to modern issues tends to emerge from consideration of specific laws, *through* the derived principles, thence to the matter in hand.

Christians often experience the difficulty of applying very broad principles to very specific issues; Jews are more often faced with having to extrapolate from a very specific instance, through a derived principle, to another specific instance, often radically different from that in mind when the law was formulated.

1.5 Our Heritage is Everything that has Come before Us

There are many theories about truth – correspondence, coherence, and so on – and I can live with most of them. But I refuse to live with a theory that the criterion of truth is whether the person who wrote or said it was Jewish (Christian, Muslim etc. – the disease afflicts all religions). Truth comes to us from many sources, and is to be warmly welcomed, not grudgingly recognised.

Indeed, we are a fortunate generation. We are not limited to a small number of classical sources of our own tradition, but have access to all that has been preserved from earlier generations, in whatever language (except for the few that remain undeciphered) as well as to the whole of modern learning. This deeply affects our identity. If I identify myself as a Jew this cannot mean that I relate to the sources of one tradition only. My total heritage is everything now available to me, and that does not exclude the other religious traditions. My special relationship with Judaism is to do with which set of people I feel I belong with in family and historical and religious perspectives, and to some extent to do with truth claims; it is not a delineation of the resources available to me for spiritual and intellectual – or for that matter social – growth.

If a Jew, or someone from some other tradition, isolates him- or herself today, this is voluntary act, a wilful rejection of all other sources of knowledge. It is, I believe, an evil and destructive act.

1.6   Attitude to Texts

Our attitude towards sacred texts, in particular the Bible and the Talmud, has changed under the impact of modern scholarship. We have learned to see them as the record of the Israelite and Jewish response to God over a period of some thousands of years, and in varying cultural environments. We therefore try to relate statements to their social–historical contexts, and we recognise the views which then emerge as attempts, not always perfectly executed and by no means always mutually consistent, to grapple with major issues. Bible and Talmud are not 'proof texts' but guides to life, aids to our rediscovery and reformulation of the teachings and insights they enshrine.

1.7   There is a Jewish Mission

One of the most widely peddled distortions of Judaism is that it is
some sort of 'ethnic' religion. As Jews themselves, sometimes even
the learned amongst them, are principally responsible for this
notion getting about, I cannot follow my gut reaction of blaming it
on antisemitism. But it about as wrong-headed as can be.

Judaism combines a world religion with a prototype people.

If, by the time he puts this book down, the reader has not
learned that Judaism is a missionary (though not necessarily proselytising) religion, with deep concern for the world and a profound contribution to make to resolving its present problems, I
shall have failed in my main task.

1.8   The Existence of God and the Authenticity of Revelation

It will be obvious that these are unproven assumptions throughout
this book. I might ask questions about them in another book, but,
so far as this one goes, (a) in chapter 8, in particular, I spell out
some of the difficulties of God-talk and revelation-talk, and (b) I do
not commit myself to particular views about God and revelation,
but only examine the consequences of some such views.

Part I
Society

2

Conservation[1]

2.1 Introduction

2.1.1 Aim of this chapter

The aim here is to provide a structured guide to the main traditional Jewish sources which relate to the great ecological problems of our time. Some of these sources, namely the books of the
Hebrew scriptures, are shared with Christians; but they are often
read quite differently. Most sources – the Talmud and other rabbinic writings – are peculiar to Judaism; they determine the traditional way of understanding scripture and in addition offer
insights of their own.[2]

It should go without saying that Judaism did not stop in the first
century; it is a living religion constantly developing in response to
changing social realities and intellectual perceptions. At the present time, it is passing through one of its most creative phases;
however, within the limited scope of this chapter only a few
references can be made to the contemporary literature.

Traditional Jewish thought is expressed in several complemen-
tary genres. The most distinctive is *halakhah*, or law, but history,
myth, poetry, philosophy and other forms of expression are also
significant. Our focus here is not on the contributions made by
individual Jews, for instance scientists and economists, to the
modern ecological movement – though this would make an
interesting study in itself – but on the religious sources, which
demonstrate the continuity between traditional Jewish thought
and a range of contemporary approaches.

2.1.2 Which problems are addressed?

There is a worry prevalent today that people are destroying the
environment on which living things depend for their existence.
Many species are endangered as a result of human activity, the

11

planetary climate may already have been destabilised, the protective ozone layer has been damaged, forests have been destroyed, species threatened or made extinct, and pollution in forms such as acid rain and other forms of water contamination is widespread.

Much of this destruction arises from the level of economic activity demanded by a rapidly increasing world population which is locally raising its living standards faster than ecologically sustainable levels of production.

In addition, there is a permanent worry that stockpiles of highly destructive weapons might actually be used, and that the use of even a small part of the available arsenal would cause irreversible damage to the planetary environment, perhaps rendering impossible the survival of *Homo sapiens* and many other species.

2.1.3   *How is religion relevant?*

It is not at first sight clear what these problems have to do with religious beliefs. After all, the only belief necessary to motivate a constructive response to them is a belief in the desirability of human survival, wedded to the perception that human survival depends on the whole interlinking system of nature. The belief is not peculiar to religions, but part of the innate self-preservation mechanism of humankind; the perception of the interdependence of natural things arises not from religion, but from careful scientific investigation.

Moreover, the discovery of which procedures would effectively solve the problems of conservation is a technical, not a religious one. If scientists are able to offer alternative procedures of the same or different efficiency the religious may feel that the ethical or spiritual values they espouse should determine the choice. But few choices depend on value judgements alone, and no judgement is helpful which is not based on the best available scientific information.

These considerations will be borne in mind as we examine the relevance of traditional Jewish sources to our theme.

2.2   Attitudes to Creation

2.2.1   *Goodness of the physical world*

'God saw that it was good'[3] is the refrain of the first creation story of Genesis (1:1–2:4), which includes the physical creation of humankind, male and female. The created world is thus testimony to God's goodness and greatness.[4]

The second 'creation' story (Genesis 2:5–3:24) accounts for the psychological make-up of humankind. There is no devil, only a 'wily serpent', and the excuse of being misled by the serpent does not exempt Adam and Eve from personal responsibility for what they have done. Bad gets into the world through the free exercise of choice by people, not in the process of creation, certainly not through fallen angels, devils, or any other external projection of human guilt; such creatures are notably absent from the catalogue of creation in Genesis 1.

Post-biblical Judaism did not adopt the concept of 'the devil'. In the Middle Ages, however, the dualism of body and spirit prevailed, and with it a tendency to denigrate 'this world' and 'material things'. The Palestinian kabbalist Isaac Luria (1534–72) taught that God initiated the process of creation by 'withdrawing' himself from the infinite space he occupied; this theory stresses the 'inferiority' and distance from God of material creation, but compensates by drawing attention to the divine element concealed in all things. The modern Jewish theologian who wishes to emphasise the inherent goodness of God's creation has not only the resources of the Hebrew scriptures on which to draw but also a continuous tradition based on them.

ANTHROPOCENTRISM

Certain theologians[5] are greatly exercised to replace traditional anthropocentric, fall–redemption, hence guilt-laden theologies with a 'creation spirituality' of 'original blessing'. They invoke spirits, demons and earth goddesses, and do not rest satisfied until they have appropriated scripture itself to their purposes.

Perchance they redress an imbalance in Catholic theology. But by what arbitrary whim do they confer authority on earth-centred Genesis 1–2:4 and deny it to people-centred Genesis 2:5–3:24? And by what further wilfulness do they ignore the culmination of Genesis 1–2:4 itself in the creation of humankind in the image of God, at the apex of creation?

Do they not acknowledge that the Hebrew scriptures are a polemic against idolatry, and that the most significant feature of Genesis 1:2–4 is its denial, by omission, of the very existence of sprites, hobgoblins, demons, gods, demigods, earth spirits and all those motley beings that everyone else in the ancient world sought to manipulate to their advantage? There is only one power, and that is God, who is *above* nature (transcendent).

The Bible encompasses three realms: of God, of humankind, of nature. It does not confuse them. There is 'original blessing', indeed – 'God saw all that he had made, and it was very good' (Genesis 1:31) – but that includes people, maintains hierarchy, excludes 'earth spirits', and remains subject to succeeding chapters of Genesis as well as to the rest of scripture. As Aaron Lichtenstein remarked at a conference at Bar Ilan University (Tel Aviv) on Judaism and ecology, 'Our approach is decidedly anthropocentric, and that is nothing to be ashamed of.'[6]

Below, in section 2.2.4, we shall speak of the hierarchy within nature itself.

2.2.2   Biodiversity

I recall sitting in the Synagogue as a child and listening to the reading of Genesis. I was puzzled by the Hebrew word *leminehu* ('according to its kind') which followed the names of most of the created items and was apparently superfluous. Obviously, if God created fruit with seeds, the seeds were 'according to its kind'!

As time went on I became more puzzled. Scripture seemed obsessive about 'kinds' (species). There were careful lists and definitions of which species of creature might or might not be eaten (Leviticus 11 and Deuteronomy 14). Wool and linen were not to be mixed in a garment (Leviticus 19:19; Deuteronomy 22:11), ox and ass were not to plough together (Deuteronomy 22:10), fields (Leviticus 19:19) and vineyards (Deuteronomy 22:9) were not to be sown with mixed seeds or animals cross-bred (Leviticus 19:19) and, following the rabbinic interpretation of a thrice-repeated biblical phrase (Exodus 23:19; 34:26; Deuteronomy 14:21), meat and milk were not to be cooked or eaten together.[7]

The story of Noah's Ark manifests anxiety that all species should be conserved, irrespective of their usefulness to humankind: Noah is instructed to take into his Ark viable (according to the thought of the time) populations of both 'clean' and 'unclean' animals. That is why the 'Interstellar Ark' is the model, amongst those concerned with such things, for gigantic spaceships to carry total balanced communities of living things through the galaxy for survival or colonisation.[8]

The biblical preoccupation with species and with keeping them distinct can now be read as a way of declaring the 'rightness' of God's pattern for creation and of calling on humankind not only not to interfere with it, but to cherish biodiversity by conserving species.

Scripture does not of course take account of the evolution of species, with its postulates of (a) the alteration of species over time and (b) the extinction (long before the evolution of humans) of most species which have so far appeared on earth.[9] Yet at the very least these Hebrew texts assign unique value to each species as it now is within the context of the present order of creation; this is sufficient to give a religious dimension, within Judaism, to the call to conserve species.

'PEREQ SHIRA'

Pereq Shira (the 'Chapter of Song')[10] affords a remarkable demonstration of the traditional Jewish attitude to nature and its species. The provenance of this 'song' is unknown, though in its earliest form it may well have emanated from mystical circles such as those of the *hekhalot* mystics of the fourth or fifth centuries CE.

Though occasionally attacked for heterodoxy it is clearly rabbinic not only in its theology but even in the detail of its vocabulary and allusions, and only in a general sense can it be compared with Christian and Muslim works such as the Syriac Testament of Adam, the *Ikhwan al-Safa*, or Francis of Assisi's hymn in chapter 120 of *The Mirror of Perfection*.

More significant than its origin is its actual use in private devotion. It has been associated with the 'Songs of Unity' composed by the German pietists of the twelfth century, who undoubtedly stimulated its popularity. At some stage copyists prefaced to it exhortatory sayings which were erroneously attributed to talmudic rabbis: for instance, 'Rabbi Eliezer the Great declared that whoever says *Pereq Shira* in this world will acquire the right to say it the world to come.'[11]

As the work is printed today it is divided into five or six sections, corresponding to the physical creation (this includes heaven and hell, Leviathan and other sea creatures), plants and trees, creeping things, birds, and land animals (in some versions the latter section is subdivided). Each section consists of from 10 to 25 biblical verses, each interpreted as the song or saying of some part of creation or of some individual creature. The cock, in the fourth section, is given 'seven voices', and its function in the poem is to link the earthly song, in which all nature praises God, with the heavenly song.

We shall see in section 2.2.4 that the philosopher Albo draws on *Pereq Shira* to express the relationship between the human and the animal; yet *Pereq Shira* itself draws all creation, even the inanimate, even heaven and hell themselves, into the relationship, expressing a fullness which derives only from the rich diversity of things, and which readily translates into the modern concept of biodiversity.

2.2.3   *Stewardship or domination*

There has been discussion amongst Christian theologians as to whether the opening chapters of Genesis call on humans to act as stewards, guardians of creation, or to dominate and exploit the created world. There is little debate on this point amongst Jewish theologians,[12] to whom it has always been obvious that when Genesis states that Adam was placed in the garden 'to till it and to care for it' (2:15) it means just what it says. As Rav Kook[13] put it,

> No rational person can doubt that the Torah, when it commands people to 'rule over the fishes of the sea and the birds of the sky and all living things that move on the earth' does not have in mind a cruel ruler who exploits his people and servants for his own will and desires – God forbid that such a detestable law of slavery [be attributed to God] who 'is good to all and his tender care rests upon all his creatures' (Psalm 145:9) and 'the world is built on tender mercy' (Psalm 89:3).[14]

So perverse is it to understand 'and rule over it' (Genesis 1:28) – let alone Psalm 8 – as meaning 'exploit and destroy' (is that what people think of their rulers?) that many Christians take such interpretations as a deliberate attempt to besmirch Christianity and not a few Jews have read the discussions as an attempt to 'blame the Jews' for yet another disaster in Christendom.

2.2.4   *Hierarchy in creation*

'God created humans[15] in his image . . . male and female he created them' (Genesis 1:27). In some sense, humankind is superior to animals, animals to plants, plants to the inanimate. There is a hierarchy in created things.

The hierarchical model has two practical consequences. First, as we have seen, is that of responsibility of the higher for the lower, traditionally expressed as 'rule', latterly as 'stewardship'. The second is that, in a competitive situation, the higher has priority over the lower. Humans have priority over dogs, so, for instance, it is wrong for you to risk your life to save that of a dog, though right, in many circumstances, for you to risk your life to save that of another human. Contemporary dilemmas arising from this are described in section 2.5.1.

The Spanish Jewish philosopher Joseph Albo (1380–1435) places humans at the top of the earthly hierarchy, and discerns in this the possibility for humans to receive God's revelation.[16] This is just a mediaeval way of saying what we have remarked. God's revelation, *pace* Albo and Jewish tradition, is the Torah, from which we learn our responsibilities to each other and to the rest of creation.

According to Albo, just as clothes are an integral part of the animal, but external to people, who have to make clothes for themselves, so are specific ethical impulses integral to the behaviour of particular animals, and we should learn from their behaviour. God 'teaches us from the beasts of the earth, and imparts wisdom to us through the birds of the sky' (Job 35:11) – as the Talmud puts it, 'R. Yohanan said, "If these things were not commanded in the Torah, we could learn modesty from the cat, the ant would preach against robbery, and the dove against incest."'[17] The superiority of humans lies in their unique combination of freedom to choose and the intelligence to judge, without which the divine revelation would have no application. Being in this sense 'higher' than other creatures, humans must be humble towards all. Albo, in citing these passages and commending the reading of *Pereq Shira* (see under section 2.2.2), articulates the attitude of reverent stewardship towards creation which characterises rabbinic Judaism.

A DIVERGENCE BETWEEN EAST AND WEST?

With regard to the hierarchical model there appears to be a radical difference of approach between Jews, Christian and Muslims on the one hand and Hindus and Buddhists on the other.

The difference may be more apparent than real. Consider the following:

I recall that with God's grace in the year 5665 [1904/5] I visited Jaffa in the Holy Land, and went to pay my respects to its Chief Rabbi [Rav Kook]. He received me warmly . . . and after the afternoon prayer I accompanied him as he went out into the fields, as was his wont, to concentrate his thoughts. As we were walking I plucked some flower or plant; he trembled, and quietly told me that he always took great care not to pluck, unless it were for some benefit, anything that could grow, for there was no plant below that did not have its guardian[18] above. Everything that grew said something, every stone whispered some secret, all creation sang. . . .[19]

Rav Kook, drawing on a range of classical Jewish sources from Psalm 148 to Lurianic mysticism, and without doubt accepting the hierarchical view of creation, nevertheless acknowledges the divine significance of all things – the immanence of God. Conversely, although Buddhists and Hindus teach respect for all life they do not conclude from this that, for instance, the life of two ants takes precedence over the life of one human being; in practice, they adopt some form of hierarchical principle.

2.2.5 Concern for animals

Kindness to animals is a motivating factor for general concern with the environment, rather than itself an element in conservation.

Kindness to animals features prominently in the Jewish tradition. The Ten Commandments include domestic animals in the Sabbath rest, and the 'seven Noahide laws' are even more explicit.[20] Pious tales and folklore exemplify this attitude, as in the Talmudic anecdote of Rabbi Judah the Patriarch's contrition over having sent a calf to the slaughter,[21] and the folk tale of the rabbi and the frog.[22]

A. CAUSING PAIN OR DISTRESS TO ANIMALS

In rabbinic law this concern condenses into the concept of *tzaar baalei hayyim* ('distress to living creatures').[23] An illuminating instance of halakhic concern for animal welfare is the rule attributed to the third-century Babylonian Rav that one should feed one's cattle before breaking bread oneself;[24] even the Sabbath laws are relaxed somewhat to enable rescue of injured animals or milking of cows to ease their distress. Recently, concern has been expressed about intensive animal husbandry including battery chicken production, and about animal experimentation.[25]

B. MEAT-EATING

The Torah does not enjoin vegetarianism, though Adam and Eve were vegetarian (Genesis 1:29). Restrictions on meat-eating perhaps indicate reservations; amongst the mediaeval Jewish philosophers of the Iberian peninsula Joseph Albo (1380–1435) wrote that the first people were forbidden to eat meat because of the cruelty involved in killing animals.[26] Isaac Abravanel (1437–1508) endorsed this,[27] and also taught that when the Messiah comes we would return to the ideal, vegetarian state.[28] Today the popular trend to vegetarianism has won many Jewish adherents though little official backing from religious leaders.[29]

Judah Tiktin[30] cites the kabbalist Isaac Luria as saying, 'Happy are they who are able to abstain from eating meat and drinking wine throughout the week.' This has been cited as support for vegetarianism, but is irrelevant. The context is that of abstaining from meat and wine on Mondays and Thursdays (the traditional penitential days), a custom akin to the widespread Roman Catholic practice of not eating meat on Fridays. The goal is self-denial, or asceticism, not vegetarianism, as may be inferred from the fact that the very same authorities endorse the eating of meat and the drinking of wine in moderation as the appropriate way to celebrate the Sabbath and Festivals. There have, indeed, been some holy men whose asceticism has led them to abstain entirely from eating meat and drinking wine – Rabbi Joseph Kahaneman (1888–1969)[31] for instance – but this provides no basis in principle for vegetarianism.

C. HUNTING

On 23 February 1716 Duke Christian of Sachsen-Weissenfels celebrated his fifty-third birthday by a great hunting party. History would have passed by the Duke as well as the occasion had not J. S. Bach honoured them with his *Hunting Cantata*. The text by Salomo Franck, secretary of the upper consistory at Weimar, is a grand celebration of nature and its priest, Duke Christian, with no sense that hunting sounds a discordant note, and the cantata includes one of Bach's most expressive arias, 'Schafe können sicher weiden' ('Sheep may safely graze').

Hunting, it is clear, enhances appreciation of nature. Moreover, the hunter does not oppose conservation: he destroys only individual prey and has an interest in preserving the species.

Conditions of Jewish life in the past millennium or so have rarely afforded Jewish princes the opportunity to celebrate their birthdays by hunting parties. But it has happened from time to time, and led rabbis to voice their censure.

Nahum Rakover[32] sums up the halakhic objections to hunting for 'sport' under eight heads.

1   It is destructive/wasteful (see section 2.3.2).
2   It causes distress to animals (section 2.2.5A).
3   It actively produces non-kosher carcasses.[33]
4   It leads to trading non-kosher commodities.
5   The hunter exposes himself to danger unnecessarily.
6   It wastes time.[34]
7   The hunt is a 'seat of the scornful' (Psalm 1:1).[35]
8   'Thou shalt not conform to their institutions' (Leviticus 18:3).[36]

From this we see that, although Jewish religious tradition despises hunting for sport, this is on ethical and ritual grounds rather than in the interest of conservation.[37]

2.3 The Land and the People: A Paradigm

Judaism, whilst attentive to the universal significance of its essential teachings, has developed within a specific context of peoplehood. In the Bible itself the most obvious feature of this is the stress on the chosen people and the chosen land.

This has meant that Judaism, both in biblical times and subsequently, has emphasised the interrelationship of people and land, the idea that the prosperity of the land depends on the people's obedience to God's covenant. For instance,

If you pay heed to the commandments which I give you this day, and love the Lord your God and serve him with all your heart and soul, then I will send rain for your land in season . . . and you will gather your corn and new wine and oil, and I will provide pasture . . . you shall eat your fill. Take good care not to be led astray in your hearts nor to turn aside and serve other gods . . . or the Lord will become angry with you; he will shut up the skies and there will be no rain, your ground will not yield its harvest, and you will soon vanish from the rich land which the Lord is giving you.   (Deuteronomy 11:13–17)

Two steps are necessary to apply this link between morality and prosperity to the contemporary situation.

1 The chosen land and people must be understood as the proto-type of (a) all actual individual geographical nations (including, of course, Israel) in their relationships with land, and of (b) humanity as a whole in its relationship with the planet as a whole.
2 There must be satisfactory clarification of the meaning of 'obedience to God' as the human side of the covenant to ensure that 'the land will be blessed'. The Bible certainly has in mind justice and moral rectitude, but in spelling out 'the command-ments of God' it includes specific prescriptions which directly regulate care of the land and celebration of its produce; some of these are discussed below.

To sum up: the Bible stresses the intimate relationship between people and land. The prosperity of land depends on (a) the social justice and moral integrity of the people on it, and (b) a caring, even loving, attitude to land with effective regulation of its use. Conservation demands the extrapolation of these principles from ancient or idealised Israel to the contemporary global situation; this calls for education in social values together with scientific investi-gation of the effects of our activities on nature.

2.3.1   Sabbatical year and Jubilee

When you enter the land which I give you, the land shall keep sabbaths to the Lord. For six years you may sow your fields and for six years prune your vineyards but in the seventh year the land shall keep a sabbath of sacred rest, a sabbath to the Lord. You shall not sow your field nor prune your vineyard. . . .   (Leviticus 25:2–4)

The analogy between the Sabbath (literally, 'rest day') of the land and that of people communicates the idea that land must 'rest' to be refreshed and regain its productive vigour. In contemporary terms, land resources must be conserved through the avoidance of over-use.

The Bible pointedly links this to social justice. Just as land must not be exploited so slaves must go free after six years of bondage or in the Jubilee (fiftieth) year, and the sabbatical year (in Hebrew *shemittah* – 'release') cancels private debts, thus preventing exploitation of the individual.

The consequence of disobedience is destruction of the land, which God so cares for that he will heal it in the absence of its unfaithful inhabitants:

> If in spite of this you do not listen to me and still defy me . . . I will make your cities desolate and destroy your sanctuaries . . . your land shall be desolate and your cities heaps of rubble. Then, all the time that it lies desolate, while you are in exile in the land of your enemies, your land shall enjoy its sabbaths to the full. . . . (Leviticus 26:27–35)

If in Israel today there is only a handful of agricultural collectives which observe the 'Sabbath of land' in its biblical and rabbinic sense, the biblical text has undoubtedly influenced the country's scientists and agronomists to question the intensive agriculture favoured in the early years of the state and to give high priority to conservation of land resources.

2.3.2   *Cutting down fruit trees*

> When you are at war, and lay siege to a city . . . do not destroy its trees by taking the axe to them, for they provide you with food. . . . (Deuteronomy 20:19)

In its biblical context this is a counsel of prudence rather than a principle of conservation; the Israelites are enjoined to use only 'non-productive' – that is, non fruit-bearing – trees, for their siege works.

In rabbinic teaching, however, the verse has become the *locus classicus* for conserving all that has been created, so that the very phrase *bal tashchit*[38] is inculcated into small children to teach them not to destroy or waste even those things they do not need. In an account of the commandments specially written for his son, Rabbi Aaron Halevi of Barcelona (*c.* 1300) sums up the purpose of this one as follows:

> This is meant to ingrain in us the love of that which is good and beneficial and to cleave to it; by this means good will imbue our souls and we will keep far from everything evil or destructive. This is the way of the devout and those of good deeds – they love peace, rejoice in that which benefits people and brings them to Torah; they never destroy even a grain of mustard, and are upset at any destruction they see. If only they can save anything from being spoilt they spare no effort to do so.[39]

2.3.3 *Limitation of grazing rights*

The Mishnah rules, 'One may not raise small cattle [sheep, goats, etc.] in the land of Israel, but one may do so in Syria or in the uninhabited parts of the land of Israel.'[40] The history of this law has been researched[41] and there is evidence of similar restrictions from as early as the third century BCE.

The Mishnah itself does not itself provide a rationale for the law. Later rabbis suggest (a) that its primary purpose is to prevent the 'robbery' of crops by roaming animals, and (b) that its objective is to encourage settlement in the land. This latter reason is based on the premise that the raising of sheep and goats is inimical to the cultivation of crops, and reflects the ancient rivalry between nomad and farmer; at the same time it poses the question considered by modern ecologists of whether animal husbandry is an efficient way of producing food.[42]

2.3.4 *Agricultural festivals*

The concept of 'promised land' is an assertion that the consummation of social and national life depends on harmony with the land.

The biblical pilgrim festivals all celebrate the land and its crops, though they are also given historical and spiritual meanings. Through the joyful collective experience of these festivals the people learned to cherish the land and their relationship, through

God's commandments, with it; the sense of joy was heightened through fulfilment of the divine commandments to share the bounty of the land with 'the Levite, the stranger, the orphan and the widow'.[43]

2.4   Specific Environmental Laws

Several aspects of environmental pollution are dealt with in traditional *halakhah*. Although the classical sources were composed in situations very different from those of the present, the law has been, and is, in a continuous state of development, and in any case the basic principles are clearly relevant to contemporary situations.

2.4.1   *Waste disposal*

Arising from Deuteronomy 23:13, 14, *halakhah* insists that refuse be removed 'outside the camp' – that is, collected in a location where it will not reduce the quality of life. The Talmud and codes extend this concept to the general prohibition of dumping refuse or garbage where it may interfere with the environment or with crops.

It would be anachronistic to seek in the earlier sources the concept of waste disposal as threatening the total balance of nature or the climate. However, if the rabbis forbade the growing of kitchen gardens and orchards around Jerusalem on the grounds that the manuring would degrade the local environment,[44] one need have no doubt that they would have been deeply concerned at the large-scale environmental degradation caused by traditional mining operations, the burning of fossil fuels and the like. I would like to think that their response, had they been faced by the problem of disposal of nuclear wastes, would have led them to weigh up the evidence very carefully rather than to rush into an emotional judgement.

Smell (see also section 2.4.2) is regarded in *halakhah* as a particular nuisance, hence there are rules regarding the siting not only of lavatories but also of odoriferous commercial operations such as tanneries.[45] Certainly, rabbinic law accords priority to environmental over purely commercial considerations.

2.4.2 *Atmospheric pollution and smoke*

Like smell, atmospheric pollution and smoke are placed by the rabbis within the category of indirect damage, since their effects are produced at a distance. They are nevertheless unequivocally forbidden.

The Mishnah[46] bans the siting of a threshing floor within fifty cubits of a residential area, since the flying particles set in motion by the threshing process would diminish the quality of the air.

Likewise, the second-century rabbi Nathan[47] ruled that a furnace might not be sited within fifty cubits of a residential area because of the effect of its smoke on the atmosphere; the fifty-cubit limit was subsequently extended by the Gaonim to whatever the distance from which smoke might cause eye irritation or general annoyance.[48]

The Hazards Prevention Law passed by the Israeli Knesset on 23 March 1961 contains the following provisions:

#3   No person shall create a strong or unreasonable smell, of whatever origin, if it disturbs or is likely to disturb a person nearby or passerby.

#4   a No person shall create strong or unreasonable pollution of the air, of whatever origin, if it disturbs or is likely to disturb a person nearby or passerby.

The subjectivity of 'reasonable' in this context is apparent. Meir Sichel, in a recent study[49] on the ecological problems that arise from the use of energy resources for power stations to manufacture electricity, and from various types of industrial and domestic consumption such as cooking, heating and lighting, has drawn on the resources of traditional Jewish law in an attempt to define more precisely what should be regarded as 'reasonable'. Citing rabbinic responsa from an 800-year period, he concludes that *halakhah* is even more insistent on individual rights than the civil law (of Israel), and that *halakhah* does not recognise 'prior rights' of a defendant who claims that he had established a right to produce the annoyance or pollutant before the plaintiff appeared on the scene.

It seems to me that in an exercise such as Sichel's there is no difficulty in applying traditional law to the contemporary context with regard to priority of rights, and also in clarifying the relationship between public and private rights. However, it is less clear that one can achieve a satisfactory definition of 'reasonable', since ideas of what is acceptable vary not only from person to person but in accordance with changing scientific understanding of the nature of the damage caused by smells and smoke, including the 'invisible' hazards of germs and radiation unknown to earlier generations.

2.4.3   *Water pollution*

Several laws were instituted by the rabbis to safeguard the freedom from pollution (as well as the fair distribution) of water. A typical early source:

> If someone is digging out caves for the public he may wash his hands, face and feet; but if his feet are dirty with mud or excrement it is forbidden. [If he is digging] a well or a ditch [for drinking water], then [whether his feet are clean or dirty] he may not wash them.[50]

Pregnant with possibilities for application to contemporary life is the principle that one may claim damages or obtain an appropriate injunction to remove the nuisance where the purity of one's water supply is endangered by a neighbour's drainage or similar works. It is significant that the Gaonim here also rejected the Talmudic distance limit in favour of a broad interpretation of the law to cover damage irrespective of distance.[51]

2.4.4   *Noise*

Rabbinic law on noise pollution offers a fascinating instance of balance of priorities. The Mishnah lays down that in a residential area neighbours have the right to object to the opening of a shop or similar enterprise on the grounds that the noise would disturb their tranquillity. It is permitted, however, to open a school for Torah notwithstanding the noise of children, for education has priority. Later authorities discuss the limit of noise which has to be tolerated in the interest of education,[52] and whether other forms of religious activity might have similar priority to the opening of a school.[53]

2.4.5 Beauty

Much could be said of the rabbinic appreciation of beauty in general. Here we concern ourselves only with legislation explicitly intended to enhance the environment, and we discover that it is rooted in the biblical law of the Levitical cities:

> Tell the Israelites to set aside towns in their patrimony as homes for the Levites, and give them also the common land surrounding the towns. They shall live in the towns, and keep their beasts, their herds, and all their livestock on the common land. The land of the towns which you give the Levites shall extend from the centre of the town outwards for a thousand cubits in each direction. Starting from the town the eastern boundary shall measure two thousand cubits, the southern two thousand, the western two thousand, and the northern two thousand, with the town in the centre. They shall have this as the common land adjoining their towns.   (Numbers 35:2–5)

As this passage is understood by the rabbis, there was to be a double surround to each town: first a 'green belt' of 1000 cubits, then a 2000-cubit-wide belt for 'fields and vineyards'. Whilst some maintained that the 1000-cubit band was for pasture, Rashi[54] explains that it was not for use, but 'for the beauty of the town, to give it space' – a concept reflected in Maimonides' interpretation of the Talmudic rules on the distancing of trees from residences.[55]

The rabbis debate whether this form of 'town planning' ought to be extended to non-Levitical towns, at least in the land of Israel, designated by Jeremiah (3:9) and Ezekiel (20:6, 15) 'the beautiful land'.

The rabbinic appreciation of beauty in nature is highlighted in the blessing they set to be recited when one sees 'the first blossoms in spring':

> You are blessed, Lord our God and ruler of the universe, who have omitted nothing from your world, but created within it good creatures and good and beautiful trees in which people may take delight.[56]

2.5   Sample Ethical Problems relating to Conservation

2.5.1   *Animal versus human life*

Judaism consistently values human life more than animal life. You should not risk your life to save an animal: for example, if you are driving a car and a dog runs into the road, it would be wrong to swerve, endangering your own or someone else's life, to save the dog.

But is it right to take a human life – for instance, that of a poacher – to save not an individual animal but an endangered species? I can find nothing in Jewish sources to support killing poachers in any circumstances other than those in which they directly threaten human life. If it be argued that the extinction of a species would threaten human life because it would upset the balance of nature, it is still unlikely that Jewish law would countenance homicide to avoid an indirect and uncertain threat of this nature.

Even if homicide were justified in such circumstances, how many human lives is a single species worth? How far down the evolutionary scale would such a principle be applied? After all, the argument about upsetting the balance of nature applies just as much with microscopic species as with large cuddly-looking vertebrates such as the panda, and with plants as much as with animals.

Judaism, true to the hierarchical principle of creation (section 2.2.4), consistently values human life more than that of other living things, but at the same time stresses the special responsibility of human beings to 'work on and look after' the created order (Genesis 2:15 – see section 2.2.3).

2.5.2   *Procreation versus population control*

The question of birth control (including abortion) in Judaism is too complex to deal with here, but there is universal agreement that at least some forms of birth control are permissible where a potential mother's life is in danger and that abortion is not only permissible but mandatory up to full term to save the mother's life.[57] Significant is the value system which insists that, even though contraception may be morally questionable, it is preferable to abstinence where life danger would be involved through normal sexual re-lations within a marriage.[58]

What happens where economic considerations rather than life danger come into play? Here we must distinguish between (a) personal economic difficulties and (b) circumstances of 'famine in the world', where economic hardship is general.

On the whole, *halakhah* places the basic duty of procreation above personal economic hardship. But what about general econ-omic hardship, which can arise (a) through local or temporary famine and (b) through the upward pressure of population on finite world resources?

The former situation was in the mind of the third-century Pales-tinian sage Resh Lakish when he ruled, 'It is forbidden for a man to engage in sexual intercourse in years of famine.'[59] Although the ruling of Resh Lakish was adopted by the codes,[60] its application was restricted to those who already have children, and the de-cision between abstinence and contraception is less clear here than where there is a direct hazard to life.

Upward pressure of population on world resources is a concept unknown to the classical sources of the Jewish religion, and not indeed clearly understood by anyone before Malthus. As David M. Feldman remarks,

> It must be repeated here that the 'population explosion' has nothing to do with the Responsa, and vice versa. The Rabbis were issuing their analyses and their replies to a specific couple with a specific query. These couples were never in a situation where they might aggravate a world problem; on the contrary, the Jewish community was very often in a position of seeking to replenish its depleted ranks after pogrom or exile. . . .[61]

Feldman goes on to say, 'It would be just as reckless to overbreed as to refrain from procreation.' Although I am not aware of any explicit traditional rabbinic source for this, I certainly know of none to the contrary. Indeed, as the duty of procreation is expressed in Genesis in the words 'be fruitful and multiply and fill the earth', it is not unreasonable to suggest that 'fill' be taken as 'reach the maximum population sustainable at an acceptable standard of living but do not exceed it'. In like manner the rabbis[62] utilise Isaiah's phrase 'God made the earth . . . no empty void, but made

it for a place to dwell in' (45:18) to define the minimum requirement for procreation – a requirement, namely one son and one
daughter, which does not increase population.

Of course, there is room for local variation amongst populations.
Although as a general rule governments nowadays should discourage population growth, there are instances of thinly populated
areas or of small ethnic groups whose survival is threatened where
some population growth might be acceptable even from the global
perspective.

2.5.3   *Nuclear, fossil fuel, solar energy*

Can religious sources offer guidance on the choice between nuclear
and fossil, and other energy sources?

It seems to me that they can have very little to say and that –
especially in view of the extravagant views expressed by some
religious leaders – it is vitally important to understand why their
potential contribution to current debate is so small.

The choice among energy sources rests on the following parameters.

1   Cost-effectiveness.
2   Environmental damage caused by production.
3   Operational hazards.
4   Clean dispotal of waste products.
5   Long-term environmental sustainability.

Let us consider these parameters. Cost-effectiveness cannot be
established without weighing the other factors. There is no point,
however, at which religious considerations apply in establishing
whether a particular combination of nuclear reactor plus safety
plus storage of waste and so on will cost more or less than
alternative 'packages' for energy production.

It is equally clear that religious considerations have no part to
play in assessing environmental damage caused by production,
operational hazards, whether waste products can be clearly dis-
posed of, or what is the long-term environmental sustainability of
a method of energy production. These are all technical matters,
demanding painstaking research and hard evidence, and they
have nothing to do with theology.

The religious might perhaps have something to say about overall strategy. For instance, a religious viewpoint might suggest that scientists should pay more attention to finding out how to use less energy to meet demands for goods than to finding out how to produce more energy. However, unless the religious are actually aiming to persuade people to demand less goods, such advice – i.e. to seek more energy-sufficient ways to do things – is merely the counsel of prudence, not dependent on any characteristically religious value.

It is a matter of sadness and regret that religious leaders are so prone to stirring up the emotions of the faithful for or against some project, such as nuclear energy, which really ought to be assessed on objective grounds. Much of the hurt arises from the way the religious 'demonise' those of whom they disapprove, and in the name of love generate hatred against people who seek to bring benefit to humanity.

2.5.4 *Global warming*

A very similar analysis could be made of the problems relating to global warming – problems of which scientists have been aware since Arrhenius in the late nineteenth century, though only recently have pressure groups developed and governments become alarmed. The fact is that in mid 1990 no one knows the extent, if any, to which global temperatures have risen as a result of the rise in atmospheric carbon dioxide from 290 parts per million in 1880 to 352 parts per million in 1989, and no one knows what would be the overall effects of the projected doubling of atmospheric carbon dioxide by the middle next century (I leave aside the question of other greenhouse gases). Some consequences, indeed, may be beneficial, such as greater productivity of plants in an atmosphere with more carbon dioxide. Unfortunately, neither the techniques of mathematical modelling used to make the projections, nor the base of global observations at 500-kilometre intervals, can yield firm results.[63]

So how can a government decide whether to spend hundreds of thousands of millions of dollars on reducing atmospheric carbon dioxide, and vast sums in aiding Third World countries to avoid developing along 'greenhouse' lines, when the draconian measures required greatly limit personal freedom and much of the expenditure might be better diverted to building hospitals, improving education and the like?

Essential steps, including better research, must be initiated, but it would be a lack of wisdom to rush into the most extreme measures demanded. From our point of view, however, it is clear that the decisions must be rooted in prudence, not in theology. Theology tends to absolutise and call for radical solutions where we have only relative and uncertain evidence, or, conversely, to commend us to faith in God when we ought to be taking practical initiatives.

2.5.5   Who pays the piper?

Our observations on the response to the possibility of global warming raised the question of paying for conservation. The dilemmas involved in this are exceedingly complex. Should rich nations pay to 'clean up' the technology of poorer nations (for instance, Western Europe for Eastern Europe)? Should governments distort the free market by subsidising lead-free petrol and other 'environment-friendly' commodities? How does one cost out social and environmental efficiency, and how should such costs be distributed between the taxpayer and the manufacturer? Several of these problems will be addressed in our chapters on economics.

2.5.6   Directed evolution

After writing about the progress from physical evolution through biological evolution to cultural evolution, Edward Rubinstein continues,

> Henceforth, life no longer evolves solely through chance mutation. Humankind has begun to modify evolution, to bring about nonrandom, deliberate changes in DNA that alter living assemblies and create assembles that did not exist before.
>
> The messengers of directed evolution are human beings. Their messages, expressed in the language and methods of molecular biology, genetics and medicine and in moral precepts, express their awareness of human imperfections and reflect the values and aspirations of their species.[64]

These words indicate the area where religions, Judaism included, are most in need of adjusting themselves to contemporary reality – the area in which modern knowledge sets us most apart from those who formed our religious traditions. Religion as we know it has come into being only since the Neolithic revolution, and thus presupposes some technology,[65] some mastery of nature. But it has also assumed that the broad situation of humanity is static, and this is now seen to be an illusion.

All at once there is the prospect, alarming to some yet challenging to others, that we can set the direction of future development for all creatures in our world. The ethics committees of our hospitals and medical schools are forced to take decisions; although the religious take part – and Judaism has a distinctive contribution to make to medical ethics[66] – it has yet to be shown that traditional sources can be brought to bear other than in the vaguest way ('we uphold the sanctity of life') on the problems raised even by currently available genetic engineering.

Will religions, as so often in the past, obstruct the development of science? They need not. We shall see in section 3.4.1 that Jewish religious attitudes have ranged from Isaac Abravanel, who opposed in principle the development of technology,[67] to Abraham bar Hiyya, who in the twelfth century played a major role in the transmission of Graeco-Arab science to the West. If Judaism (or any other religion) is to contribute towards conservation it will need to be in the spirit of bar Hiyya, through support for good science, rather than through idealisation of the 'simple life' in the spirit of Seneca and Abravanel.

2.6 Conclusion: Religion and Conservation

There is no doubt that Judaism, along with other religions, has resources which can be used to encourage people in the proper management of Planet Earth. We shall now review the interaction of religion with conservation with special reference to the sources cited.

1   We saw in section 2.2.1 how Judaism interprets the created world, with its balanced biodiverse ecology, as a 'testimony to God', with humankind at the pinnacle holding special responsibility for its maintenance and preservation. Certainly, this attitude

is more conducive to an interest in conservation than would be emphasis on the centrality of the 'next world', on the spirit versus the body, or on the 'inferior' or 'illusionary' nature of the material world.

2   One of the priorities of conservation at the present time is to control population so as not to exceed resources. Although Judaism stresses the duty of procreation, we learned in section 2.5.2 that it offers the prospect of a constructive approach to population planning, including some role for both contraception and abortion.

3   We have noted several specific areas in which Judaism has developed laws or policies significant for conservation. Prime among them (section 2.3) are the laws regulating the relationship between people and land, for which the 'chosen people' in the 'promised land' is the model. Care of animals (section 2.2.5), waste disposal, atmospheric and water pollution, noise, and beauty of the environment (section 2.4) are also treated in the classical sources. It would be neither possible nor fully adequate to take legislation straight from these sources; but it is certainly possible to work in continuity with them, bearing in mind the radically new awareness of the need for conserving the world and its resources as a whole.

4   Religions, Judaism included, discourage the pursuit of personal wealth. Whilst in some instances this may be beneficial to the environment – if people want fewer cars and fewer books there will be fewer harmful emissions and fewer forests will be chopped down – there are also many ways in which poverty harms the environment: for instance, less research and development means that such technology as remains (presumably for hospitals and other welfare matters) will be less efficient and the problems of environmental pollution less effectively addressed. Only rich societies can afford clean disposal of wastes.

5   Some religions remain strongly committed to evangelistic or conversionist aims which inhibit co-operation with people of other religions. Judaism is not currently in an actively missionary phase; some would say that it is unduly introspective, and needs to proclaim its values in a more universal context. All religions, however, must desist from ideological conflicts and espouse dia-

logue; conservation cannot be effective without global co-operation.

6   Mere information can motivate, as when someone who per-ceives a lion ready to pounce reacts swiftly. If ecological disaster were as clearly perceived as a crouching lion, ideological motiva-tion would be unnecessary. It is better that religions support conservation than oppose it, but the world would be safer if people would act on the basis of rational collective self-preservation rather than on the basis of confused and uncontrollable ideologies.

7   Several times, particularly in discussing energy sources in sec-tion 2.5.3 and global warming in section 2.5.4, we had to stress the need to distinguish between technological and value judgements. Whether or not nuclear reactors should be built must depend on a careful, dispassionate assessment of their hazards; shrill condem-nation of the 'hubris of modern technology' merely hinders judge-ment, though it is right and proper that religious values be consid-ered when an informed choice is made.

Of course, the same need for objective assessment before value judgements are made applies to all other major conservation ques-tions, such as how to reverse deforestation, control the greenhouse effect, restore the ozone layer.

8   Towards the end of section 2.5.6 we noted a characteristic religious ambivalence towards science. In the interests of conserva-tion it is essential that the 'pro-science' attitude of Abraham bar Hiyya, Gersonides and others be encouraged. The craziness of 'simple life' proponents must be resisted. For a start, the present world population could not be supported if we were to revert to the simple life. Moreover, who would wish to do without sanita-tion, communications, electric light, books, travel, medical services and all those other benefits of 'complex' civilisation? The small population which would survive the 'return to Eden' would live a very dull and insecure life.

If science has got us into a mess (which I would dispute) the way out is not *no* science but *better* science, and science performed with a sense of moral responsibility.

Finally, let us note that Judaism, like other religions, has a vital role to play in eradicating those evils and promoting those values in society without which no conservation policies can be effective. The single greatest evil is official corruption, frequently rife in precisely those countries where conservation measures must be carried out. Next in line is drug addiction with its associated trade. Religions must combat these evils and at the same time work intelligently for peace, not only between nations but amongst religions themselves.

3

Ethics of Commerce

Whereas there has been little systematic coverage of conservation in the Jewish sources, economic topics have received such extensive treatment that here it is only possible to set out a framework for critical assessment of the sources and to suggest some simple guidelines.

3.1 Economic Preliminaries: Why are there Problems?

Economics is a very hard subject to pin down. Trying to grasp it is like trying to grasp a handful of loose sand: the harder you squeeze, the more falls out. Thus, in attempting to come to grips with economic theory, the harder you squeeze with apparently hard scientific techniques such as those of econometrics, the more you lose hold of the broad subject you originally set out to understand.

Fortunately we do not need to be too concerned about theory here. The essential thing for present purposes is to demystify what money is, why we have it, and why there is so much fuss and trouble over it.

3.1.1 *Money and commerce*

Social life is only possible where goods and services flow amongst people. This is true of social units of every size, whether it be the mother from whom the milk flows to the baby, or the entire world with its complex web of economic relationships.

The flow must be orderly, predictable within practicable margins, to ensure a stable society. That is, goods and services must change hands according to definite, mutually accepted rules. People must know that promises are highly likely to be kept.

David Hume summed this up as 'the three fundamental laws of nature, *that of the stability of possession, of its transference by consent,* and *of the performance of promises'.*[1]

Money – gold, silver, tobacco, cowrie shells or any other agreed range of objects – is a means of rendering the flow of goods and services orderly. It works by establishing one or a very small number of agreed standards by which people measure how much they want each object or service. 'Value' is not some quality inherent in an object, but a summation of a large number of individual psychologies, how much people want this or that and what they are prepared to do to get it; it is not surprising economists cannot agree an exact way to measure 'value'.

Reducing the number of standards of value measurement to one or two, for instance silver and gold, makes possible a simpler and hence more orderly system than barter for the flow of goods and services amongst people.

Goods and services may indeed flow where no money changes hands and there is no barter – within the family, for instance, or in acts of benevolence. Religions are very interested in this sort of flow. Indeed, the ethics of commerce is largely necessary to counteract the hardships (not necessarily injustices) which arise from the system by which the flow of goods and services is regulated. It may be that no better system than a money-based one is possible; money, the simplified measure of value which is necessary to facilitate the flow of goods and services must, because it is a simplification, be imperfect.

GRESHAM'S LAW – OF GOOD MONEY AND BAD

Gold, silver, tobacco, cowrie shells, even paper notes, can themselves be commodities (things you buy or sell), and this sometimes causes confusion, especially where one and the same item may function as either money or commodity. Hence the Mishnah tells us,

> Gold acquires silver, but silver does not acquire gold; brass acquires silver, but silver does not acquire brass; bad coins acquire good, but good ones do not acquire bad.[2]

This means that the handing-over of money for a commodity does not finalise the transaction, whereas the handing-over of the commodity does. It is the commodity, not the money, which 'acquires'. Hence one must know which is which, and this may depend on circumstances.

Meir Tamari states,

Gresham's law – that bad money (in other words, inferior, inflated, currency) drives out good money – was formulated by the rabbis of the Talmud some 1,500 years prior to its formulation by Gresham.[3]

Gresham's law means that people will use bad money in preference to good, driving the good out of circulation. The Mishnah, on the other hand, is making the point that 'bad coins' – that is, coins which are no longer valid currency – are to be treated in law as a commodity (lumps of metal) rather than as money. It is an ethical statement, to the effect that people should desist from cheating by using inferior coins. This is not the same as Gresham's law. Indeed, it presupposes the tendency noted by Gresham, and attempts to counteract it. Tamari appears to have been misled by a fortuitous similarity of phrase.

3.1.2 'The law of the country is law'

Jewish law, like other legal systems, is reticent in its acknowledgement of alternative jurisdictions. For instance, a marriage contracted under some other system of law would not be recognised; someone guilty of an offence under another system of criminal jurisdiction, but which was not an offence under Jewish law, would not be held guilty under Jewish law.

Nevertheless, alternative jurisdictions are recognised in matters concerning money and ownership of property. Four times in the Talmud[4] the view of the Babylonian Samuel of Nehardea (177–257 CE) is cited that *dina de-malkhuta dina* ('the law of the country is law'), and this became the accepted norm.[5] It is the basis on which, for instance, Jewish subjects accept as obligatory taxes levied by a non-Jewish government, and as such has played a crucial part 'for the entire history of Judeo-Gentile symbiosis in the dispersion'.[6]

Likewise, a Beth Din (a properly constituted Jewish court) has a power of *hefqer bet din hefqer*[7] – that is, of annulling ownership.

This power of court or of government to alter proprietary rights has no counterpart in other spheres of law. For instance, a Beth Din cannot, other than as explicitly sanctioned by the law, change personal status or decide that a criminal act has or has not taken place.

What makes the bond between owner and owned particularly

subject to intervention is that ownership is essentially a social convention rather than a physical reality. In legal terminology, it is contractual. Society – 'everybody' – agrees to acknowledge me as the owner of this desk or this dinner. The court or government acting in the interests of society can modify or suspend this agreement. The moralist or preacher discoursing in the interests of the poor who need the desk or the dinner more than I cannot himself modify or suspend the agreement, but can urge me to do so.

Most of the ethics of commerce and economics arises from the contractual nature of ownership, for this renders the relationship between owner and owned infinitely manoeuvrable.

3.2 Personal Ethics: The Basics

As we consider complex issues of commerce right up to the global level we must not lose sight of the simple but powerful rules and values that our religions teach us to apply at all levels in transactions amongst people. It is precisely these simple and obvious things, such as 'love your neighbour as yourself' (Leviticus 19:18) which tend to be ignored and overlooked in practice, and so we have to re-emphasise them constantly.

Legitimate dealings with other people fall into two categories. Some are 'according to law', just, correct, reflecting an equal and agreed exchange between persons; for instance, one enters a shop and purchases a bicycle, paying the just price requested by the vendor. Other dealings are unequal, proceeding from the wish of one party to benefit the other; for instance, when you give alms to someone in need, and expect no return. This distinction relates to that between justice and love, though to some extent both values should enter into both types of transaction.

Let us look first at what the Torah has to say about correct dealing, and then at its teaching on benevolence.

3.2.1 *Correct dealings*

A third-century rabbi, Resh Laqish, listed six questions one would be asked on the Day of Judgement; the very first of these was *nasata ve-natata be'emunah* – 'Did you act with integrity in all your [business] dealings?'[8]

Values which affect interpersonal behaviour include mutual concern and consideration, love, respect, goodwill, and trust-worthiness.

Rules include not stealing, not cheating, not deceiving, not overcharging, not delaying payment, not bribing, and so on.

To both Hillel (early first century CE) and Rabbi Akiva are attributed statements affirming the centrality in Torah, and hence in interpersonal relationships, of the Levitical commandment 'Thou shalt love thy neighbour as thyself' (Leviticus 19:18).[9]

Values and rules are expressed in the traditional sources as *mitzvot* – the biblical roots, or 'commandments'.

Moshe Hayyim Luzzatto (1707–47) devotes the eleventh chapter of his ethical classic *Mesillat Yesharim*[10] to the concept of *neqiyyut* (literally 'cleanliness', i.e. from sin). Scrupulous honesty in business lies at the heart of this:

> Although most people are not overt thieves, that is, they do not actually put out their hands and help themselves to their neigh-bours' belongings, they taste theft in their dealings by convinc-ing themselves that it is all right to profit from another's loss. But indeed many of the commandments relate to stealing – 'do not oppress you neighbour' [Leviticus 19:13], 'do not rob' [19:13], 'do not steal' [19:11], 'do not deny' [19:11],[11] 'do not lie one to another' [19:11], 'do not cheat one another' [25:14], 'do not remove your neighbour's landmark' [Deuteronomy 19:14][12] – all these comprise details which are commonly ignored in commer-cial transactions . . . even the distribution of sweets and nuts to children was permitted by the sages only on the grounds that others may do likewise.[13]

The concept of bribery is broadened by the Talmud and later moralists to include any instance of putting one's judgement at risk by accepting favours. It is vigorously condemned, regardless of whether the resulting judgement is correct, in law.

BEYOND THE LAW

Although a court cannot demand more than correctness or justice, the individual should seek to exceed this, by, for instance, refraining from making the full legal demand on the other party, demanding the 'pound of flesh'.[14] This restraint is known as *lifnim mishurat ha-din* and has a major role in Jewish ethics. The third-century Palestinian rabbi Yohanan said, 'Jerusalem was destroyed only because people did not act beyond the strict requirement of law.'[15] The exasperation of legislators who knew that the boundaries they could legitimately define were inadequate to the Torah's moral standards in expressed in the traditional *mi shepara'*:

> If [the purchaser] had handed over the money but had not yet taken possession of the goods [the vendor] has the right to withdraw from the sale; but he who punished [*mi shepara'*] the generation of the flood and the generation of the tower [of Babel] will punish him who does not stand by his word.[16]

The relationship between law and ethics has been a major issue in Judaism. Does the concept of *lifnim mishurat ha-din* indicate that the law is not always just, or is *lifnim mishurat ha-din* itself part of one's legal responsibility? Perhaps, as Menachem Elon suggested, it has evolved from one to the other.[17]

3.2.2 Benevolence

Alms-giving features prominently in Jewish teaching and practice, and the rabbis constantly impressed on their followers the need for compassion and charity. One of the Hebrew words for alms-giving is *tzedakah*, derived from a root meaning to be right, fair or correct. Alms-giving is not so much an act of piety as one of fairness, ensuring correct distribution of the wealth God has entrusted to us.

The overall concept within which alms-giving is contained is, however, *hesed*, a biblical Hebrew word which can be translated by 'love' or 'compassion' and has frequently been translated 'loving-kindness'.

Isadore Twersky has well stated,

> If, as Whitehead aphorized, all of western thought is a footnote to Plato, one might suggest that western *humanitas* is a footnote to the Bible – and then proceed indolently to luxuriate in this flattering fact.[18]

Few scholars can be less indolent than Twersky himself, who proceeds to develop a theory of benevolence on the basis of the following Talmudic tale:

> It has been taught: R. Meir used to say: The critic [of Judaism] may bring against you the argument, 'If your God loves the poor, why does he not support them?' If so, answer him, 'So that through them we may be saved from the punishment of Gehinnom.' This question was actually put by Turnus Rufus to R. Akiba: 'If your God loves the poor, why does He not support them?' He replied: 'So that through them we may be saved from the punishment of Gehinnom.' 'On the contrary,' said the other, 'it is this which condemns you to Gehinnom. I will illustrate by a parable. Suppose an earthly king was angry with his servant and put him in prison and ordered that he should be given no food or drink, and a man went and gave him food and drink. If the king heard, would he not be angry with him? And you are called "servants", as it is written, *For unto me the children of Israel are servants.*' R. Akiba answered him: 'I will illustrate by another parable. Suppose an earthly king was angry with his son, and put him in prison and ordered that no food or drink should be given to him, and someone went and gave him food and drink. If the king heard of it, would he not send him a present? And we are called "sons", as it is written, *Sons are ye to the Lord your God.*' He said to him: 'You are called both sons and servants. When you carry out the desires of the Omnipresent, you are called "servants". At the present time you are not carrying out the desires of the Omnipresent.' R. Akiba replied: 'The Scripture says, *Is it not to deal thy bread to the hungry and bring the poor that are cast out to thy house?* When "dost thou bring *the poor who are cast out to thy house*"? Now; and it says [at the same time], is it not to deal thy bread to the hungry?'[19]

The first inference Twersky derives from this passage is that God has, so to speak, abdicated to people part of a function of his own in order to enable them to transcend mere biological existence, to escape damnation. In the practice of *hesed* one does not merely 'imitate' God, one shares directly in his work.

The second is that we are all equal, all 'children' of God; even our sin and temporary disgrace does not abrogate this relationship.

Third, the fact that God's judgement has condemned an individual to poverty does not allow us to sit in judgement on that person and to desist from giving help; on the contrary, we are challenged to vigorous ethical response to his situation.

Fourth, we cannot 'dismiss a destitute person with a counterfeit expression of faith: "Rely on God . . .! He will help you."'' To the poor, faith, or trust (*bitahon*), means trusting in God's mercy; to the rich, on the other hand, 'it suggests the obligation of sustained and gracious liberality'.[20]

Twersky finally adverts us to the 'dialectic' nature of the halakhic approach to charity. Whilst the essential achievement of *halakhah* is the system of rules by which a principle of faith is anchored into a detailed ethical code, it sought 'to combine the thesis of free, spontaneous giving with the antithesis of soulless, obligatory contribution and produce a composite act which is subjective though quantified, inspired yet regular, intimate yet formal'. This dialectic is indicated in the polarities between the attitude and manner of giving and the determination of the amount of giving, as well as between individual and community responsibility; both of these polarities are delicately handled within *halakhah*.

RULES AND VALUES
Like the rules and values for correct dealing, those for benevolence are expressed in terms of *mitzvot*. Here are some of them.

'After the Lord your God shall you walk . . .' (Deuteronomy 13:5) is interpreted as *imitatio dei*:

> Said Rabbi Hama bar Hanina: How can a person walk after God? Is it not written 'For the Lord your God is a consuming fire' [Deuteronomy 4:24]? But follow God's attributes. As he clothes the naked . . . as he visits the sick . . . comforts the bereaved . . . buries the dead . . . so should you.[21]

'Do not be vengeful, do not bear a grudge' (Leviticus 19:18) is given precise practical application:

> What is vengeance and what is a grudge? If A said to B, 'Lend me your scythe', and he refused, and the next day B asked A for his axe and A said, 'No, I will not lend it to you, just as you would not lend me [your scythe]', that is vengeance. What is a grudge? If A said to B, 'Lend me your axe', and he refused, and

the next day B said to A, 'Lend me your cloak', and A replied, 'Here it is, I am not like you', that is a grudge.[22]

Rav Dimi cited 'If you lend money . . . do not act like a creditor' (Exodus 22:24) to rule that a creditor should take care to keep out of the way of one who owes him money if he knows he is not in a position to pay it back,[23] a ruling endorsed and carefully expressed in the codes:

> It is forbidden to press a borrower to repay when he does not have the means. Moreover, one should avoid being seen by him in case he is embarrassed. . . .[24]

'Thou shalt not harden thy heart, nor shut thy hand from thy needy brother . . . thou shalt surely open thy hand . . .' (Deuteronomy 15:7, 11).

Much of the Jewish philosophy of benevolence is wittily summed up by Zangwill in his novel *The King of the Schnorrers* in the figure of the beggar who, far from humbly requesting favours from those he importunes, maintains his dignity as he condescends to afford them the opportunity to fulfil the great *mitzvah* of benevolence.[25]

3.3 Attitudes to Wealth and Industry

3.3.1 *The pursuit of wealth*

Psalm 24 opens with the words 'The earth is the Lord's and the fulness thereof' (Authorised Version); we and all we possess belong absolutely to God. Poverty, the rabbis taught, 'is a wheel that rolls around the world'.[26] Rags or riches can be anyone's lot, for ownership of material goods is a temporary trusteeship granted by God. The privilege of ownership carries the responsibility of right use.

A decree passed at Usha in Galilee in the second century advises anyone not to give away 'more than a fifth' of his assets at one time and thus become dependent on others;[27] as Maimonides puts it, one who brings poverty on himself by dissipating his resources and becoming dependent on others is a fool.[28] Nevertheless, the rabbis condemned the pursuit of wealth for its own sake as a major evil, responsible through envy and greed for human conflict and for turning people away from God.

Riches and poverty are not intrinsically good or bad: both challenge people's moral commitment. This attitude is rooted in biblical wisdom, as in the prayer of Agur bin Jakeh:

> give me neither poverty nor wealth,
> provide me only with the food I need.
> If I have too much I shall deny thee
> and say, 'Who is the Lord?'
> If I am reduced to poverty, I shall steal
> and blacken the name of my God.
>   (Proverbs 30:8)[29]

Rabbi Simon the son of Yohai, in early-second-century Palestine, debated with Rabbi Ishmael. Ishmael maintained that it was right and proper for a man of piety to engage in a worldly occupation; does not scripture say, 'You shall gather your corn, your wine and your oil' (Deuteronomy 11:14)? But Simon retorted, 'How can a man plough in season, sow in season, reap and thresh and winnow in season, and still devote himself adequately to Torah?'[30] The argument reflects the constant human tension in facing the demands and opportunities of the material world. Ishmael's more worldly attitude predominates in subsequent Jewish teaching, yet Simon's influence endures. Religious teachers persistently proclaim the pursuit of material wealth for its own sake a vice; wealth calls for justification in terms both of its method of creation and of the use to which it is put.

The 'heroes' whose lives are celebrated amongst traditional Jews are not the scientists, writers, musicians, business people and the like who are best known to the 'world outside', but people of learning, of holy life, who give of themselves and of what they possess to those in need. Jeremiah epitomises the ideal:

> Let not the wise man boast of his wisdom
>   nor the valiant of his valour;
> let not the rich man boast of his riches;
> but if any man would boast, let him boast of this.
> that he understands and knows me.

For I am the Lord, I show unfailing love.
I do justice and right upon the earth . . .

(Jeremiah 9:23–4)

Meir Tamari writes that, 'despite certain Talmudic sayings to the contrary, no anticommercial tradition existed in Judaism as existed in Christian social thought',[31] and he cites Aquinas as holding that 'the occupation of the merchant and all that surrounds it is to be justly condemned, since it serves only the lust of gain and Mammon'. This is at the very least an overstatement of the difference, if any, between Jewish views (broadly speaking) and Christian views (broadly speaking). There is a strong tradition in Jewish moralistic literature discouraging individuals from engaging more than absolutely necessary in commerce; one should seek one's basic needs, that is all (*histapkut*). Luzzatto is able to draw on a wide range of rabbinical models for his advocacy of *perishut*, and offers this advice:

> For there is no worldy pleasure upon whose heels some sin does not follow. For example, food and drink when free from all dietary prohibitions are permitted, but filling oneself brings in its wake the putting off of the yoke of Heaven, and drinking of wine brings in its wake licentiousness and other varieties of evil. . . . If he is once made to lack his usual fare he will be painfully aware of the fact and will thrust himself into the heat of the race for possessions and property so that his table will be spread in accordance with his desires. He will thence be drawn on to wrongdoing and theft, and thence to taking oaths and to all the other sins that follow in its wake; and he will depart from the Divine service, from Torah and from prayer. . . .[32]

Admittedly, this stops short of the glorification of poverty – poverty and asceticism[33] are not seen as ends in themselves. Conversely, Aquinas is not alone even in the scholastic tradition in commending liberality and magnificence in commercial life. Pius XI, taking up this aspect of Aquinas's teaching in a 1931 encyclical, says,

> The investment of rather large incomes, so that opportunities for gainful employment may abound, provided that this work is

applied to the production of truly useful products (we gather this from a study of St Thomas Aquinas) is to be considered a noble deed of magnificent virtue, and especially suited to the needs of our time.[34]

Tamari commits an error all too common in religious apologetics of assuming a systematic difference between religions where what in fact exists is an overlapping range of options.

3.3.2   *The dignity of labour*

> Happy are all who fear the Lord,
> who live according to his will.
> You shall eat the fruit of your own labours,
> you shall be happy and you shall prosper.
>   (Psalm 128:1–2)

This Psalm and other biblical passages of similar import gave rise to a bucolic trend in Zionist ideology, secular as well as religious, from the late nineteenth century onwards. The return of the people to the land is seen as the restoration of an idealised biblical scenario of 'each man beneath his vine and beneath his fig-tree' (I King 5:5 and elsewhere), labouring with dignity on the beloved soil, free from exploitation, at peace with God and man. It is a romantic picture owing much to nineteenth-century nostalgia for the simple life and would be rightly scorned by those who actually face the rigours and indignity of unremitting toil in non-industrialised society. In a highly industrialised technological society such as modern Israel the economics of agriculture have undermined the ideal of everyone tilling his own patch of beloved soil.

In any case, the Bible speaks not so much of the dignity of labour as in praise of the contentment which comes to those who are blessed with self-sufficiency, who are free from dependence on the 'gifts of flesh and blood'. Ben Zoma, in the second century, commented, 'Who is rich? He who rejoices in his portion.'[35] Ben Zoma knew that one had to have a portion in which to rejoice. He would have understood well the malaise of the unemployed even where they were not actually suffering extreme deprivation. Their unease lies in the feeling of dependence their situation engenders, in the loss of expectation of fulfilment of the Psalmist's blessing. Social welfare may provide for them, and they do not starve; but they lack what Ben Zoma so aptly calls a 'portion'.

3.3.3 *The Protestant work ethic and 'Faith in the City'*

The rabbis of the Talmud showed appreciation of the craftsman's or artisan's satisfaction in creative work, as well as of that of the agricultural worker whose 'partnership with God' was more obvious. They exhorted people to prayer and faith, for worldly prosperity is the gift of God (cf. Psalm 128). At the same time, they considered carefully what the human contribution should be. The Talmud discusses the responsibility of a father to prepare his son for a worldly occupation. Such now-popular Jewish careers as that of medicine are rejected – the doctor is led to sin by neglecting his poor patients in favour of the rich. Other occupations are variously rejected as unpleasant, as disruptive of family life, as tending to dishonesty or immorality. In the end we are advised to train our sons to be tailors, for, so the rabbis judged, tailoring is an honest, not too demanding trade.[36]

Does Judaism present any parallel with the 'Protestant work ethic'? Max Weber argues that this attitude of thrift and independence had particular appeal to small farmers and craftsmen moving up in society.[37] These were not the typical roles of Jews in most areas in which they lived in the eighteenth and nineteenth century, though there is more than a hint of a similar attitude in the *Torah im derekh eretz*[38] philosophy of the German rabbi Samson Raphael Hirsch (1808–88), who headed a small community in Frankfurt-am-Main in the mid nineteenth century.

A late echo of Hirsch's views was heard in Chief Rabbi Jakobovits's response to the Archbishop of Canterbury's 1985 report on areas of urban deprivation ('Urban Priority Areas') in Britain. The Archbishop's report effectively abandoned the Protestant work ethic, and, instead of calling on the deprived to be thrifty and independent, called on the government and business to pour money and resources into the inner cities; the Chief Rabbi, however, to the delight of the government of the day, put forward Jewish experience in Britain as a paradigm of how the individual could succeed by thrift and determination. There was irony in the spectacle of a Chief Rabbi defending the Protestant work ethic against the Archbishop of Canterbury.[39]

Faith in the City does devote a chapter[40] to the question 'What is the place of theology in our argument?' The answer it tenders perfectly exemplifies the limitations of theology in confronting economic problems. It admits that no theology is required to drive home 'Jesus' call to show compassion to those in need', and it then agonises as to whether

> the acknowledged Christian duty to 'remember the poor' should be confined to personal charity, service and evangelism directed towards individuals, or whether it can legitimately take the form of social and political action aimed at altering the circumstances which appear to cause poverty and distress.[41]

In Jewish teaching there is no question that the Torah requires us to address the institutional causes of poverty as well as individual cases of distress – after all, much of *halakhah* concerns institutional models – and indeed it is hard to conceive that pre-Protestant Christianity, which had not learned a rigorous separation between Church and state, would have taught otherwise.

But, even if we accept that theology should lead to social and political action – as the theologians of liberation, whom we discuss in the next chapter, emphatically do – how do we move from that general principle to specific recommendations of the type which actually emerge from the report? In point of fact, such recommendations are based not on theological principle, but on economic and administrative considerations. By and large, the Chief Rabbi, like many Christian critics, was not challenging the theological generalities, the broad moral theology of the report, but disputing its social analysis and the predicted effect of its recommendations.

3.4 Competitive Enterprise and Traditional Religious Teaching

In a very obvious sense, Copernicus's dethronement of earth from its centrality in the universe, and the geological and biological demonstrations of organic evolution in the eighteenth and nineteenth centuries, shattered the world picture of traditional Christianity and Judaism. It is less obvious that the understanding of wealth creation and economic competition expressed in the works of Adam Smith and others seriously undermined traditional religious teaching on how people ought to conduct their affairs. It is a matter of taste whether one regards *The Wealth of Nations* as a new, capitalist revolution or as the culmination of the evolution which had set aside the prohibition of usury and replaced feudal by mercantilist economy in Europe.

3.4.1 Industrial growth, technological innovation

Mediaeval and early-modern rabbis exemplify a wide range of attitudes to technological innovation and industrial growth. In the twelfth century Rabbi Abraham bar Hiyya published many scientific works and was one of the most important figures in the movement which made the Jews of Provence, Italy and Spain the intermediaries between Muslim science and the Christian world, seeding the Age of Discovery and our whole modern scientific and industrial development. On the other hand, Isaac Abravanel (1437–1508), despite living at the height of the great Age of Discovery, preferred the simple life. Drawing more on the Roman philosopher Seneca than on Jewish tradition, Abravanel pictured the age of the Messiah as one of bucolic simplicity, without houses, ships, or even organised government, for he saw all government as the instrument of despotism.[42]

3.4.2 Wealth creation, self-interest and social well-being

The Industrial Revolution was not a single invention or event but an accelerating process of innovation, and so brought a new understanding of the concept of the *creation*, rather than the *amassing*, of wealth. The traditional concern of religious teachers is with the distribution of wealth – with envy, with greed, with extortion and injustice, all of which bear upon the way wealth is apportioned amongst people. Wrongful distribution is the subject matter of their sermons and moral judgements.

It was first clearly perceived in the eighteenth century that, subject to certain necessary restraints, the pursuit of self-interest resulted in the enhancement of social well-being. According to Adam Smith the pursuit of self-interest, far from undermining the moral fabric of society, as all the religions seem to have taught, resulted in the maximisation of social well-being. The idea is central to Smith's economic philosophy, but it is as well to remember that this classical advocate of *laissez-faire* economics also formulated the classical expression of the need for appropriate government intervention:

> The sovereign has only three duties to attend to . . . first, the duty of protecting the society from the violence and invasion of independent societies; secondly, the duty of protecting, as far as possible, every member of the society from the injustice or oppression of every other member of it, or the duty of establishing an exact administration of justice; and, thirdly, the duty of erecting and maintaining certain public works and certain institutions, which it can never be for the interest of any individual, or small number of individuals, to erect and maintain, because the profit could never repay the expense to any individual or small number of individuals, though it may frequently do much more than repay it to a great society.[43]

Much of the subsequent economic history of Western countries has been bound up with the manner and extent in which these duties should be implemented.

Karl Marx rejected Smith's concept that the pursuit of self-interest results in the maximisation of social well-being. Marx argued that the 'dominant mode of production' – that is, the ownership of the means of production – meant that 'inevitably' (one of his favourite but most dangerous terms) workers would be 'exploited' (another dangerous key term) by entrepreneurs.

Those who seek a formal refutation of Marxist economics should consult specialist works; my purpose is not to demonstrate the soundness or otherwise of any particular economic theory, but to assess whether or not theological premises are relevant to such a demonstration. The next chapter will assess whether a choice of economic 'system' – say, capitalist or socialist – can be determined on theological premises; for now we merely ask how traditional theology, with its antipathy to the pursuit of wealth, can come to terms with the idea that the pursuit of self-interest results in the enhancement, if not maximisation, of social well-being. Let Adam Smith again be the spokesman:

> [an individual who] intends only his own gain is led as if by an

invisible hand to provide an end which was no part of his intention. Nor is it always the worse for the society that it was not part of it. By pursuing his own interests, he frequently promotes that of the society more effectually than when he really intends to promote it. I have never known much good done by those who affected to trade for the public good.[44]

The rejection of communism in much of Central and Eastern Europe adds to the evidence suggesting that the nations with the freest markets have produced, with the surplus wealth they have generated, the best living conditions for their citizens. Traditional theology would have forecast only disaster from such unchaining of self-interest.

It is a profound and disturbing challenge for traditional theology, which has constantly preached the evils of avarice and the evil or at least irrelevance of technology, to see that the well-regulated avarice of free enterprise, coupled with industrial progress, has been far more successful than any previous movement in society in providing precisely those good things that religion demands – care for the poor and the sick, education, housing and sanitation, benefits for the retired and the unemployed, and the other things modern Western society regards as universal human rights.

3.4.3 *Moral aims of economic activity*

Even those religious teachers who decry material pursuits as evil agree that it is right to feed the hungry and to clothe the naked and to administer medicine to the sick; they would say that their own spirituality is enhanced through conferring material benefits upon others.

One must not lightly conclude that because the creation of wealth enhances our ability to do better things for our fellow humans it is in itself a desirable activity and it does not matter how it is pursued. The end does not justify any and every means by which it may be attained. There are conflicts between industrial justice and economic efficiency, and hence a need for balancing priorities.

The religious backing available in Judaism for recognition of the role of the industrialist and entrepreneur in society is allied with a call for the thorough moralisation of commercial activities at personal, national and international level. Both law and education have their part to play in bringing this about.

Religious-based ethics may help clarify the broad moral aims of economic policy. Are we satisfied with the utilitarian outlook generally assumed by economists until very recently? Is it enough to seek the 'greatest happiness of the greatest number', as Hume, Bentham and Mill would have it? Should we perhaps recast our economic theories to achieve the 'maximin' aims outlined by Rawls?[45] Rawls argues that the true principles of justice are those that individuals would choose if they did not know what chance they had of being born rich or poor, healthy or unhealthy, intelligent or stupid; on this basis, he calls for higher taxation and greater spending on health and education, with the less-privileged members of society the principal beneficiaries. Or is the common assumption that it is a good thing to allow all people the maximum options to 'fulfil their potentialities' intelligible, let alone morally sound?

Specific social policy issues will be discussed in section 3.6.

3.5   In Business

In section 3.2.1 we reviewed the demand for integrity in dealings between individuals. Our classical sources were formulated with such small-scale operations in mind. As we move to consider the operations of large companies the definition of integrity becomes more complex, and it is not always clear how and whether to extrapolate from the earlier sources.

3.5.1   *Managers*

The manager, whether a sole trader, a partner, or a director of a limited company or state-owned corporation, has a special range of responsibilities. According to the size and nature of the enterprise he will be concerned with some or all of the following.

1   Integrity, in the narrow sense of honesty, openness and reliability.

2 Environment – how does the product affect the environment?

3 Product safety.

4 Employees' welfare, for instance the provision of sports facilities and health screening.

5 Workplace safety.

6 Confidentiality, including ensuring the security of company records; refraining from using confidentially acquired knowledge for personal gain, as in 'insider trading'.

7 The 'hard sell'. Clearly, all advertisements should be balanced and accurate. But how does one assess promotional techniques? At what point is one bringing undue pressure or persuasion to bear on a potential customer?

8 Conflict of interests, for instance balancing the interest of the firm against some private benefit.

9 Prioritising claims of shareholders, employees, customers, suppliers, society in general (e.g. the environment).

10 Costing – not only balancing the interests of shareholder, employee and customer, but also assessing social and environmental costs.

Some of these matters will be discussed in section 3.6 under the heading of social policy. Some which do not fall under that heading will be examined now.

3.5.2 Shareholders

No one should actively acquire shares in an enterprise before checking that its activities are conducted on an acceptable moral basis. Involvement, even without direct responsibility, in a dishonest or otherwise wrongful enterprise is complicity in wrongdoing. Even passively leading others to take part is 'putting a stumbling-block before the blind'.[46]

Shareholders with a controlling interest, as owners of the company, would normally exercise their responsibility through the appointment and monitoring of suitable professional management. Shareholders without a controlling interest have only to ensure that they relinquish their shares if the company fails to meet adequate moral standards.

People who promote 'ethical trusts' and the like must beware not only of self-righteousness and hypocrisy but also of a peculiar kind of 'hard sell' which unfairly plays on the emotions of their clients. They must also be sure that by promoting their trust as 'ethical' they do not imply that other trusts, not so labelled, are not ethical.

3.5.3   *Employees*

Employees' rights will be referred to in several parts of section 3.6. Here we note that employees have responsibilities arising from their contract of employment, and the additional moral responsibility of doing the best job they reasonably can, even where this is not contractually enforceable.

They are morally obliged also to consider the nature of the enterprise in which they are involved. This leads to charming dilemmas. What should a worker at a cigarette factory do if he becomes convinced that (a) smoking cigarettes is harmful and (b) there is no other form of employment open to him by which he could sustain his family?

This is not the only dilemma to confront the morally inclined worker. Suppose it is the custom in his workplace to engage in some petty dishonesty, such as helping oneself to stores or signing on on behalf of colleagues in order to mislead payroll management about the time actually spent at work? On the one hand, one should be honest. On the other hand, one should be loyal to one's workmates. More than that, one would not wish, for instance, to cause a fellow worker to lose his job and thereby inflict hardship on his dependants.

3.5.4   *Buyer, seller, restrictive practices*

A business is not, of course, run solely for the benefit of employer and employee. No customer, no business. A very large part of rabbinic writings is concerned with buyer–seller relations, with the ethics as well as the law of contract.[47]

The Jewish communities dependent for their existence on guarantees of protection afforded by local rulers were constrained to impose a series of restrictions, the *herem ha-yishuv*, on non-members of the community who wished to become residents, in order to protect their own members from the effects of trade competition by newcomers. Rabbinic law had long recognised the need to protect traders from ruinous competition. Later authorities try to reconcile this protectionism with the public interest, as where a new competitor is ready to provide goods at a lower price than the one with the established right.[48]

3.5.5 *Priorities: subordination of religious decision to market regulation*

The rabbis occasionally modified a religious requirement in order to benefit the public economically. For instance, in the regulations governing the institutuion of public fasts for rain it is laid down that special fasts may not be ordained on Mondays on Thursdays, the normal market days, lest traders, anticipating people's anxiety to buy food for the termination of the fast, would raise prices.[49]

There are clear priorities. A religious decision may be subordinated to market regulation only if (a) the market regulation itself serves some higher, religious purpose, for instance the prevention of profiteering, and (b) the religious decision is of a category clearly defined as minor.

3.5.6 *Banker and client*

Those responsible for banking decisions have not only the usual responsibilities of management at their level but a group of special responsibilities arising from the fact that they handle money rather than commodities. Similar considerations apply to other financial operators, such as stockbrokers and investment-trust managers.

How should a banker advise a client ('I go to the bank for advice on my money, not on my morals')? Assuming there is no illegality, does 'good advice' mean 'profitable', or 'profitable and moral', and does it include 'with due consideration for the benefit of human-kind and the environment'?

Under what conditions should a banker extend or refuse credit or credit facilities? How should he weigh up the interests of the bank, the customer, other potential borrowers, the general public, the shareholders?

Are banks acting morally by promoting loans with no other consideration than ensuring repayment?

What is the morality of marketing credit cards on the basis of the company giving a small percentage of their profit to charities? Is this unfair exploitation of people's moral susceptibilities, and would it not be morally better simply to charge a lower rate for use of the card?

Orthodox Jews and Muslims object in principle to lending on interest. But, if charging interest be allowed, what moral constraints are there on the rate of interest? Is there a valid distinction between interest and usury? We return to this at the end of Chapter 4.

3.6   Social Policy

In section 3.4.3 we discussed the overall aims of economic activity, and noted how industrial justice and economic efficiency might conflict. We now look at specific issues of social policy, and to provide an overview of the sort of topic involved let us first set down in order the items listed in the proposed Social Charter of the European Economic Community:[50]

1 *Mobility*. Free movement and equal treatment for workers throughout the European Community.
2 *Work conditions*. Better working conditions, annual paid holiday, weekly break from work.
3 *Wages*. Decent wages, restrictions on withholding of wages, free placement services.
4 *Social protection*. Adequate social security for the unemployed.
5 *Freedom of association and collective bargaining*. Right to join a trade union (or not to join) and to make collective agreements and to strike.
6 *Training*. Vocational training.
7 *Equality*. Equal treatment and opportunity for men and women; information, consultation and participation of workers.
8 *Health and safety*. Health and safety at work and the protection of children and adolescents.
9 *Retirement*. Decent standard of living for the retired.
10 *Disablement*. Helping the disabled achieve integration at work, at home and in the community.

Looking at this from the point of view of traditional Jewish religious sources, the following observations may be made.

Worker mobility, in the modern European sense, was not an issue. However, people did move, often as a result of expulsions, and as we saw in section 3.5.4 the *herem ha-yishuv* was devised to protect the rights of local workers against those of immigrants. This 'protectionism' has to be set against the gross interference in the market by Christian authorities who (a) restricted the Jewish population and the number of its workers, and (b) did not allow Jews to compete freely in the markets. As soon as competition became free the *herem ha-yishuv* was dropped.

On the broad issues of *work conditions*, proper wages, prompt payment and equal treatment (though not, in the pre-modern sources, for women) there is no doubt as to the positive stance of the *halakhah*. Placement services,[51] training, and even help for the disabled find precedents (see section 3.6.2).

Vocational training was in the talmudic period regarded as a parental responsibility – 'one who does not teach his son a trade, it is as if he taught him robbery'.[52] With the development of community structures came *taqqanot* (local ordinances), which enlarged the base for this responsibility; in modern conditions, it is logical to extend it to large employers.

Holidays are hardly new to a religion which invented the Sabbath and the sabbatical year, nor is retirement a new concept when scripture itself (Numbers 4) set fifty as the age of retirement for Levites. In their modern sense, holiday and retirement provision would be treated as contractual obligations which, nowadays, are part of the 'normal' contract of employment, and as such enforceable according to local usage.

There seems no clear traditional provision for consultation and *participation of workers* in decision-making.

The Mishnah reports that a certain Rabbi Yohanan ben Matthew sent his son to engage some workers, and the son contracted to provide them with food. 'Even if you feed them as Solomon feasted in his time [of glory],' remarked the rabbi, 'you will not have fulfilled your obligation, for they are the children of Abraham, Isaac and Jacob.'[53] The halakhic implication of this statement is that one needs to spell out the terms of a contract between employer and employees clearly and unambiguously. Also significant is its stress on the dignity of the worker. The contract is viewed as limiting the natural right of the worker to that which is economically practicable, though never below the minimum stipulated in Torah and rabbinic law; but the right is recognised, and affords a basis for the contemporary demand for improved working conditions and contractual arrangements.

There follow observations on some specific topics within the range of social policy.

3.6.1 *Unions and strikes*

The emergence of guilds in Central Europe had the effect of excluding Jews from all productive labour, for guilds were established as religious fraternities with patron saints; for instance, in Austria in 1316 Jews were excluded from the manufacture of clothes. (This, and their exclusion from ownership of land, were major factors in driving Jews into money-lending.)

Though the older sources are meagre on questions of organised labour, more recent rabbis have developed Torah law in relation to unions and strikes. Rav Kook (1865–1935) maintained that the strike was a legitimate means of forcing an employer either to submit a labour grievance to demand or arbitration or to adhere to a labour arbitration decision. According to the late Rabbi Moshe Feinstein,

A majority vote by members of a union to strike binds the decision on all members of the union, including the dissenting minority. While both union demands and the decision to strike are not binding on non-union members, the striking union members are entitled to judicial protection against the intrusion of strike-breakers. Offer to work for less advantageous terms than the demands of the striking workers amounts to encroaching upon the latter's livelihood and is therefore prohibited. . . .

Rabbi Tchursh rules that

Strikes endangering the public health and safety . . . cannot be countenanced under any circumstances. Labour disputes in such industries must, therefore, be settled by means of compulsory arbitration.[54]

3.6.2 *Labour relations*

This is how Edward Zipperstein sums up the *halakhah* on employer – employee relations:

An employer must not impose superfluous hardship on employees, nor may he demand that the workers exceed their capabilities or strength . . . local custom is a prime consideration in many instances.

Workers must be enabled to come home prior to sunset on the Sabbath and holidays. The pregnant maidservant is to be extended special consideration. . . .

An employer is not permitted to embarrass, insult, belittle or degrade an employee. An employer is not permitted to withhold a worker's pay in order to recover a debt. . . . Promptness of (wage) payment is stressed by Biblical edict (Leviticus 19:13).

Providing employment is a most significant form of benevolence. Placing a person's job in jeopardy is considered an evil act. In hiring an employee, preference is to be granted to the applicant less capable of performing the task, since the more capable person will no doubt be able to obtain employment, but the employment possibilities of the less capable may be questionable.

For compensation (sc. payment) received, the worker is expected to render proper, capable and efficient service to the employer. The employee is not permitted to waste time, slack off in his performance interrupt his work, leave his work, or engage in unnecessary time-consuming conversations. . . . Jewish law does not favour the protection of any particular group, employer, or employee, rich or poor. Equal rights and justice is demanded from all parties.[55]

But how do we move from the talmudic and mediaeval sources summarised by Zipperstein to the realities of contemporary life? The generalities are easy enough – we can go on proclaiming that employers have responsibilities to employees and vice versa – but what about the specifics?

Perhaps within the framework of the mediaeval Jewish community it was feasible, when hiring an employee, to grant preference 'to the applicant less capable of performing the task'; is this still possible or even desirable when we move from the small 'family-type' business, and a situation of assured employment for the more skilled worker, to today's large, impersonal firms, skill-based efficiency, and serious unemployment? We have to recognise socio-economic changes, and instead of slavishly applying a rule in a very different situation learn how to abstract that which is relevant. For instance, the rule mentioned might be regarded as a prototype of 'affirmative action', or of the sort of requirement which now exists in law in Britain that businesses over a certain size must employ a minimum quota of disabled people. However, it is no light thing to make these extrapolations to different circumstances, and there are many other ways in which the earlier rules might be interpreted and applied.

3.6.3 *Public welfare provision*

Having agreed in principle that workers and others should benefit from improved health care and the like, it is still necessary to decide whether it should be paid for out of public money (national or local taxes) or private sources (insurance schemes paid for by employer, employee, or a combination). There is ample precedent in the responsa and in the *taqqanot* of mediaeval communities to support the notion that people might be communally taxed for 'charity', under which heading most of what now goes for welfare would classified.[56] However, it might be argued that the main thing is that provision be made, and the decision as to what sources it comes from should be decided in the light of what is most efficient in the particular context.

3.7 Who is Responsible?

There are three levels upon which ethics can be implemented: that of government through the laws it enacts, that of the voluntary code adopted by a profession or organisation for its self-regulation, and that of individual personal choice.

These levels form a continuum. Any given society at a given time may seek to influence a specific form of behaviour at any of these levels. For instance, 'insider trading' has only recently, and only in certain countries, become subject to legal restrictions; previously, and even now in other countries, it was a matter of personal ethics, or at most subject to a voluntary professional code. How much and by whom ways of behaviour should be controlled is one of the major issues of politics. Anarchists seek the maximum personal responsibility and the minimum control by authority, whilst at the other extreme religious governments have sought to determine virtually every aspect of their citizens' lives, even in very private matters of a kind which would not matter to a secular despot.

Voluntary pressure groups are, in contemporary Western society, a major influence on the three levels of decision, and it is often through their campaigning that a particular ethical issue is moved from one level to another of personal, professional and legislative. The movement can be in either direction. Pressure groups, through their influence on public opinion and through that on legislators and the judiciary, have brought it about that homosexuality and blasphemy are by and large, in Britain, matters of personal ethic; at the same time, environmental misdeeds, which were previously matters of private conscience, have become statutory offences.

Support can easily be found, in traditional Jewish sources, for the interplay of levels of responsibility. Legislation, in Bible, Talmud and mediaeval and later orthodox practice, extends to realms, such as those of sexual relationships, or of religious ritual, which the modern legislator would regard as more appropriate to the private sphere. Still, there is a private sphere where ethical demands are made without the backing of law, as we saw in section 3.2.1 (under 'Beyond the Law'). And there is ample scope for voluntary professional codes, from the version of the Hippocratic oath, regulating medical practice, in the so-called Book of Asaph,[57] to the regulations of communal institutions such as the *hevrah qadishah* (Burial Society) and Welfare Board.

A vast number of voluntary codes on business ethics exist in Britain today, principally to do with advertising and marketing. CABE (the Christian Association of Business Executives) produced an excellent general code in 1974,[58] and one might have hoped that Jewish businessmen in Britain would follow suit. But perhaps they have taken to heart CABE's statement that their 'Code is respectfully offered to men of all creeds and none', seeing that the Christian view of the nature of man and society 'is consistent, if not congruent, with the views of all who observe the more obvious facts of our common humanity'.

3.8 Social Efficiency

Resources are never adequate to fulfil all of everybody's demands. This is not because there are too many people and too little to go

round, but because, so long as there are at least two people in the
world, A might want what B has. That is why the Ten Commandments do not merely enjoin us not to steal, but go on to prohibit
coveting; we may already have a house, or a spouse, but still want
our neighbour's house or spouse.

So, resources are 'scarce', and have to be allocated.

Amongst the resources which are scarce are not only manufactured products, but labour and services of all kinds, quality of life,
and environmental factors such as healthy air and pleasant sur-
roundings. Classical economics tended to omit from its calculations environmental factors not directly involved in the process
of production, but nowadays they are often considered; thus the
costs for building a rail link from the Channel Tunnel into central
London include not only the acquisition of buildings and land on
the route and the labour and materials for the track but further
amounts to avoid environmental degradation – for instance, for
routing the track underground rather than through the countryside.

But there are also purely 'social' factors which have to be calcu-
lated. Still on the subject of railway lines there are many situations
where, if one were to ignore social factors, it would be cost-
effective to close down a particular line, perhaps because it oper-
ates in remote country with few passengers; but if it proves
possible to quantify the social effects of axing the line it may
transpire that the overall loss from closure is greater than the cost
of keeping it open. The question may still remain of who should
pay for the line – the passengers who use the rest of the system,
the local authority, the central government, or perhaps tourists
whose enjoyment is enhanced by the working presence of the few
who live in that remote region.

The aim of any economic policy must be to ensure the best
possible allocation of resources, including those of environment
and quality of life. In fact, even those religious-minded people who
think we would all be better off if we had fewer material goods
rather than more work on this assumption; they differ from standard economists only in placing a higher premium on, for instance, facilities for meditation than on improved diet, housing,
medical care, travel and entertainment. Even those who see this
world only as a preparation for the next seek to ensure the optimal
allocation of resources bearing in mind the needs of the next
world.

Certainly, theology interacts with economic policy in evaluating the goods that people might choose or be encouraged to choose. This presents us with a political dilemma. Should economic policy be formulated in terms of theological evaluations of goods, or should theology have its impact on economic policy indirectly, through its influence in forming public attitudes and desires which in turn affect market forces? To me it is obvious that the latter method is preferable, for unlike the former it allows freedom of conscience to the individual.

Wealth creation means that it is often possible for somebody to get more without depriving anyone else of anything; for instance, when Jacques Cousteau invented a new 'commodity', the possibility of cheap underwater swimming, far from depriving anyone of anything he was creating new possibilities for large numbers of people. Ideally, all changes in the economy should be of this nature – that is, they should make at least some consumers (of manufactured articles, services, environmental amenities, rewards in the next world, or whatever people wish and expect to consume) better off without making any others worse off. When resources are allocated in such a way that, apart from the creation of new resources, nobody can be better off without someone else becoming worse off, we refer to the distribution of resources as a 'Pareto-optimal allocation'.

Technical and behavioural imperfections as well as defective flow of information cause disequilibrium in the market, so authorities and mechanisms have to be designed to achieve the closest approximation to Pareto optimality. Technical imperfections include external effects such as pollution, the provision of public goods (i.e. those where the addition of a consumer does not reduce the quantity available to others), as well as economies of scale. Behavioural imperfections which undermine efficient competition include excess supply and demand, or monopoly situations.[59]

A major aim of economic policy has to be to achieve Pareto optimality on a global scale. Such a project is bedevilled by political rivalries, protectionism, and perhaps most of all by the fact that the world's countries do not start at an equal or even comparable economic base. We shall now glance at some of the problems which confront any attempt to achieve the free-market conditions within which Pareto optimality would be possible, whilst 'cushioning' transitional effects on the less well-off economies.

3.8.1   *'We are poor because you are rich'*

This is how Isa el Mahdi, leader of the landless poor of Africa, confronts Claire Fitzgerald, Commissioner for Development for the European Community, in the BBC fictional drama *The March*, broadcast on 20 May 1990 for 'One World' week, Reminding her that many Europeans spend more on keeping their cats alive than is spent on keeping Africans alive, el Mahdi proposes a simple solution: 'You can come and live here. I could come and live in your house.'

In similar vein, Marc Ellis, following a popular liberation-theology line, writes, 'Capitalism, as practised, may represent affluence for the few; it means unemployment and poverty for many'. Ellis at least recognises that not capitalism *per se*, but malpractice, contributes to Third World poverty.

If one makes the erroneous assumption that underlies most traditional religious talk and much uninformed talk today – that the finite amount of wealth in the world is already all in the hands of individuals – it would follow that amassing wealth could only be done at the expense of somebody else in whose hands the wealth already existed. If it were impossible to make anyone richer without making someone else poorer in the process, we would be right to blame the rich for the poverty of the poor – the rich would be holding on to wealth which ought, in simple fairness, to be in the hands of the poor.

In our discussion of social efficiency at the beginning of section 3.8 we did indeed suggest that Pareto optimality, in which no one can be allocated more resources without someone else being allocated less, is an ideal at which economic policy should be directed. But Pareto optimality only applies, strictly speaking, in a closed system within which additional wealth is not generated. When more is generated this need not be to anyone's loss, though it creates a new set of goods for allocation, and Pareto optimalisation will indicate appropriate reallocations.

It is misleading, if not tendentious, to blame Third World deprivation on the riches of the industrialised world. Many theories have been advanced to explain why the poor nations are poor.[60] One hears the *cri du coeur* of the desperately poor who see what Europeans spend to keep their cats alive, and it is not too far-fetched to say that, too often, the poor have been 'robbed' of their labour. The great danger of this metaphor, though, is that it points to the wrong solution, redistribution of goods, rather than to beneficial paths such as genuinely free trade, the elimination of corruption and the control of population.

3.9 Macro-Economic Questions

Classical Jewish sources were not in a position to consider the ethics of trans-national commercial activities. Yet the general tenor of Jewish ethics is such as to make it necessary nowadays to give the most serious attention to such problems as the following.

3.9.1   *Rich and poor nations: debt crisis*

Should one lend sums of money to underdeveloped countries or extend repayment terms, when this is likely to lead to long-term indebtedness?

3.9.2   *Multinationals*

How should the activities of multinational corporations be controlled? The problem here is to allocate responsibilities between the corporation itself, and local and international jurisdictions. Unfortunately theologians, environmentalists and Marxists have conspired to regard multinational corporations as sinister entities wilfully despoiling the planet and robbing the poor. On the contrary, multinational corporations are the most efficient means yet devised of producing and distributing goods and services; sadly, the world's political and legal structures are not always adequate to the task of international regulation. It is governments and the international community, not corporations, who have the primary responsibility for deciding how much rain forest it is acceptable to chop down for timber; the corporations will perforce obey the regulations imposed on them.

3.9.3   *Different countries, different conditions*

Should one exploit cheap foreign labour or materials? If not, how can one decide the 'right' wage level for a foreign, and different, economy? Some economists, notably the Friedmans,[61] have argued resolutely for a totally unrestricted international market, and have persuaded some governments to follow them part of the way, but none to be entirely consistent (see section 3.9.4). Theologians and moralists tend to call for everyone to be paid the same everywhere, or else for preference to be given to the poor – certainly for intervention of some kind, none of it very practical or likely to be of long-term benefit. Clearly, it is economics rather than theology or moral philosophy which has to decide how to create the most efficient market. Unfortunately, economists cannot agree on this, and the moralists are left with a double task: first, to choose, perhaps arbitrarily, which school of economic thought to follow; and, secondly, to decide how to modify the recommendations of that school to make special provision at least for those in urgent need, but without upsetting the market mechanism. Unfortunately, this does not allow for rational decision-making.

3.9.4 *Protectionism*

How does one extrapolate guidelines on the balance between protectionism and free trade to the international situation?

Britain subsidises food production and actually produces a net surplus of food. Government subsidies have been used to support a range of nationalised industries and continue, if disguised as tax and other concessions, to subsidize the production of armaments. This follows from a political decision, not necessarily overt, that self-sufficiency in food and defence are essential to the nation's independence.

The Friedmans have argued stridently against government subsidies to industry, and in particular against farming subsidies. For people in Britain, where Milton Friedman has influenced government policy, it is bewildering that the government spent £2000 million on farm subsidies in 1989 whilst urging the Russians to put up the price of bread! At last, on 11 July 1990, the leaders of the world's seven richest industrialised nations agreed in Houston on the principle of reduction in European farm subsidies, though specific timetables were not set. Yet there is probably no measure, and no aid programme, which would do so much to help Third World and East European economies as the rapid achievement of world free trade in agriculture; and, if Friedman's analysis is right, the short-term dislocation caused to the West European economies would be more than compensated for by removal of trade barriers.

3.9.5 Cartels (price-fixing)

When an OPEC (Organisation of Petroleum-Exporting Countries) cartel quadrupled the price of oil in 1967 the obvious motive was political blackmail against Israel. For all the talk of an 'oil weapon', the actual weapon wielded was not oil at all but the power of the cartel.

Many countries have adopted anti-trust or anti-monopoly legislation, and one of the main arguments against nationalisation has been that it leads to inefficient monopolies. The Friedmans[62] argue that anti-trust laws are of doubtful merit in preserving an open market, and that the real quarantee of free competition is an open international market. This argument fails on the planetary level, for in the absence of political intervention what is to prevent world monopolies from forming? OPEC indeed seemed to approximate that position in 1967, and industries such as the manufacture of aeroplanes or of silicon chips could conceivably become world monopolies if there were no anti-trust legislation. We do not as yet have interplanetary competition which might limit the power of an 'earth monopoly'.

It would thus seem that there is a strong economic argument for intervention to prevent conglomerates growing to world monopoly size, or even to a size comparable with the largest effective market. Whether there is a moral argument is unclear. A moral argument would have to take the form of an objection to a private person or group achieving a certain level of wealth or power, and the level at which private wealth or power becomes morally unacceptable would not be easy to define. Is it morally wrong for an individual to have a monopoly, or does such a position only become morally wrong when it is abused? If it is wrong even to have a monopoly, why have religious leaders not objected in the past when kings, princes and high prelates exercised monopolies? When Isaiah castigated those who 'join house to house and field to field' (5:8) was he objecting to wealth *per se* or to rapacity?

3.9.6   *Boycotts and the arms trade*

Are there states with whom it would be wrong to trade because their social or political policies are so repugnant? South Africa is the common example, but there are surely countries today with far more odious regimes. Should France or the United States, for example, refuse to co-operate with a measure such as the Arab boycott of Israel, to the possible detriment of its own economy?

Unfortunately, the moral high ground has often been taken by people who are highly selective in their political judgements, and political and economic pressures combine to make governments much more ready to 'bully' small countries, such as Cuba, than large ones, such as the Soviet Union. But there would seem to be a strong moral case for the application of economic pressure where appropriate and feasible, and an even stronger one for limiting the spread of arms, even though these actions interfere with the operation of the free market.

3.9.7   *Limits to growth, pollution, population*

These topics were dealt with in Chapter 2, on conservation, and population growth is again dealt with in section 4.3, on Brazil.

4

Economic Topics

4.1 Liberation Theology and Economics

4.1.1 Liberation theology and Judaism

Liberation theology is a reform movement within the Roman Catholic Church, rooted in the soil and experience of Latin America. When those of us 'outside' seek to apply its insights to our own very different situations we must not merely echo its powerful vocabulary; we must carefully take stock of realities both in South America and in our own areas of direct concern.

Some interest has been shown by Jews in the theology of liberation: witness the books by Dan Cohn-Sherbok[1] and Marc Ellis[2] and a dedicated issue of the journal *Christian Jewish Relations*.[3] In 1968 – towards the end of the 'revolutionary decade' – the Latin American Bishops' Conference (CELAM) met at Medellín and called for Christians to be involved in the transformation of society, thus unwittingly providing a Magna Carta to the liberation-theology movement. Not much later, in January 1975, the World Council of Churches and the International Jewish Committee on Interreligious Consultations – neither of them Catholic or predominantly South American – met in London for a dialogue of Jews and Christians on the concept of power, at which many of the themes of the theology of liberation were aired. I cite the words of the Israeli professor Shlomo Avineri on that occasion:[4]

> The just struggle for liberation unfortunately has been often too narrowly conceived, as if it dealt merely with the *transfer* of power, while power itself remained a constant factor. Such a purely political conception of liberation . . . can become self-defeating and may result in the mere substitution of one class of masters by another: that this substitution may mean a change in the racial background of the masters may perhaps enhance the legitimacy of the new rulers; nevertheless it cannot solve the dilemma of power, since society has not yet created new

71

structures that should themselves be free from the dichotomy between masters and slaves.

Professor Avineri is aware that, in Ellis's words, 'we often confuse empowerment with liberation'.

Liberation theologians rely heavily on the central biblical themes of freedom from oppression, justice, and the role of the saving remnant. Their extensive use of Tanakh ('Old Testament') and the concern for the 'real', historical Jesus – a concern found in the writings of Leonardo Boff and other liberation theologians – echo in Jewish hearts. As against that, there is the danger (certainly recognised by Boff) that Christian typological exegesis will cancel the 'bond' established with Judaism through the Hebrew scriptures; it is too easy for Christians to read the 'Old Testament' as having no significance other than as preparing the way for the 'New'. There is also the pitfall in which many have stumbled of reading from Genesis to Exodus 12 and then skipping to Matthew as if nothing – not Torah at Sinai, nor the land of Israel – came between.

Some have stressed the emphasis on praxis as parallel with traditional Jewish emphasis on *halakhah* rather than theology. Perhaps, but then Karl Marx spoke of the 'self-emancipation of the proletariat through consciousness-forming praxis', and rather more liberation theologians have read Marx than have read the Talmud.

The new attitude to poverty is akin to the Jewish. Where Christians in the past have tended to make a virtue of poverty, Gutiérrez and others claim that the poverty idealised by Christians is not the dehumanising lack of material goods, but humility of spirit and commitment to solidarity with the poor.

BIBLICAL MODELS

Liberation theologians have made much use of the Exodus and prophetic paradigms of the Hebrew scriptures. Let us see what these paradigms are and what might be their relevance to critiques of the 'socio-economic system'.

(a)   The Exodus paradigm   There have been some very sophisticated analyses of Exodus theology. It would be fascinating to compare, for instance, John Pawlikowski's four-stage model of liberation (faith in God's saving acts in history, communitarian

spirituality, link between liberation and Torah and *mitzvot*, movement from political to inner freedom) with Leon Klenicki's model,
based on S. R. Hirsch's philosophy, of 'overcoming inner and
outer bondage' (experience of God's redeeming presence, freedom
to become a covenantal community in one's own land, the service
of God through Torah and *mitzvot*): all the same elements appear to
be present.

Our task is, fortunately, a simpler one. What essentials emerge
from a plain reading of the Exodus text? How does the account in
Exodus of the bondage of the Hebrew slaves in Egypt correspond
with the state of the desperately poor in Brazil?

The Hebrew slaves in Egypt were an oppressed class. They were
in some sense 'conscientised' by Moses; they were freed from
bondage; they were brought to Sinai and given a 'message' there
by God.

All this suggests some parallels with the South American situation, but there are significant differences.

The Israelites in Egypt were a minority, unlike the masses of the
poor in Latin America. They were foreigners, which on the one
hand was an alienating factor contributing to the sense of home-
lessness and deprivation, but on the other hand meant that, unlike
the South American poor, they did not have the experience of
being persecuted primarily by their own brethren. The 'conscientisation' they received through Moses had nothing to do with 'the
causes of poverty', but centred on their identity as children of
Abraham, Isaac and Jacob, with whom God had bound himself by
the promise of a land of their own. The 'freedom' promised and
given was a freedom from subjection to the taskmasters of Egypt.
The 'message' at Sinai was a detailed constitution for their society;
it is significant that the 'new order for society' – the Torah – was
proclaimed by God himself, and did *not* arise from the 'basic
community' of Israelites. Indeed, the Israelites themselves seem to
have done very little at any stage to bring about their own redemption; God – not the community, not even Moses – is the prime actor
on the stage, and the very name of Moses is omitted from the
account of the Exodus read at Passover.

The Exodus text of the story of the Egyptian bondage does not
offer an explicit paradigm for a critique on 'the causes of poverty'.
Exodus does not seem concerned with explaining causes, other
than historical ones, for the oppression. And when Ezekiel (16:4–7)
takes up the theme he offers no critique of the Egyptian economic

system, only a condemnation of Israel's sins. Theologians of liberation do not engage in scathing denunciation of the sins of the South American poor, attesting it as the cause of their oppression, and quite rightly so; though surely the ancient Israelites were no more if no less sinful than the present-day South American poor.

It is true that the Israelites were not 'conscientised' to their situation before Moses and Aaron came, and only as they became more aware did they 'cry out unto the Lord'. But, as already noted, the 'conscientisation' they received through Moses had to do not with 'the causes of poverty', but with their identity as children of Abraham, Isaac and Jacob to whom God had made his promise. It is legitimate for us to argue that the Egyptian 'system', if that can be blamed for Pharaoh's work of self-aggrandisement and the accompanying forced labour, was a 'cause' of the Hebrew bondage. The Bible itself, however, does not assign it as the cause.

Is there, then, nothing in the Exodus story which would indicate a concern with 'the system'? Quite the contrary. The Torah, whether specifically at Sinai or in the numerous sections of legislation in the Hebrew Bible, is at great pains to delineate a 'system' in which injustices shall not prevail; the constant concern of the prophets is that it shall be implemented. But the system does not *arise from* the people; it is *addressed to* the people by God, as the terms of his covenant with them.

That the 'system' of Torah is concerned with macro- as well as micro-economics there is no shadow of doubt. The sabbatical year, the cancellation of debts, the return of slaves in the Jubilee are all measures clearly designed to prevent or ameliorate the exploitation of smallholders and individuals by wealthy landowners, and indeed to prevent the growth of a class of wealthy landowners. Typically, they are specific legislative acts rather than generalised prophetic calls.

(b) Prophetic models All biblical prophets agree that sin is the cause of evil and suffering, and that the root sin is idolatry, which is essentially 'unfaithfulness' to God. Beyond that, there are three levels in the prophetic response to poverty.

1 Elijah represents the 'Band-Aid' level of concern. He acts on specific problems, be it the nationally significant 'case' of Naboth's vineyard (1 Kings 21), or the private 'case' of the poor widow of

Zarephath in Sidon (1 Kings 17:8–24). Elijah is the master of the *ad hoc* miracle.

2   Amos performs no miracles. Instead, he ruthlessly exposes the heart of social injustice:

> . . . because they sell the innocent for silver
>   and the destitute for a pair of shoes
> They grind the heads of the poor into the earth
>   and thrust the humble out of their way. . . .
>
> (Amos 2:6, 7)

Amos wants to change people, rather than 'the system':

> Seek good and not evil
>   that you may live. . . .
> Hate evil and love good
>   enthrone justice in the
> courts. . . .
>
> (5:14, 15)

3   Moses alone is concerned with what we might call 'the system'. He is sent to free the slaves and provide them with a land *and* with a constitution, the Torah. The Torah is 'the system'. Whether this 'system' lends itself to development in a capitalist fashion only, or whether in Marxist fashion must 'inevitably' progress with history to feudalism, capitalism and communism, is perhaps not a fair question to put in relation to economic structures of early in the first millennium BCE.

4.1.2   *Disagreements with liberation theology*

Disagreements on economic principles are of the essence of the following sections (to 4.2.4), in which it will be argued that the views of liberation theologians on this subject are not really dependent on their theology. Where I have criticised some liberationist view in general theology, I have often found myself agreeing with mainstream Catholic thought; my words are therefore not a Jewish critique of a Christian philosophy, but an individual contribution to debate amongst both Jews and Christians about matters of shared concern.

4.1.3   The questions to be asked

In their concern with politics and power structures liberation theologians too easily slip into the error of assuming that, if power (political) structures are changed, the economic problems – the creation and distribution of wealth – will somehow solve themselves. Economics and politics cannot indeed neatly be separated, but we must focus on the former.

Besides being on our guard against the slipshod assumption that some unspecified change of power structure will magically assure the generation and just distribution of wealth, we must seek answers to the following questions.

1   What are the ultimate economic aims formulated for society by theologians of liberation?
2   Granted that liberation theologians are justified in their complaints about economic exploitation in Latin America and elsewhere, does it follow that 'the [economic] system' as such is not the best available? Does the fault lie in the people who operate it, rather than in the system itself?
3   If 'the system' is not the best available, what is proposed to replace it with?
4   Can theology decide between the competing claims of different economic systems to achieve the ultimate aims the theologians have formulated?

4.1.4   Does liberation theology require a distinctive economics?

Is it perhaps missing the whole point of liberation theology even to ask such questions? A superficial glance at the writings of liberation theologians – most of whom would in any case maintain that their praxis rather than their theorising is what matters – reveals such headings as 'liberation and salvation', 'eschatology and politics', 'the scandal of poverty' and 'liberation praxis and Christian faith', none of which would figure in a standard textbook of economics.

On the other hand, a closer inspection will undoubtedly yield statements with serious economic import; there will be talk of a 'preferential option for the poor', and in many cases there will be a liberal sprinkling of Marxist jargon, even if the writer denies being a Marxist. Indeed, there is no way one can express solidarity with the poor – and 'poor' in the context of liberation theology includes, if it is not exhausted by, those lacking material goods – without involving economic consequences. If one complains about the maldistribution of wealth one *ipso facto* calls for its more just distribution. If one views the maldistribution as a consequence of 'the system' rather than of the failings and greed of individuals, one is in effect calling for either a modification or a replacement of the system. It is the prophetic role of religion to criticise society, even in a radical way. If, as Gustavo Gutiérrez claims,[5] Latin America is a 'sub-continent of oppression and pillage', then religious people, together with all who care, should shout aloud and spare no efforts to achieve change. Everyone should admire the courage and the moral fire of the Latin American religious who have given up their comfortable lives in city and religious community to go out into the wilderness wastelands to identify with the poor and the oppressed. The basic communities they have created are a symbol of light and hope for our times.

But the question addressed here is not whether the basic communities are symbols of hope and light for our times, but whether they, or the theology of liberation in general, constitute the most effective response to the maldistribution of wealth, or to the other major issues they highlight. It may well be that theologians, or prophets, are not the right people to solve such problems, even if they are an appropriate group to demand a solution. But, if they cannot, *qua* theologians or prophets, solve the problems, they should be careful not to give the impression that they are solving them, or by loose talk to lead people to think that they have committed themselves to particular economic or political viewpoints.

4.1.5 *Compassion or effective help?*

We shall return in section 4.1.7A to a consideration of the 'preferential option for the poor'. Here I must pose, but not attempt to answer, the radical question of whether an option for the poor is the answer to the problem of injustice. Gregory Baum has defined the preferential option for the poor as 'the double commitment, implicit in Christian discipleship, to look upon the social reality from the perspective of the marginalised and to give public witness of one's solidarity with their struggle for justice'.[6] Whilst not questioning the second of these commitments, or the compassion of the first, I am asking whether the first provides the right vantage point for effectively combating injustice. If my neighbour has a leaky tap, my sharing his suffering will not get the tap mended. Sufficient (but not excessive) compassion is necessary to see that something is amiss; my next task is not to share the leaking tap but to send for an expert plumber. Why should economic problems require a different approach?

4.1.6 *Is poverty inevitable?*

There was a time when people believed that poverty was inevitable. Bachya ben Asher, in his thesaurus of Jewish themes written round about the year 1300, expresses an attitude he would have shared with Christians and Muslims:

> Moreover, [one should always depend on God for sustenance because] poverty is an existing feature of human society, as it is written, *For the poor shall never cease out of the land* [Deuteronomy 15:11].[7]

Liberationists apparently share the optimism of the modern scientific outlook that poverty can be eradicated. Actually the rabbis, noting the discrepancy between the verse just cited from Deuteronomy and a verse earlier in the same chapter, 'For there shall be no poor among you' (Deuteronomy 15:4), remark that the latter would become true were Israel to act in accordance with God's will.[8] But a talmudic anecdote about two third-century Palestinian sages graphically illustrates the moral dilemma that remains:

> Ilfa and Rabbi Yohanan were studying Torah together, but were suffering great [economic] hardship. They said, 'Let us get up and do some trade and fulfil of ourselves the verse *For there shall be no poor among you.*' They went and sat under a shaky wall. As they were eating their bread two Ministering Angels came by. Yohanan heard one say to the other, 'Let's throw this wall down on them and kill them, for they cast aside everlasting life and occupy themselves with transitory life.' The other said, 'Leave

them alone, for one of them will succeed.' Rabbi Yohanan heard: Ilfa did not. . . . [Yohanan] said, 'So, let us now go and fulfil of ourselves the verse *For the poor shall never cease out of the land.*'[9]

In plain words, is it worthwhile pursuing wealth and raising living standards, or would it be better to accept poverty and devote oneself to 'spiritual' concerns?

4.1.7   *The option for the poor*

A. WHAT IS THE 'PREFERENTIAL OPTION'?
In 4.1.5 we cited Gregory Baum's definition of the 'preferential option'. The editors of a recent collection of papers state,

> The preferential option for solidarity with the poor is nothing short of a Copernican revolution for the Church. The protagonist in history and society who henceforth implements the Christian mission will be the poor . . . who are the privileged bearers of the message.[10]

I cannot pass judgement on whether the preferential option is a Copernican revolution in Christianity, though one wonders whether such Christians as Francis of Assisi were not at least precursors. So far as Judaism is concerned, however, the 'preferential option' is not startling. The Talmud states, for instance,

> Take care with the children of the poor – it is from them that Torah shall come forth to Israel. If any poor person shall claim [in extenuation on the Day of Judgement] 'I was poor and distracted by the need to obtain food' they [i.e. the heavenly judges] will reply to him, 'You were certainly no poorer than Hillel.'[11]

It is worth recalling, in these days when the affluence of North American Jewry forms the popular image of what Jews are, that the historical reality of Jewish communities has generally been of intense poverty; even today the affluence of the few should not be allowed to obscure the deprivation of the many.

B. THE NEED FOR BALANCED PERSPECTIVES

One must, however, place the 'preferential option' in a balanced context. Is Baum suggesting, when he instructs Christians 'to look upon the social reality from the perspective of the marginalized', that one should look upon the social reality *exclusively* from the perspective of the marginalised? God, and even we humans, are not so simple-minded that we are limited to one perspective. Situations are rarely so simple that one individual is in all respects 'the marginalised' and another 'the oppressor'. In the context of the Middle East, for instance, Israel, with respect to the neighbouring states which wish to undermine or destroy her, is 'marginalised'; this is perfectly consistent with the perception of the Palestinian that he is 'marginalised' by Israel. Likewise women, in virtually all known societies, are 'marginalised' by men; children and animals are 'marginalised' by all humans, including women. To state, as an absolute, that one should 'look upon the social reality from the perspective of the marginalized' is to ignore the limited nature of all perspectives other than the divine, which is infinite.

When we are told 'You shall love the stranger, for you were strangers in Egypt' (Deuteronomy 10:19), we are taught to *appreciate* the perspective of the stranger, the 'marginalised'; but we are not taught that this is the *exclusive* perspective from which to view the world.

Once anything becomes exclusive, it is an idol. We must reject idolatry of the poor as surely as we reject the idolatry of riches or power.

Does God show favour to the poor? Surely he shows favour to those who love him and obey his commandments, irrespective of whether they are rich or poor. His 'principle', if so we may put it, is to help those in need, those who suffer oppression; this is the theme of many of his commandments.

God's Torah does not favour one social stratum over another. The rich and the poor are equal in God's eyes. Hence scripture insists, in its legislative sections, on attention to the marginalised elements within society – the women, the orphans, the Levites, the strangers – so that the special attention given them might lead to *equal* treatment. 'You shall not pervert justice, either by favouring the poor or by subservience to the great' (Leviticus 19:5).

Identification exclusively with the poor leads to confrontation, hatred and strife, 'either–or' attitudes, divisions, onesidedness.

Identification exclusively with the poor leads to absorbing the prejudices of the poor, such as that the wealthy are wicked, or that 'those in power' – the United States, the multinationals, the employers, the government – are wicked. Some of them are wicked, no doubt. But so are some of the poor.

In his 1981 encyclical *Laborem Exercens* the Pope argues strongly for solidarity of workers:

> Therefore, one must continue to investigate the 'subject' of labour and the conditions in which he lives. To create social justice in different parts of the world, in different Countries and their interrelationships, there is always a need for *new movements of solidarity with* working people *and for solidarity with* working people. Such solidarity must always be present where the social degradation of the subject of work, the exploitation of the workers, and the increasing burdens of misery, even famine, require it. The Church is strongly pledged to this cause, for she considers it her mission, her service, as she confirms her faith in Christ, truly to be 'the Church of the poor'. And 'the poor' appear in many guises . . . often as a *consequence of the violation of the dignity of human labour* . . . the plague of unemployment . . . the devaluation of . . . the right to a just wage, to personal security. . . .[12]

A proper balance ought to have led to his calling unequivocally for solidarity of workers and management. In the later *Sollicitudo Rei Socialis* he seems more clearly to recognise the inherent divisiveness of calls to workers' exclusive solidarity when he draws attention to the broader groupings of society:

> By virtue of her own evangelical duty the Church feels called to take her stand beside the poor, to discern the justice of their requests, and to help satisfy them, without losing sight of the good of groups in the context of the common good.[13]

In this last phrase, 'without losing sight . . .', John-Paul II wisely, if not with great emphasis, acknowledges the need for a plurality of perspectives in addressing the problems of society.

C. THEOLOGY AND SOCIAL PERSPECTIVES

The concern of liberation theologians with the 'historical Jesus'

Judaism and World Religion

82

attracts a warm response from Jews, for this is a level upon which
they feel they can 'handle' the Jesus story.

However, as is natural for Christian theologians but anathema to
Jews, this historical, suffering Jesus is seen as the incarnation of
God. A new Christology ensues, that of the suffering god identified with the poor. This becomes the rationale for Baum's call to
the 'double commitment, implicit in Christian discipleship, to look
upon the social reality from the perspective of the marginalized
and to give public witness of one's solidarity with their struggle for
justice'.

The argument proceeds backwards, as liberation theologians
have based their Christology on their social theories rather than
vice versa. The ideology has become an epiphenomenon of the
social struggle, to use Marxist terms; perhaps this is what is meant
when we are told that theology is a 'reflection on praxis'. If they
had started with Christology they could scarcely have failed to
notice that Catholic Christianity has a Christ in Majesty as well as a
Suffering Servant. As strongly as I reject all forms of incarnational
Christology, it seems clear enough that, if one is to express one's
understanding of God in incarnational terms at all, there must
either be multiple incarnations, as in Indian religions, or a multi-
faceted incarnation, as provided by the varied images of Christ
which figure in traditional Christian thought. The Suffering Servant figure – the 'marginalised' historical Jesus – can be part of the
imagery, but does not of itself express the wholeness of God.

In the Hebrew scriptures there is no such problems, as the
incarnation-free imagery of God is protean in expression, ranging
from the 'mighty man of war' to the 'compassionate father' to the
shepherd who accompanies the walker through the valley of the
shadow of death (Psalm 23). Anthropomorphism abounds, pointing to a wholeness in the vision of God which precludes identification with a particular section of society. Certainly, God is with
the poor. But was he not also with David and the kings so long as
they walked in his ways?

Few rabbinic passages more convincingly demonstrate the biblical balance in the concept of God and hence of society than the
following:

Rabbi Yochanan said, In every passage where thou findest the
greatness of God mentioned,, there thou findest also his humility. This is written in the Torah, repeated in the Prophets,

and a third time stated in the Writings. It is written in the Torah, For the Lord your God, he is God of gods, and Lord of lords, the great, mighty and revered God, who showeth no partiality, nor taketh a bribe. And it is written afterwards, He doth execute justice for the fatherless and widow, and loveth the stranger, in giving him food and raiment. It is repeated in the Prophets, as it is written, For thus saith the high and lofty One that inhabiteth eternity, and whose name is Holy, I dwell in the high and holy place, with him also that is of a contrite and humble spirit, to revive the spirit of the humble, and to revive the heart of the contrite ones. It is a third time stated in the Writings, Sing unto God, sing praises unto his Name: extol ye him that rideth upon the heavens whose name is the Lord, and rejoice before him. And it is written afterwards, A father of the fatherless, and a judge of the widows, is God in his holy habitation.[14]

4.2 Changing 'the System'

4.2.1 'Structures of sin'

Liberation theologians are divided between those who unequivocally wish to 'change the system' and those who favour working with the basic communities rather than tackling 'the system' head-on.

'The system' has to be changed because it is a 'structure of sin'. But is 'structure of sin' a helpful concept? A 'structure of sin' is not a particular type of socio-economic system, defined in socio-economic terms, but a socio-economic system in which people are motivated by greed, lust and sinful impulses generally. This is a very confusing way to categorise socio-economic systems. People living under any known socio-economic system may individually and in specific instances act through altruistic or through selfish motives; but these are characteristics of people, not of socio-economic systems.

What seems to underlie the concept is the Marxist idea that the nature of the capitalist system is such that capitalists are bound to exploit labour, hence greed is actually built into the system; in a classless, socialist society this would not happen. The refutation of this simplistic notion may be observed daily in socialist societies; they are no more free from greed, envy, corruption and other human evils than are capitalist societies. Just at the time of writing, when East Germany is casting off its communist heritage, accusations of corruption are being made against high officials of the *ancien régime*. It would be sad if the East Germans were to delude themselves into thinking that their devoutly sought new democracy will guarantee freedom from corruption. At best it will provide checks and balances of a kind not available in an authoritarian regime; but this has to do with the difference between accountable and non-accountable governments, not with the difference between economic systems *per se*.

It is a cornerstone of theology that where there are human relations there is the opportunity to sin. The more complex that set of relationships – as in world trade at the present time – the more complex are the opportunities to sin.

No one has designed a sin-proof system. Surely the Church itself, viewed as a social structure, is not claimed to be a sin-proof supranational structure, and the same goes for the 'establishments' of all religions. Leonardo Boff argues that liberation theologians seek a *participatory democracy*, not actual socialism as it is in force in any existing country; but this evades the question by implying that the new economic order can only be formulated by the participatory democracy,[15] so Boff in effect calls for a revolution which has no clearly defined programme.

There are three principal dangers in calling for radical revision of the system when one cannot say what is to be put in its place and how. First, such a call destabilises society, thus providing opportunity for the strong-armed and the unscrupulous (of left or of right) to take charge. Second, it distracts people from constructive criticism of the existing system. Third, the absence of a clearly formulated alternative generates confusion and false hopes.

There may be some difference of opinion between Jews and Augustinian Christians as to whether mankind is *inherently* evil (carries a burden of sin from Adam), but there is no disagreement that mankind has a considerable *propensity* to evil. If one is not convinced of this on theological grounds one need only turn to Freudian and subsequent depth psychology for confirmation (though 'evil' is itself a theological rather than a psychological category).

Of course, some 'systems' lend themselves to particular types of evil. A system might depend on slavery (in the literal old-fashioned though not yet obsolete sense rather than the metaphorical 'wage-slave' sense of the Marxists). It is interesting that the Bible (and indeed the Church, until recently) did not oppose this system, though it certainly modified it and sought to ameliorate its harshness; the actual abolition of slavery was the achievement of modern Western industrialised society.

Isaac Abravanel (1437–1508/9) held that there would be no government in the days of the Messiah, for all forms of government lead to domination of one human being by another, and are by nature restrictive and repressive; government is only required at the present time owing to the sinfulness of mankind.[16] He did realise that this would mean a return to a very primitive sort of existence, where people would live directly on the bounty of nature, abandoning all technology and presumably trade. Clearly liberation theologians share with me the rejection of this ideal, and would like those whom they serve to partake in the benefits – health services, good food, clean water, education, and the like – that are now the prerogative of the wealthier nations. There is no way this can be attained without complex economic and hence political structures.

The way ahead lies not in the revolutionary substitution of novel socio-economic systems for the present ones, but in the difficult and painstaking evolutionary process of curbing abuses which arise within the system. Moralists and preachers have a dual role in this process. They must persuade individuals to act in an upright and moral fashion, explaining how traditional values can be upheld in a modern society. They must also urge legislators to enshrine appropriate values in their laws. As we saw in Chapter 3, this point was well appreciated even by that great apostle of the free market, Adam Smith.

Can the classical debates of economics be settled on a genuinely theological basis? Curiously, amongst both Jews and Christians there have been found thinkers who would maintain that socialism is the true expression of their faith, and also thinkers diametrically opposed to this view, to whom only a free-enterprise system harmonises with the values taught by their faith. On the socialist side, we have the liberationist Mexican ex-Jesuit José Porfirio Miranda.[17] Miranda is presumably unacquainted with the writings of the early religious socialist Zionists, but his conviction that socialism is the only just system and is therefore what his religion is all about is matched by theirs. What they also have in common is the lack of a serious critique of socialism or a serious examination of alternative and mixed systems. Their argument seems to be: socialism is the most just possible system for the organisation of human society; faith demands social justice; therefore faith demands socialism. In this way, one is bamboozled into thinking that their socialism is based on their theology. In fact it is not, for the truth of the first premise – that socialism is the most just possible system for the organisation of human society – is precisely what remains unproven. Moreover, the only relevant ways to demonstrate the truth of this premise are non-theological.

4.2.2 *Wealth creation and identification with the poor*

Julio de Santa Ana remarks in an impassioned essay[18] how, 'during the sixties, hardly anyone spoke about the situation of the poor. Poverty seemed simply something that was inevitably about to be eradicated.' The rich nations were about to help the developing nations to become rich themselves. The hopes proved illusory. Santa Ana, following Furtado (and at some distance, Marx), explains that the poor nations remained poor because the rich nations used mercantile means to extract surplus value from them. He seems to think that this is inevitable: 'So we have to say that *development and underdevelopment are two faces of the same coin*' (his emphasis).

Santa Ana has every right to be passionate, as he has before him the memory of the exploitation of the native Americans by the *conquistadores* – and the reality of present-day poverty. But one must be careful in suggesting comparisons. The *conquistadores* quite openly set out to plunder, conquer, take over the lands of the Americas for themselves, and with some honourable exceptions were unconcerned with the welfare and culture of the conquered. But the nations who assembled at Bretton Woods in 1944 to set up a new world economic order had already, by and large, rejected exploitative imperialism, even though paternalistic attitudes persisted. The World Bank and the International Monetary Fund (IMF) may have failed, as Santa Ana claims, to halt the growth of poverty in Brazil and other countries, but there is no doubt that, whatever their profit motives and their errors of economic judgement, they have also had the consistent aim of stimulating the Third World economies in which they have invested.

Is it true, as he claims, that 'the *international order agreed at Bretton Woods is incapable of eradicating poverty from our societies*' (his emphasis again)? From anyone's point of view, Bretton Woods was long ago seen to be inadequate to its stated purpose of stabilising the world's currencies. Santa Ana is hitting wildly at an obsolete target. Let us take it that what he means is that that cause of persistent poverty in Third World countries lies in the present 'economic order' (one need not be very cynical to say 'disorder') of the affluent countries. I disagree strongly with this assertion and believe that the causes of persistent poverty in Brazil and other countries lie elsewhere – after all, countries such as South Korea have successfully evolved from underdeveloped to developed under the same external conditions. J. K. Galbraith, in his critique of Raoul Prebisch, exposes the lack of clear relationship between external conditions, including the availability of natural resources, and economic development.[19] I shall return to the theme in section 4.3 with special reference to Brazil. The point I wish to make here is that, whatever the reasons for the failure of the rich nations, despite their honourable intentions, to rescue the undeveloped nations from poverty, these reasons can only be ascertained by careful economic argument and analysis, not by theology.

I therefore feel wronged when I hear that in the name of religion in general, or Christianity in particular, poor and previously uneducated men and women are being 'conscientised' into a realisation of 'the causes of poverty' by being exposed to this type of economic philosophy. They do not yet have the education and critical training to assess what they hear, and can too easily be led into hatred of and confrontation with the 'devil' who is alleged to be the source of all their ills. This is bad in itself, like all causeless hatred; it also diverts them from discovering the real causes of their poverty. The so-called 'Freire Method'[20] cheats by pretending to work in a 'bottom–up' manner; ideas on power structure are implicit in the very language with which the teachers cajole 'spontaneous' responses from their pupils, and from a political point of view at least there is a clear 'top–down' indoctrination.

Santa Ana argues his whole case on economic grounds. 'Argues' may not be the right word, as he assumes rather than argues Marxist principles; his detailed and reasoned arguments are *within* rather than *for* his system of thought. Be that as it may, there remains an unbridged gap between liberation theology *as theology* and the economic doctrines espoused by its advocates. Inevitably. For there is in reality *no connection* between theological views on poverty and specific economic analyses of the causes of poverty.

4.2.3   *Hinkelammert's critique of capitalism*

Franz J. Hinkelammert's *The Ideological Weapons of Death*[21] has attracted attention as a serious attempt by a theologian of liberation to come to grips with complex economic realities. Unfortunately for a work pretending to critical economic analysis it is marred by a passion and righteous indignation which make one feel guilty and uncomfortable to disagree with its arguments and conclusions even when it is manifestly wrong. Still, in the interest of truth let us not be frightened into submission; in the aftermath of the 1989 rejection of Marxism in much of Central and Eastern Europe we can afford to be a little less squeamish in defending capitalism. We can now openly wince and admit to feeling 'conned' when Pablo Richard and Raul Vidales, introducing the English version of Hinkelammert's book, glowingly promise readers the discovery that the 'capitalist production process excludes freedom and individual independence from the labor processes'.[22]

Let us by all means allow Hinkelammert his imaginative transformation of Marx's three-stage analysis of 'fetishism' – commodity fetishism, money fetishism and capital fetishism – into the theological category of idolatry, or into the 'hypostasis' of property. After all, even capitalist preachers readily condemn their congregations for making money, or property, an idol, though for this they need have no recourse to Hinkelammert's detailed analysis of the conditions under which commodities are produced and money is generated, but need simply refer to the story of the Golden Calf;[23] whether or not one treats money and commodities like idols depends not at all on which economic theory one espouses. Freud, indeed, came closer to accounting for the phenomenon of fetishism than Marx, for at least he perceived that a psychological rather than an economic explanation was required.

In his attack on Pierre Bigo and Lopez Trujillo in the latter part of his book Hinkelammert reveals that fetishism consists in the absolutising of values, and that to absolutise values is to destroy them. For instance, absolutising 'Thou shalt not kill' comes to mean 'Kill those who refuse to absolutise values.'[24] Values cannot be made absolute, insists Hinkelammert, for 'in their abstract form there is no way to ensure that they be observed. . . . They must always be made concrete.' Certainly Hinkelammert is saying something important here: though he does not know it, he is urging the concept which underlies the whole system of *halakhah*, with its balances, checks, assessments of the relative weight of competing values, and its preference for real-life cases rather than abstractions. This is curious, for one would have thought that here, if anywhere, there has been in the past a major difference of orientation between Judaism and Christianity; Hinkelammert's approach is the traditional Jewish one, even though he has not worked out its implications or attempted to create a system based on it, and has not explored the relationship between this aspect of his thinking and his earlier observations on law, morality and the human subject.[25]

We may mildly endorse Hinkelammert's rejection of an extreme instance of Milton Friedman's non-interventionism[26] whilst reserving judgement on whether he has correctly understood Friedman: how serious is he when he informs us that, in Friedman's view, 'the free exercise of the freedom to murder (which has relinquished the use of physical force) coexists alongside the exercise of the freedom to live'?[27] But extreme non-interventionism is in no way characteristic of capitalism, and, as we saw in Chapter 3, Adam Smith himself set down the three main areas for government intervention.

On the other hand, Hinkelammert's blanket rejection of Hayek does not convince. Now, there are many reasons which could be adduced to refute this, that or the other contention of Hayek. But Hinkelammert, grandiose and sweeping, does not stoop to details. Enough for him that Hayek commends humility. The passage he cites from Hayek is indeed so beautiful that we cannot let it pass:

The fundamental attitude of true individualism is one of humility toward the processes by which mankind has achieved things which have not been designed or understood by any individual and are greater than individual minds. The great question at this moment is whether man's mind will be allowed to continue to grow as part of this process or whether human reason is to place itself in chains of its own making.[28]

Hinkelammert distorts the 'humility' in Hayek's statement into an attitude of devotion towards 'collective reason', whereas Hayek is really thinking of the individual's appreciative wonder of that which has been achieved, without deliberate overall design and without coercion, by others. It is ironic that a passionately Catholic theologian should concentrate his ire precisely on that aspect of Hayek's teaching which most closely corresponds to religious ideas of virtue. Humility, in the sense of valuation of others above self, was the great virtue of Moses (Numbers 12:3), and permeates the ethical literature of Judaism, Christianity and other faiths.

Of course, the demand for others to be humble can be abused by those who wish to dominate. But, once again, what has this to do with economic theory, least of all with Hayek, who would certainly count himself amongst the 'humble' in the sense in which he is speaking? If the real object of ire is people who dominate others, it is quite arbitrary to single out economic structures rather than any other form of human domination, such as the family, tribe or church. Indeed, in the latter part of his book Hinkelammert criticises the historical involvement of the Church in slavery, rightly pointing to the facile way in which theologians justified the enslavement of the indigenous South Americans on the basis that the 'external' state of slavery was the counterpart of the 'inner' sin of these un-Christianised peoples. There was certainly an economic rationale for the enslavement of the South American peoples, but the demand for their 'humble submission' to their degrading state was justified by reference to their lack of Christianity – in other words, in terms of the Church's own power structure. Hinkelammert ought to have given us a general theory of human domination, but he has allowed himself to be misled by Marx's contention that domination is an aspect of class structure arising from economic relationships only.

Cornel West, in his Foreword, observes that 'Hinkelammert's book provides neither full-fledged solutions nor panaceas to the broad range of issues it raises'. This is a damning comment, for, unless a viable alternative economic structure to capitalism can be proposed, we simply have to make the best of what we have. In fact, Hinkelammert sounds as if he is against private property, and even thinks Thomas Aquinas was against it, which will surprise many even when they realise that he argues that Thomas was writing in a feudal society, and that in feudal society the organisation of the production process did not necessitate pauperisation.[29]

But a dislike for private property is not a fully-fledged alternative to the present state of affairs, nor does the idea that 'esteem for real life has always been the starting point for the ideologies of the oppressed'[30] take us any further towards a new economic structure.

Hinkelammert's wholesale rejection of the way mainstream Christians interpret Christianity leads the reader to conclude that Hinkelammert's economic critique determines his reading of Christian sources rather than vice versa. Once again, we are brought to the conclusion that the theological premises on which a critique of 'the system' is based are not primarily theological at all, since all the theological sources can be, and usually are, read differently. The driving force behind Hinkelammert, as behind so many theologians of liberation, is his passionate concern with the poor; since his personal identity is a Catholic one, he interprets that identity – that is, constructs his theology – to fit.

4.2.4   *False utopianism*

As to 'the system', I have made clear that I favour evolution, not revolution. Judgements in politics, economics and other technical subjects must be grounded in specialist knowledge of those subjects. Theology may lay down broad aims – help the poor, seek peace, cease exploitation – but these aims must be implemented through the increasing knowledge available to us in the social and natural sciences, not through woolly ideologies and ignorance of the 'facts on the ground'.

In this, it is unlikely that my views differ at all from those of any Christian of similar temperament and cultural background. We can both share in learning from the deeds of 'men seized by the spirit', as we recognise so many liberationists to be. We can also share in disentangling true insight from false ideology, and specifically in disentangling theology from politics and economics – which is not to deny the former a role in shaping the broad aims of the latter.

We must be on our guard against any form of 'utopian heresy'. And those of us who think of ourselves as theologians would do well to heed the words of Cardinal Joseph Ratzinger, who, in a letter criticising liberation theology, writes,

liberation is first and foremost liberation from the radical slavery of sin. . . . As a logical consequence, it calls for freedom from many different kinds of slavery in the cultural, economic, social and political spheres.[31]

I do not share the Cardinal's views on sin and atonement, but my Jewish heritage teaches me that ultimately the success of any social or economic system depends not so much on how well it is drafted as on the sinfulness or otherwise of those who operate it.

And in point of fact no one knows how to draft the utopian economic system. If the new order cannot yet be described, what basis is there for the critique of present economic practice other than that it results in deprivation for many? Even this is questionable; without the present economic order the poor would presumably be deprived anyway, though they might not notice it as no one would be rich. 'All men and women of good will' agree that we ought to help the poor, and that in economic (though not judicial) matters they should have some form of 'preferential option'. If theology gets us no further than that it is superfluous. What we really need to know is how to combine effective wealth creation with just distribution, and this demands the specialised knowledge of economists, sociologists and politicians rather than the prescriptions of theologians or newly 'conscientised' peasants.

4.3　Excursus: On the Special Problems of Brazil

I shall in no way presume to tell the Americas, or any part of them, how to work out their future. But I may at least be permitted to note down some of the considerations which appear from the other side of the Atlantic to be pertinent.

I refer to Brazil because Brazil exemplifies the conditions with regard to which the theology of liberation was first formulated. But how can I possibly comprehend Brazil? If I were to visit the country as a tourist or as participant in some academic conference, I have no doubt that I should meet wonderful people and be made comfortable; would this help me to grasp the enormity that on my planet there is a region which millions of children are said to die each year from causes related to malnutrition? But maybe even if I were a native, living sheltered and comfortable in a 'respectable' suburb of Rio, I would not grasp the reality any better; perhaps that is an element in the situation, and 'conscientisation' should start amongst the affluent in the cities rather than amongst the poor in the *barrios*.

The fact that I have no definitive answer to the question 'How can the poor of Brazil be liberated?' is only secondarily due to ignorance. Even if I knew far more about Brazil and about economics and politics and the human soul than I do, I would not expect to be able to formulate a definitive answer. To do so would be a false utopianism. Such progress as is made in tackling the problems of human society is piecemeal, two steps forward and one backwards; one problem is solved, another appears. The right approach is a pragmatic one, where there is feedback and learning from errors.

4.3.1 *Population*

The population of Brazil was 53,400,000 in 1950 and 144,440,000 in 1988. It is expected to reach 233,800,000 by 2020. This statistic alone suggests that Malthus rather than Marx points the way forward. The Church does not permit Catholics actively and openly to promote birth control in the *barrios*, but this does not alter the fact that population control is a prerequisite for economic improvement and long-term stability.

There is no way that the country can indefinitely support a population which grows by 2 per cent per year. Even if all the other problems of Brazil were overcome and land and forests returned to their pristine state, it would be very difficult to support the population of 233,800,000 anticipated by 2020. Yet a simple calculation shows that the same rate of increase would produce 1000 million people by 2086 (less than a century away) and reach the present world population of 5000 million by 2167. We are already witnessing precisely the type of social and environmental breakdown that population experts have warned about for decades.

Of course the population will not actually reach 5000 million by 2167. Something will happen. War? Starvation? Disease? Shall we leave it to AIDS to decimate the population? Surely planned birth control is preferable to any of these.

Emigration on any useful scale is impossible. Movement within the country does not work either. Rondônia sounded like a good idea, but it has already exceeded its capacity in absorbing about a million people, a mere third of the annual population increase, and even this has only been achieved by widespread destruction of forest habitat and Indian tribal life.

4.3.2　Environment

One of the consequences of ignoring population growth is the destruction of the environment. Brazil is a vast country, and to anyone who flies across it appears to support lush tropical growth. But appearance deceives: the vast forests of the Amazon grow mostly on land too poor for agriculture, and we now know something about the climatological and ecological effects of deforestation.

Deforestation and exhaustion of the land have driven people to the cities, destroying the city environment. 400 shanty towns have come into being in the neighbourhood of Rio, and there is no way the city can cope. Millions of children are said to die every year from causes related to malnutrition.

Yet for the long term – not just for aesthetic or even moral reasons, but for the plain economics of survival – it is imperative that the environment be protected *now*, before it is too late. This can only be accomplished by government in co-operation with international agencies; it demands legislation, international co-operation, and effective administration. Special-interest groups and 'basic communities' can by all means initiate schemes and make government aware of what has to be done, but only governments have the control and the resources to solve the problems.

4.3.3　Wealth distribution

Statistics can mislead. Brazil is sometimes referred to as a middle-income country, its per capita income far below that of Japan or the United States, but higher than that of India or China. Joelmir Beting calls his country 'Belindia' – 30 million or so enjoy a Belgian standard of living, and maybe the same number just get by, but the rest are as seriously deprived as the poor of India.

However, the statistic does demonstrate that *there is sufficient wealth in the country to raise the standard of living of the poorest significantly, even at the present population level.*

How can the redistribution of wealth be accomplished? More,

how can it be accomplished in such a manner that the redistribution will not undermine the wealth-creation capabilities of the wealthier part of society? It is a fallacy to think that taking the wealth from those who have it and distributing it among those who do not, even if politically possible, would produce an *economically* viable solution. It would be more likely merely to destroy the wealth-producing ability of the country. Redistribution – presumably through public expenditure financed by taxation – has to be a more careful and finely tuned process, and once again we come up against the problem of a population exploding so rapidly that it is not administratively feasible to create the necessary infrastructures to channel wealth in these ways. For instance, with a workforce growing even faster than the general population, industry cannot be organised to create sufficient new jobs fast enough.

Of course, mistakes have been made in the past. With hindsight, perhaps Brasilia ought never to have been built, and various other prestige projects should not have been accorded priority over infrastructure. Mistakes will be made in the future. We must learn from them, and not justify ourselves by imputing malevolence to those who took the risks and made the mistakes.

4.3.4 *The external debt*

Santa Ana climaxes his essay with the dramatic statement that 'in reality, it is not the rich who are "owed". They have seized the value produced by the poor. It is really the poor to whom repayment is due.'

Not so. First, the rich have not 'seized' anything. They have lent their wealth, and indeed there is a moral preference for lending with dignity over giving outright (cf. Leviticus 25:35, but note that the next verse bans the taking of interest!). No one knew that interest rates would escalate, or that an OPEC cartel would quadruple the price of oil out of political spite in 1967 (see section 3.9.5). The general idea, which worked in other countries, for instance South Korea, was to enable underdeveloped countries to develop their own resources. If it didn't work, it was not on account of malevolence on the part of the IMF or even because of 'the system'. There was corruption, and honest mistakes were made as well, such as spending money on 'prestige' rather than 'seed' projects.

The answer is not to drum up hatred against the helping hand, but to eradicate corruption and invest wisely.

Santa Ana's words 'This international usury is designed to consolidate the security of the rich' are tendentious; the payment of interest is designed to facilitate borrowing and hence commerce, and the non-payment of debt simply leads to the non-availability of credit. Recently, rescheduling not having enabled repayment, international banks have been 'writing off' a large part of the debt. But this is a double-edged sword. Without credit, commerce is inhibited; barter is not an adequate substitute. The point was well understood by Hillel, 2000 years ago, when he circumvented the biblical cancellation of debt in the seventh year by the institution of the *prosbul*, explicitly in order 'that the door be not shut before borrowers'; Hillel moreover limited the *prosbul* to debts placed in the hands of the courts, thereby ensuring that his legal device could not be abused for extortion.[32]

The poor suffer, as well as the rich, if credit is withheld.

4.3.5 Social divisions

I do not know, and pass no judgement. But it is said that the division between rich and poor eats into the heart of society. Pervasive racism and ingrained sexism are alleged. If one could reach the vast numbers, one could educate. But how can this be done when (in 1989) only 14 per cent of all Brazilian children finish primary school?

And, as the number of children in Brazil increases annually by about half a million, how will enough schools ever be built and teachers trained to cater for them?

I fear that 'conscientisation', if not carefully enough handled, will lead to hatred on the better-off and to hatred of the very institutions, such as those of 'big business', which might be able to help. Attacking the rich might make the rich poorer, but it won't make the poor any richer.

Social divisions are overcome by love, by the sense of belonging together and facing problems together; not by Marxist-style confrontation, which aims to destroy. 'Conscientisation' must accordingly awaken people to the wholeness of society.

4.3.6   *Corruption*

Greed, envy, lust, ambition – these are perfectly 'normal' human motives. They do not arise out of a 'system', but out of the hearts of people, as explained in section 4.2.1.

The right leadership helps. The perceived patterns of leaders' behaviour (not always the same as the actual patterns) influence people, for good as well as for bad. Also, good leaders will tinker with the system, a little at a time, and make the pursuit of evil less convenient, less profitable.

One cannot state categorically that changing 'the system' is wrong. The problem, though, is that, without a known and tested alternative system and a known and tested process for change, changing the system is dangerous and potentially destructive. Was it better to live under Stalin than under Tsar Nicholas? Even where, as in Eastern Europe at the present time, imperfect socialist systems are being changed to known and tested (though imperfect) capitalist or mixed systems, the process is uncertain and destabilising.

4.3.7   *The contribution of the priests*

Priests (Catholic, Protestant, Jewish) must raise the consciousness not just of the poor, but of rich and poor alike, to the appalling suffering of the majority of people of the country. But they must be careful not to set rich and poor against one another, or to set up any foreign government or transnational institution as 'the devil'. Always, always, demonising wreaks injustice on its objects and distracts attention from the real faults, which so often lie within ourselves. For close on 2000 years Jews have been cast in the role of the devil. We have suffered, and nobody has gained. When the Great Plague came upon Europe, we were maliciously and falsely accused of poisoning the wells. How did this help the situation? Did it make the waters any sweeter? Did it not rather set back the time when people would look to hygiene and to cleanliness to assure their health?

Once *the whole people* has been 'conscientised' to the suffering *of the whole community, whether rich or poor*, corruption must be addressed. Real corruption is difficult to detect and boring when

98	*Judaism and World Religion*

found. Corruption is not the multinational corporation trying to
get the highest market price for its goods or to pay the lowest
wages the local government permits (after all, it is governments
who regulate these things); it is the minor local official lining his
pockets, the high official accepting a bribe to award a contract, the
weak and fearful youth who gets lured into drug-trading, the
policeman who connives, the judge who turns a blind eye. It
gnaws the liver of a nation and saps its strength.

Above all, there is education. Whether it is better for the priests
to operate government planned and sponsored schemes or to 'do
their own thing' in the basic communities I cannot say; certainly
the communities have highlighted the need and the problems. The
education which is needed is not theological and doctrinal, of
course, but basic and practical.

4.4   Excursus: Interest-Free Banking in Judaism and Islam

4.4.1   *Christians and usury*

Judaism, Christianity and Islam have all at some stage expressed
horror at the notion of somebody lending something and getting
more of the same back in return. However, in recent times,
although orthodox Jews abstain from interest transactions and
some Israeli banks lend on the basis of a document (the *hetter 'isqa*)
that converts all loans into business participation, it is the Muslim
world which has led the call for the worldwide abolition of
interest-based banking.

Yet Psalm 15 and Ezekiel 18 lavish praises upon him 'who does
not put his money out to usury' and Exodus, Leviticus and Deuteronomy all contain express prohibitions.[33] The Council of Nicaea in
325 forbade clergy to engage in usury and Leo I, in the fifth
century, extended this to all Christians, so that usury became
regarded as a 'mortal, enduring and inexcusable sin'. Gratian,[34] in
the mid-twelfth century, and Thomas Aquinas,[35] in the thirteenth,
upheld the ban and developed the underlying moral theology,
notwithstanding the fact that they lived in a world already heavily
dependent on capital and credit. To such an extent had commercial
life burgeoned by the thirteenth century that, even had Jews,
Lombards and Cahorsins been exempted from the canonical pro-

hibition, it is inconceivable that they could have coped with the need for credit.[36]

Many attempts were made by theologians to devise ways to recompense creditors whilst avoiding usury. Methods proposed included the concept of partnership without participation in losses, which was rejected by the rabbis of the Talmud and also by Muslims. Nevertheless, some form of 'sleeping partnership' (*commendite*) was approved from the twelfth century onwards.

Eventually the Church acquiesced in the demand for credit by accepting the distinction of the jurists between usury, which remained a mortal sin, and *interesse* – a word coined by the Romanist Azo – which was fair compensation for loss, in particular for delay of payment. This distinction left the moral question of profit unsettled, but paved the way for banking and other commercial transactions.

4.4.2 *Commercial law and interest in Judaism and Islam*[37]

Al-Muwatta, 'the well-trodden path', Imam Malik's eighth-century record of the *'amal* of Medina', the record of Umar's governance of Medina, is the code *par excellence* of the Maghreb.[38]

Maimonides' twelfth-century code *Mishneh Torah* is the culmination of some centuries of Jewish juristic tradition, deriving from the pattern set almost a thousand years earlier by the Mishnah.[39]

Let us see how the sections of these codes containing the principal aspects of commercial law, including interest, are constructed.

A. CODIFICATION OF COMMERCIAL LAW IN *AL-MUWATTA*
The main sections on commercial law are books XXXI–XXXVI. Many of the matters dealt with in these books are touched upon elsewhere, and there is much – for instance, the laws on slavery and the like – which fills a number of other books, and might well be put under the heading of commercial law.

Book	Title	Details, remarks
XXXI	Business transactions	Deposit, shares, fruit of trees, money-changing, discounts, profit-sharing

Book	Title	Details, remarks
XXXII	Qirad	Investing (coin only – see XXXII.6) for share of profit
XXXIII	Share-cropping	
XXXIV	Renting land	
XXXV	Pre-emption in property	
XXXVI	Judgement	Evidence of lone witness, etc. Injury to crops and animals Defective goods, gifts, lost property, etc.

Imam Malik organised his system around the actual commercial practice of Medina as this was reflected in his sources. What were people actually doing in those 'classical' times to which so many of the *hadith* (traditions) he adduces relate? Certainly, they were working on land owned by others, paying them either in money or in kind ('share-cropping'). As merchants they were 'investing', engaging in *qirad* (though the institution itself is non-Quranic and requires harmonisation with the Quranic text), and were involved in money-changing. Significantly, it is around the actual *life of the faithful* rather than around the legal terms and concepts of the Quran itself that Imam Malik constructs his system.

This suggests a particular philosophy of religious law. It suggests that, however much *sharia* may derive and take its authority from sacred text, its final shape is defined by how it is lived, how it is expressed in the society of the faithful.

Since *Al-Muwatta* reflects the commercial practice of Medina, its most prominent concepts include *qirad*, money-changing and share-cropping, and it is in terms of these that commercial law is presented. Hence it comes as no surprise to find observations on *riba* (interest) scattered about various parts of the code – for instance XXXI.16–19, 31, 33–4, 36, 39; XXXII *passim*.

Riba emerges, in *Al-Muwatta*, as a limiting condition of *qirad* XXXII.5 illustrates this perfectly. Once legitimate *qirad* is defined once we know under what circumstances one may invest money in someone else's enterprise in the hope but without the certainty of gain, what lies beyond is *riba*, usury, and forbidden.

B. CODIFICATION OF COMMERCIAL LAW IN MAIMONIDES' CODE

Maimonides' code, the *Mishneh Torah*, is divided into fourteen books, the last four of which contain the materials relating to commercial law.

Book		*Subdivisions*
XI	*Neziqin* Damages, torts	1 Homicide and the duty to preserve life
		2 Damage to person and property
		3 Robbery and stolen property
		4 Theft
XII	*Qinyan* Transfer, acquisition	1 Sale
		2 Gifts
		3 Neighbours
		4 Agents and partners
		5 Slaves
		6 Acquisition
XIII	*Mishpatim* Judgements	1 Rent and hire
		2 Borrowing (objects) and deposit
		3 Lending and borrowing (money). Documents
		4 Plaintiff and defendant
		5 Inheritance
XIV	*Shoftim* Judges	1 Evidence
		2 Rebellion (including the authority of judges)
		3 Mourning
		4 Kings and their wars

What evidence does the selection of 'key themes' tell us about Maimonides' way of conceptualising the legal system of Judaism?[40] *Mishneh Torah* was organised as an expansion of the 613 *mitzvot* of the Torah which Maimonides had listed and explained in an earlier work,[41] but an intriguing problem in evaluating Maimonides' arrangement of books and sections arises when we consider the fourteen-fold division of the *mitzvot* he sets out in his later, philosophical work, the *Guide of the Perplexed*.[42] Though the number of major divisions is the same, their order and contents do not completely correspond. For one thing, *all* the sections on commercial practice occur in the earlier divisions in the *Guide*. For instance, the fourth *Guide* class comprises the commandments 'concerned with giving alms, lending, bestowal of gifts . . . loans and slaves . . . and all the *commandments* we have enumerated in the *Book of Seeds*'.[43] Thus, as Maimonides himself points out, he has transferred the sections on lender and borrower and on slaves from their association in the *Mishneh Torah* with transfer and judgements, respectively, to the division enumerating those commandments which 'are manifestly useful through instilling pity for the weak . . . giving strength in various ways to the poor, and inciting us not to press hard upon those in straits'.[44]

This single example points to a more general difference in the organisational principles of *Mishneh Torah* and *Guide*. In the *Guide*, *mitzvot* are organised in such a way as to show forth the ethical, moral and philosophical principles of Torah (such principles are evident in *Mishneh Torah* also, but do not form the basis of its organisation). In *Mishneh Torah* the principle of organisation is more properly juridical. The jurist does not lump cases together because their correct conduct teaches compassion, so lending and slavery on the one hand are separated from tithes and first fruits on the other. A glance at the table above will confirm that the principle of organisation is indeed juridical. Book XI contains criminal matters, divided into those involving and those not involving life. Book XII deals with civil disputes and the non-contested disposition of property. Book XIII deals mainly with non-permanent property transfer, involving the difference between ownership and possession. It ends with two sections which are not easily classifiable elsewhere and are hence placed at the end of the divisions on litigants. Book XIV moves on to the court itself: the rules of evidence, the constitution of the courts, their authority. Its concluding sections relate not so much to the legal system as to the *Mishneh Torah* as a whole.

With regard to *ribit* (interest) we have exactly the opposite situation from that in *Al-Muwatta*. *Ribit* is the fundamental (biblical) category which has to be defined, and what lies beyond it is permitted. In fact Maimonides, utilising on a small scale the organisational principle which becomes dominant in the classificatory system of the *Guide*, commences the section on lending and borrowing with an exposition of the Torah's rules on the duty of helping the poor and on the wrongness of oppressing the debtor. In chapter 4, though, he begins to expound the laws of *ribit*, and it is from this base that he considers such matters as money-changing and *'isqa*, the investment procedure analogous to *qirad*.

We have seen that, when he came to write the *Guide*, with its different perspective, Maimonides reclassified lending, including *ribit*, with the laws intended to teach compassion. A later Jewish code, the *Shulchan Arukh* of Joseph Karo (1488–1575), incorporates the laws of *ribit* not in its civil and criminal law division, but amongst 'religious' laws, between *Avodah Zarah* (idolatry) and *Niddah* (menstruant women). In this there is perhaps the reflection of another ambiguity with regard to *ribit*. Is it indeed a civil wrong to expect anyone to pay for the use of money for a period? Is he not really getting something (the use of money) for which it is reasonable to expect to pay?

It may be that the different positioning of the laws of *ribit* by Maimonides and Karo (or by Maimonides himself in his two main works) reflects a profound difference in viewpoint. The later viewpoint seems to be that the charging of interest, unlike for instance theft, in not an intrinsic moral wrong. The forgoing of interest is more akin to an act of personal benevolence, though unlike a charitable gift it is not optional, at least within the community. This is not unlike the position of Albertus Magnus and other Christians, who founded the doctrines of just price and usury on the duty of love.[45] Such a view of the nature of interest would explain why the Bible, usually so insistent on equal treatment of 'stranger' and 'native' Israelite, discriminates between them with the words, 'You may lend to the stranger on interest, but not to your brother' (Deuteronomy 23:21), and would tally with the rationale supplied by late Jewish commentators that the *mitzvah* of lending without interest was in order to 'provide a living for' one's brother, hence not directly applicable beyond the community.[46] Consistently, where benevolence would not be served by forgoing interest – for instance, where money is held on trust for the benefit of orphans – it may, even should, be lent on interest so that the orphans may be helped.

Not withstanding this Bible-based 'licence' to charge interest to the non-Jew, the rabbis discouraged such action. Commenting on the Psalmist's praise for one who 'does not put his money out on interest' (Psalm 15:5), the Talmud glosses 'even to an idolater'.[47] When economic and political conditions in the Middle Ages constrained Jews to engage in money-lending, the halakhic authorities were at some pains to justify an occupation on which the Talmud clearly frowned.

4.4.3 Interest and 'the system'

Many Muslim writers treat the avoidance of *riba* as the basis for a 'new economic system' founded on shared risk rather than interest payments. They commend 'Islamic banking' as an alternative economic system to that current in the developed world, and teach 'Islamic economics' at universities. My general suspicion of 'changing the system' in this broad sense has been expressed already in section 4.2, and I would exercise extreme caution in this instance also. Many Muslims have themselves noted the danger of overemphasis on *riba* at the expense of other elements in 'Muslim economics', such as honesty, freedom from corruption, and the other values we have stressed. Moreover, the argument that the abolition of interest-bearing loans would save nations from debt and exploitation is unconvincing. Such loans would be replaced by other trading arrangements, principally equity investment, and it need hardly be pointed out that failed equity investments create indebtedness and lead to 'exploitation'. All this presupposes that loans would genuinely be replaced by 'participatory' investments; what is more likely to happen – and this is true of the Jewish *hetter 'isqa* (section 4.4.1) also – is that loans are disguised, not replaced, as investments.

I have not found that Jewish legalists challenge 'the system' on the basis of *ribit*, though they do insist that lending transactions be covered with a *hetter 'isqa*, and Israeli banks usually comply with this requirement.

It would seem that the reason for the difference between the Muslim and Jewish approaches on this arises from the interpretation by Jews of the laws of *ribit* as a matter of benevolence rather than equity.

Part II
Politics

5

Religion, Community and State

5.1 Religion and Social Structures

What has religion to do with community, state and nation? If we could clarify this satisfactorily we would contribute greatly to the understanding of society in general, whatever the predominant religion and whatever the social structure, for religious or similar ideologies have until the present featured in all known human societies. Religion is indeed not a solitary but a social phenomenon; even the hermit is what he is by reference to a larger society.

I shall focus on Judaism and on the State of Israel, but I intend that the problems revealed should be seen as applying generally to all religions and their host societies.

The question arises in acute form in modern Western society, for three reasons.

1 Our countries have all accepted in greater or lesser measure the principle of the separation of Church and state. Such vestiges of official state religion as remain are ceremonial expressions of historical consciousness rather than exercises of power, though it would be a mistake to underestimate the influence exercised by the clergy in many European countries, or the pressure arising from residual Christian elements within European culture.

Karl Marx, in his essay *The Holy Family*, fully appreciated the significance of cultural factors in securing advantage for one religion over another. He reflected, with reference to the imposition of Sunday as the day of rest in secular French schools,

> Now according to liberal theory, Jews and Christians are equal, but according to this practice [of having the public schools open on Saturday], Christians have a privilege over Jews, for otherwise how could the Sunday of the Christians have a place in a

law made for all Frenchmen? Should not the Jewish Sabbath have the same right?[1]

2   Christianity, which is the dominant religion in Western countries, in some of its moods prefers to think of itself as concerned with matters of eternity rather than of this world, with the consequence that religion becomes a matter of individual salvation rather than public government; these moods, which on the whole have affected Protestants rather than Catholics, and are by no means an essential or permanent feature of Christianity, have facilitated the secularisation of the state; they have affected the thinking of Jews, also.

3   Western society is the birthplace of the modern concept of the nation state.

5.2   The Jewish Polity

It has proved difficult to model or name the collectivity of Jews. Nearly all those terms which were happily enough used in the past have been abandoned. Are we to use ethnic or religious criteria? If ethnic, we come up against the fact the Jews comprise a variety of peoples of all colours and many *ethne* – Judaism has always been open to converts, irrespective of colour or ethnic origin. If religious, how do we avoid the exclusion of Jews who do not 'believe' or 'practise' (let alone how do we define correct belief and practice)? If political, how do we cope with the wide spectrum of political views exhibited by Jews on almost any topic; or, if 'national', how do we account for their citizenship of many of the world's countries?

It seems that none of the conventional ethnic, religious, political or national models of human collectivities fits the Jewish reality even though all of them may have had a part in shaping it. We must therefore look carefully at what this reality has been and attempt to comprehend it in its own terms.

Daniel J. Elazar and Stuart A. Cohen have offered the first comprehensive overview of the more than 3000 years of Jewish political tradition.[2] Their study, covering fourteen epochs from the patriarchal period to the present day, reveals an extraordinary continuity and consistency. Their framework is provided by the traditional terminology of the three *ketarim*, or crowns: *keter Torah*, *keter malkhut* and *keter kehunah*, the crowns of Torah, government and priesthood. These are understood as *reshuyot* (authorities), the 'checks and balances' within the power structure of society.[3] Conditioning this are two overriding features which persist throughout the epochs. One is the religio-political goal of reformation of the existing order – *geulah*, or redemption – which means that 'the Jewish political worldview is messianic in orientation, looking toward a better future rather than a golden past'. The other is the covenantal or federal (Latin *foedus* = covenant), which leads to a concern less 'with the best structure for the regime than with the proper relationships between power and justice, the governors and the governed, and God and man'.[4] To describe this aspect as 'federal' as well as as 'covenantal' stresses the implications for inter-human relationships.

Elazar and Cohen[5] are careful to select an appropriate biblical term for the whole body politic of Israel and/or the Jewish people. The term they select is not *goy* (nation) or even *'am* (people, kinship group), but *'edah*, usually translated 'congregation', but which they understand as 'a body politic based on consent'.[6]

It is noteworthy that this framework is an essentially theological one. Let us see how Elazar and Cohen use it to categorise one particular epoch.

Epoch XII (1348–1648) is, broadly speaking, the epoch preceding emancipation. The 'crown of Torah' is represented by *yeshivot* (rabbinic colleges), *posekim* ('Those who decide' – the rabbinic legal authorities), and rabbis, the latter including, in contrast with the previous epoch, several whose authority was more than local, such as *Landesrabbiner* or chief rabbis. The 'kingly crown' or 'crown of government' sees not only the retention of the local *kehilla* (community) as the principal cell of Jewish life, with its governing committee of lay elders, but also the growth of the regional *va'ad* (lay committee), able to levy taxation, but subject to the legal rulings of the *posekim* of the 'Torah crown'. The 'priestly crown' had little power in this epoch; its representatives were the *hazzan* (prayer leader), the *magid* and the *darshan* (two types of preacher).

How can one analyse the political structure of the *'edah* in epoch XIV (1948 to the present)? Merely asking 'What is the structure of the *edah* today?' is helpful, for it forces a realisation that, with the emergence of Israel as a nation state, the virtual liquidation of Jewish settlement in Arab lands, and the pre-eminence of the US

Jewish community in the diaspora, a variety of smaller-scale structures is subsumed under the all-embracing notion of the *'edah*. Intriguingly, the *medinah*, or nation state of Israel, turns out to be a focus of the whole *'edah*, but not its summation. There is indeed no effective overall political structure to the whole, but a 'diffusion of authority as reflected in each of the three *ketarim*'.[7] The federal, covenantal nature of the *'edah* as a whole is clearly perceived, and as clearly arises on the basis of the classical biblical covenant theology; but it is an open format, able to absorb secular as well as religious Jews, Israelis as well as loyal citizens of other countries.

Clearly, there is a huge difference between the Jewish political structures of epoch XII (1348–1648) and those of epoch XIV (from 1948 onwards). It is precisely in the intervening epoch XIII that the revolutionary changes were accomplished, and it is to this epoch that we must accordingly turn for our understanding of the genesis of the new political concepts, particularly that of nationalism.

5.3   Nationhood and Nationalism

The Greeks were proud of being Greeks, the Romans of being Romans, and for all we know every nation throughout history has thought itself the best that ever was. Yet the nationalism which developed in Europe in the eighteenth and nineteenth centuries, and which is currently resurfacing in Eastern Europe, is different in kind from the ancient sense of belonging to a people. Likewise, modern Zionism, nurtured within the bosom of European romantic nationalism, has moved beyond its own roots in the traditional Jewish 'yearning for Zion'.

Elie Kedourie has stated,

Nationalism is a doctrine invented in Europe at the beginning of the nineteenth century. It pretends to supply a criterion for the determination of the unit of population proper to enjoy a government exclusively of its own, for the legitimate exercise of power in the state, and for the right organisation of a society of states. Briefly, the doctrine holds that humanity is naturally divided into nations, that nations are known by certain characteristics which can be ascertained, and that the only legitimate type of government is national self-government.[8]

Whilst this is the view of a political philosopher, a sociologist would emphasise the function of nationalism as transforming such ethnic characteristics as language and social custom into ultimate values.

Kedourie separates nationalism from both patriotism and xenophobia:

> Patriotism, affection for one's country, or one's group, loyalty to its institutions, and zeal for its defence, is a sentiment known among all kinds of men; so is xenophobia, which is dislike of the stranger, the outside, and reluctance to admit him into one's own group. Neither sentiment depends on a particular anthropology and neither asserts a particular doctrine of the state. . . . Nationalism does both . . . far from being a universal phenomenon, it is a product of European thought in the last 150 years.[9]

We must also distinguish national*ism* from nation*hood*. Nationalism depends on transforming ethnic characteristics such as language and social custom into ultimate values for which the individual citizen is prepared to kill and die. Nationhood demands no such transformation, but rather a sense of community, of belonging with others through shared history and geography, and to some extent language and social custom; such values are by all means cherished by members of the nation, but they do not define the nation exclusively nor are they transformed into absolutes. The concept of nationhood, with its associated values of loyalty and patriotism, is far older than that of nationalism, going back to ancient times.

5.3.1 *Nationhood and religion*

Does nationhood carry any implications as regards the religion of the citizen? The sociologist will want to know the extent to which a particular religion is seen as constitutive of national consciousness; are the language and customs of the religion among the cherished, if not ultimate values of the nation? And what of the predominant religion of the nation's citizens? The political theorist will want to know to what extent its norms of behaviour and definitions of status constitute the legislative structure of the state – will the prohibited degrees of marriage, for instance, be regulated in accordance with the dictates of the Church? These are not easy questions to answer, for governments and citizens have in fact generally been unsure. Hence the history of the nations of Europe in modern times is characterised by indecision as to the rights of religious minorities. An early draft of this chapter[10] was read to a gathering of British Jews and Catholics. Even now there would be a constitutional problem should a leading member of the royal family wish to convert to or even marry into either of these faiths. In many ways the British state, though it has abrogated most discriminatory legislation, manifests a Protestant Christian ethos, which one may describe as a default state for those situations in which religion or religious ceremonies are relevant.

In the tendency recently manifested in Britain to invite the comments of religious leaders on governmental matters, such as the improvement of the inner-city areas of deprivation (see section 3.3.3), we see two facets of the Church–state relationship. One is the fact that the views of religious leaders on moral questions are seen as relevant to 'secular' concerns, not merely to eternal salvation; the other is the centrality of the Church of England in the spiritual ethos of England, if not the rest of the country. To the credit of the Church of England, it not only claims no monopoly of spiritual guidance, but actively invites other denominations and faiths to express their views; but it remains, in a profound sense, the national church.

5.4 The Jewish National Movement

Arthur Hertzberg and Jacob Katz[11] have described ways in which Jewish nationalism differs from other nationalisms in modern times. Yet the similarities are also important. Undoubtedly, Jewish national*ism*, rather than nation*hood*, grew in conscious response to the development of the romantic nationalisms which arose in several European countries in the eighteenth and nineteenth centuries, and Jewish nationalists – Zionists – today still face the task of relating the age-old Bible-based 'yearning for Zion' to more modern notions of political independence and territoriality.

Let us trace some of the intellectual development of modern Jewish nationalism, or Zionism.

5.4.1 *The roots of Zionism*

Although the term 'Zionism' in its modern sense was not used until 1890,[12] the basic idea of the return of the Jewish people to their ancestral land was, of course, part of the traditional messianic belief, and it imbues the liturgy, as it imbued Jewish life, with a profound sense of hope. Throughout the period of the exile, despite hostile conditions, there had been a stream of Jews making their way, often in the face of great perils, to spend their lives in the Holy Land. For instance, in the twelfth century there was a wave of immigration from North Africa; in the thirteenth some 300 French and English rabbis went to settle there; the fourteenth century brought immigration from Spain and Germany, and the fifteenth immigration particularly from Italy – despite Pope Martin V's order forbidding Italian ships to transport Jews to Palestine. From time to time there had even been attempts at a political solution to the problem of Jewish settlement, one of the most notable being that of Joseph Nasi, Duke of Naxos, in the sixteenth century.[13] The Sabbatean movement in the seventeenth century gave a further boost to Jewish aspirations to return from exile; under its impact many actually made the journey, and many more seriously entertained the idea. Elijah, the Gaon of Vilna (1720–97) and his disciples, whilst firmly within the mystical/messianic tradition of the 'return to Zion', clearly conceived the need to cultivate the land and establish in it normal economic and governmental institutions; they afford a bridge between messianic dreaming and political realism. We shall examine their views in section 6.3.4.

5.4.2 *The context of Jewish nationalism*

The increase in antisemitism which accompanied the collapse of communist regimes in Central and Eastern Europe in 1989 is a reminder that European nationalism has a strident, exclusivist side to it. Finkielkraut has well observed that in German romantic nationalism we find the reverse of the Englightenment call to universal reason, truth and justice:

> Jurists and writers, as the privileged trustees of the *Volksgeist*, were above all concerned to resist the ideas of universal reason

and ideal law. For them the idea of culture no longer implied the driving back of prejudice and ignorance, but rather the expressing in all its indomitable singularity, of the unique spirit of the people whose guardians they were.[14]

Even Goethe, who was later to urge that art should transcend, not serve, the *Volksgeist*, was for a time seduced.[15]

The tension between nationalism and universalism which tore Europe in the nineteenth century and has not yet been resolved was of course manifested in the Jewish national movement, and with one further complication: Jews had to choose whether to lose part or all of their Jewishness by adopting the local European nationalism, and, if not, whether to opt out of Europe into a nationalism of their own. On the whole assimilation was chosen where practicable, provided that a Jewish religious identity could be maintained. But, where Jews were not accepted, or only very grudging accepted, as nationals in the countries in which they lived, and particularly where they found themselves alienated and discriminated against as in the Russian pogroms late in the century, a drive to a separate Jewish nationalism made itself felt.

Moses Hess should certainly be counted amongst the 'alienated', despite a successful career and lasting fame as a theorist of socialism. In his case it was no pogrom, but the perceived failure of the emancipation coupled with the rise of German racial antisemitism, that led him from the universalism of his early socialist writings to a rediscovery of Jewishness (one can hardly say 'Judaism') and the formulation of a solution to the 'Jewish problem' along Jewish nationalist lines. Yet his nationalism was not that of Herder and the German romantics but modelled rather on that of Mazzini,[16] combining national particularity with a universal vision, though Hess lacked the strong religious and mystical leanings of Mazzini. The two religious figures generally celebrated as pioneers of political Zionism, Judah Hai Alkalai and Zvi Hirsch Kalischer, had this dimension in full, and combined it with a practical outlook rare amongst the rabbis of the time.[17]

Hess, Alkalai, Kalischer and many others whose names are now celebrated in Zionist annals, had little influence in their own time. Heinrich Graetz (1817–91), now thought of primarily as a great historian, not only established the study of Jewish history on a scientific basis but laid the foundation for a new Jewish historical consciousness amongst Jews who, through assimilation, had lost not only contact with but pride in their Jewish roots.[18] Before he commenced his *History* he had made his intentions plain in a remarkable essay[19] in which he argued for the unity of the meta-physical, the religious and the socio-legislative, which had been separated at various epochs of Jewish history. Graetz was working towards the strongly missionary position which he later espoused, within which Israel was a 'Messiah people', and in which he proclaimed the unity of Torah, land and people.

5.4.3   On nationalism and universalism

Hermann Cohen, whose views on Messiah we shall discuss in section 6.3.5, and whose relationship with Graetz was far from cordial, has often been criticised for the apparent inconsistency between his ardent German patriotism and his complete rejection of Jewish nationalism, particularly in the form of Zionism – a criticism which is also directed against the German Jewish Reform Movement as a whole, for already in the 1840s the Reform leaders had, whilst vigorously protesting their loyalty to the (German) Fatherland, expunged from the Prayer Book all references to the physical return to Zion and Jerusalem. Cohen indeed regards Zionism and religion as mutually incompatible; for Zionism, he maintains, was a reversion to an earlier, more primitive, tribal/ nationalistic form of Judaism which had long been superseded by the universalism of the prophets.[20] Essentially, his justification of his German patriotism arises not from the notion that German nationalism is in some way superior to Jewish nationalism, but from his conviction that German idealism corresponds to the later, universalistic stage in the development of Judaism.[21] What Cohen says of German nationalism represents one trend within it, as we saw in section 5.4.2, though not the dominant one in the late nineteenth century; in fact, it corresponds rather more to Jewish nationalism as formulated by a range of thinkers from Hess to Rav Kook and beyond.

5.4.4   'Peopleness' and nationalism

If Zionism is a special expression of the Jewish sense of identity, what is the broader context of Jewish self-awareness within which it finds its meaning? Roy Eckardt, writing in the United States, and recognising that no existing term is exactly right, coined the term 'peopleness'. This is how he explains the relationship between the identity of Christians and that of Jews in the United States:

> The identity of Jews in America involves three basic elements: peopleness (a *laos*); a faith within that peopleness, yet a faith that is not an absolute condition of Jewishness; and Americanness. The identity of Christians in this country involves two basic elements: a particular faith; and Americanness.[22]

Eckardt's analysis is easily applied to the British situation. It has the advantage that, whilst allowing for the very widespread Jewish commitment to Zionism in its many forms and to Israel, it by no means lets this conflict with the reality that the actual nationality of most Jews is not in fact Israeli.

On the other hand, if Jewish 'peopleness' is not geographically restricted, why should it focus at all on some particular piece of territory? Peretz Smolenskin (1842–85) spelled out seven reasons to prefer Palestine to any other territory.

> The land of Israel is to be preferred to other lands such as America or Spain [South America] in every way:
>
> 1   Because those to whom the memory of their fathers is precious will go there joyfully if only they can be sure that they will be able to support themselves.
> 2   Because they would be looking not to some uninhabited desert which they would have to render habitable, but to a land which they can cultivate as soon as they arrive.
> 3   Because the place is not too distant from the lands in which they now live.
> 4   Because all those who leave their present homes will be able to go there together, and can continue to live in accordance with their customary ways of life.
> 5   Because those who are already there, eating the bread of sorrow and conducting themselves in disgraceful fashion to the shame of the whole nation and of the land itself, will gradually acquire the purity of heart to embrace a way of life based on honest toil, so that thousands of lives will be saved from idleness which leads to every kind of evil. Moreover,

the sums of money which are remitted to them annually from several countries will not be squandered in the support of idleness and sin.

6   Because they will not all be forced to engage solely in agriculture, but some of them will work on the land whilst others engage in profitable trade. Any intelligent person will admit that if only the land of Israel was in Jewish hands it would already be a commercial centre linking Europe with Asia and Africa. If goods would pass through it from Europe to Asia and Africa and thence back to Europe the land of Israel would quickly become a centre for international commerce; it would prosper and flourish and be a source of blessing not only to Europe but also to Asia and Africa.

7   Because there they will be able to set up factories for glass and the like, for the earth (sand) is very good, and in this way also they will prosper. On its soil they will be able to support themselves through agriculture, trade and industry. Consequently, those who go there will thrive so that as time goes on people will desire to immigrate without any (further) stimulus, for they will see the opportunity for a life of peace, a life free from shame. If the generous amongst our people wish to offer swift help to their unfortunate brethren they have no need for lengthy deliberations; let them just hurry to implement the matter by purchasing land and settling their brethren so that they might gain life.[23]

Leo Pinsker (1821–91) was clearly more interested in 'peopleness' – 'self-realisation' is his chosen term – than territory, and questions the assumption that the future Jewish homeland need necessarily be in Palestine:

If we could have a secure home, so that we may give up our endless life of wandering and rehabilitate our nation in our own eyes and in the eyes of the world, we must above all not dream of restoring ancient Judea. We must not attach ourselves to the place where our political life was once violently interrupted and destroyed. The goal of our present endeavors must be not the 'Holy Land' but a land of our own. . . .[24]

Shlomo Avineri is right when he sums up the achievement of Theodore Herzl (1860–1904) as that 'From a marginal phenomenon of Jewish life he painted the Zionist solution on the canvas of world politics – and it has never left it since.'[25] The 'founder of modern political Zionism' was prepared to consider a temporary alternative territory for the 'Jewish state'; to his proposal to negotiate with the British on the offer of a territory in East Africa his friend Max Nordau (1849–1923) responded,

> Uganda is not a station on the way to Palestine, nor can it be a land for a Jewish state; because it is not a country for settlement, but merely for exploitation.[26]

Nordau's anti-imperialist stance, not unusual amongst European liberals of his time, is nevertheless as prescient as Herzl's own concern for the welfare of the then-sparse Arab population of Palestine.[27] Both of them regarded the transfer of Jews to Palestine as a 'return home', to be accomplished in co-operation with the Jewish and non-Jewish populations already present.

Although the question of which territory would be most appropriate for a Jewish state has now been decided by events, the responses of the early political Zionists to that question are still relevant to the self-understanding of Jewish people and to the relations of the State of Israel with the Arab world.

5.4.5 Israel as a 'Jewish state'

In the world of Islam one of the most recent of several states to proclaim itself Islamic is Bangladesh. To be an Islamic state means to be a state under the guidance or jurisdiction of Islamic law, even though in many instances the law may not be applied by the *ulema* but rather by secular justices of the state. In Christian countries, where the separation of Church and state has for long been a political dogma, one does not encounter states in which jurisdiction is Christian in the sense that some form of Christian law is applied to all aspects of life; indeed, it may be argued, notwithstanding canon law, that there is no system of Christian law comparable to *halakhah* and *sharia* which could be applied as the constitution of a state. To describe a country as Christian does not say anything precise about the legal system or constitution by which it might be governed.

Israel, the only Jewish country, is Jewish in the sense that Britain is Christian rather than in the sense that Saudi Arabia is Muslim; its population is predominantly Jewish, but its legal system is basically a secular creation, inherited from the British Mandate period prior to the creation of the state. Israel has no constitution, and relations between state and 'Church' are based on a *status quo* which has four components.

1   The Jewish Sabbath and Festivals are the national public holidays. (There is no law on Sabbath observance as such, only one on 'working hours and leisure time' which determines a worker's right to Sabbath observance.)
2   *Kasher* food is the standard for public institutions.
3   Personal status (marriage, divorce and some aspects of inheritance) is subject to the jurisdiction of the rabbinical courts. (For non-Jews, personal status is governed by their own religious courts or tribunals.)
4   State schools belong either to the National Secular stream or to the National Religious stream. (Again, other religious communities have their own institutions.)

A further step was taken in July 1978 when a bill was presented to the Knesset revoking section 46 of the Palestine Order in Council 1922–47, which, with some qualifications, applied 'the substance of the common law and the doctrines of equity in force in England' to Palestine, but which had in practice been severely curtailed in operation. Under the new bill, which was enacted by the Knesset on 23 July 1980,

> Where a court finds that a question requiring a decision cannot be answered by reference to an enactment or a judicial precedent or by way of analogy, it shall decide the case in the light of the principles of freedom, justice, equity and peace of the heritage of Israel.[28]

This stops well short of referring to *halakhah* as such, let alone to adopting any form of traditional Jewish law as law of the state. Although, under this *Hoq Hayesod* – Fundamentals of Law Bill – Jewish ethics may be considered in an appeal where the matter is not determined by statute, the ultimate appeal is to the secular justices, not to the religious courts. For this reason, even in those instances where some specific element of traditional Jewish law has been incorporated into the state legislation, it would be wrong to refer to the state as being governed by Jewish law; the ultimate authority is the secular state, not the rabbis.

5.4.6   *How is religion expressed in terms of statehood?*

In the light of the preceding we see that Israel is not a Jewish state according to the ertswhile Catholic 'confessional Church' model or according to the model of those Islamic states in which the *ulema* are the final arbiters of law. Though it has no written constitution, its Declaration of Independence states,

> The State of Israel will be open for Jewish immigration and for the ingathering of the Exiles; it will foster the development of the country *for the benefit of all its inhabitants*; it will be based on freedom, justice and peace as envisaged by the prophets of Israel; *it will ensure complete equality of social and political rights to all its inhabitants, irrespective of religion, race, or sex; it will guarantee freedom of religion, conscience, language, education and culture; it will safeguard the Holy Places of all religions*; and it will be faithful to the Charter of the United Nations.   (Emphasis added)

This means that its citizens of whatever creed are all free to practise their own religion and have equal access to justice, equal status before the law. If in practice there have been occasional instances of discriminatory treatment of non-Jewish Israelis, these have for the most part arisen not from religious or ethnic reasons but as a response to Arab nationalism, which, unlike Arab *identity*, is incompatible with Israeli citizenship.

In what ways, then, can Israel be regarded as a Jewish state?

1   Its ethos and values are heavily influenced by traditional Jewish teaching. The religious leadership, or *keter Torah*, has a role akin to that of the 'public Church' or 'prophetic Church'; for instance, sections of the religious leadership have expressed views, in the name of the Torah, on how the Palestinian revolt should be handled and on whether or not territory in the land should be ceded in the interests of peace.
2   The general way of life of the state enables Jewish practices, for instance Sabbath observance, to be followed without great difficulty or inconvenience.

3 The sense of history and belonging relates to the classical expressions of Judaism in the past. There is a 'naturalness' in being Jewish which is absent in other countries.

4 Cultural and linguistic development can take place on the basis of traditional sources yet in the full richness of a vigorous national life rather than a restricted community.

5 National and international problems – international relations in peace and war, the environment, religious pluralism, treatment of minorities – all these, which the Jewish religious leadership could not effectively address under 'diaspora' conditions, can be and now are faced from within the framework of Jewish culture.

5.5 Jewish Attitudes to Israel

David Ben Gurion, in his testimony before the Peel Commission in 1937, declared, 'It is not the mandate which is our Bible, but the Bible which is our mandate.' Similarly,

> In an interview published in *Le Monde* (15 October 1971), Israel's Prime Minister, Golda Meir, declared that she felt no concern over the non-recognition of Israel by the Arabs. 'This country', she said, 'exists as a result of a promise made by God Himself. It would be ridiculous to ask for the recognition of its legitimacy.'[29]

Ben Gurion and Golda Meir were astute politicians, and so perhaps judged their audiences aright. Undoubtedly many believing Jews and some believing Christians would share the sentiment they expressed. But it is curious to hear these words fall from the mouths of secular Jews, who would certainly not regulate the details of their personal behaviour on the basis of biblical statements, and would undoubtedly be selective even in drawing on the biblical heritage for its ethical, moral and philosophical content. Certainly, Lord Jakobovits is disingenuous when he asserts that

> Even secularists recognize the relevance, if not the primacy, of Jewish religious teachings in the debate that now divides the Jewish people in Israel and the world over on asserting the claim that we have to the entire Land of Israel within its Biblical borders.[30]

One must, after all, distinguish between rhetoric and serious argument.

Theologians, who on the whole find the distinction difficult, are divided as to whether and how far to read contemporary Israel as the fulfilment of biblical prophecy. Many theologians of liberal outlook, even though they may support Israel on political and humanitarian grounds, are reluctant to commit themselves to literalism in Bible interpretation, believing that this obstructs a proper understanding of the Bible's message. Even amongst fundamentalists the position is unclear. Many Christian fundamentalists hold that the return to Zion is a fulfilment of prophecy, and there is indeed a long and significant history of Christian Zionism, with strong roots in seventeenth-century England. Some fundamentalists hold that the stage following the return to Zion is the 'rapture', in which non-Christians are destroyed, or else the wholesale conversion of the Jews – neither of these reassuring views to Israelis. Other Christian fundamentalists may deny that Israel is the fulfilment of prophecy, for they hold that Jews, since they deny Christ, are rejected, and the old promises either revoked or else transferred to Christians. In the light of such negative possibilities one sees the wisdom of the Vatican, in a recent document, in urging Catholics that 'the existence of the State of Israel and its political options should be envisaged not in a perspective which is itself religious, but in their reference to common principles of international law'.[31] The same document sensitively invites Christians, nevertheless, to understand the 'religious attachment' to the land shared by many Jews, and 'which finds its roots in biblical tradition'.

The term 'fundamentalist' must be used with caution of any Jewish group; it describes a 'mind-set' rather than a body of doctrine. Those Jewish groups to whom the term is loosely applied are characterised by a tenacious faith in the truth of rabbinic texts, fairly literally understood, and read scripture only in the light of these texts. Whilst many of these people do indeed see modern Israel as the fulfilment, or at least the beginning of fulfilment, of biblical prophecy, others, such as the Hasidim of Sotmar, say that only a state set up under the Messiah and governed in accordance with the 'true' interpretation of Torah could be the fulfilment of prophecy; something like this was a common view of the many rabbinic opponents of early political Zionism.

If fundamentalist theology, whether Christian or Jewish, is ambivalent in its attitudes to the present State of Israel, does theology have any contribution at all to make to understanding what is, constitutionally, a secular state? The following are some of the main types of religious and non-religious Jewish attitudes towards the idea of an independent Israel rather than to specific governments or policies, and are not mutually exclusive.

5.5.1 Non-religious attitudes

The attitudes listed here are essentially secular, but may be shared by many religious individuals.

1 Israel is the fulfilment of the 'national' aspirations of the Jewish people; after thousands of years of minority status, of being alienated from the host societies, and in many cases actually excluded from becoming full citizens of the lands in which they lived, they feel they have at last 'come home' and are able to control their own destiny within the normal limitations of independent statehood.

2 Israel is perceived as a secure haven for persecuted Jews; had Israel existed during the years of the Holocaust, Jews would have had somewhere to turn to.

3 Some Jews are indifferent towards the State of Israel.

4 Some are actually hostile (that is, hostile in principle, not just opposed to some policy or other of the government of the day), whether because their present national identity seems threatened by supporting Israel or because for some other reason guilt feelings are aroused. Social psychologists have drawn attention to the phenomenon of self-hatred often found in individuals belonging to minority groups.

5.5.2 Religious attitudes

1 An independent Jewish state within the borders of biblical Israel is the fulfilment of prophecy. This view is usually tempered by the recognition that there is still work to be done, that the existing Israel is by no means perfect, for it does not completely

live up to the ideals of Torah. Rav Kook expressed this in terms of the kabbalistic concept of *atchalta di-geulta* (commencement of redemption); there is a sense that something significant has begun, though it is as yet unfulfilled ('unrealised eschatology' in Christian terms).

The danger of this view is that people may lose patience and take it on themselves to complete God's work for him, possibly doing it unscrupulously. It is no coincidence that the most active religious groups in Israel seeking 'settlement of the whole land' include disciples of Kook, to the chagrin of other disciples who emphasise his desire for peace.

2   Religious Jews who do not regard Israel as the fulfilment of prophecy may take either the negative view (see above) of the Sotmar Hasidim, who actively oppose the state, or the more positive view welcoming Israel as providing the opportunity to live a fulfilling Jewish life.

3   Religious Jews differ as to whether there is a specific obligation upon all Jews to live in the land of Israel.[32]

4   Part of any national self-understanding is, as we have said, a shared sense of history. In the case of Israel the Bible is a unique part of this sense of history. The Israeli reads the Bible as part of the history of his people. Even if not religious himself, he is part of the *'edah*, he is continuous with it. This opens the way to a more liberal theology of the land, one which is meaningful even to the non-literalist.

HOW RELIGIOUS ATTITUDES RELATE TO TRADITIONAL SOURCES
In 1967 Israel, defending itself from Arab attack, occupied surrounding territory including the West Bank and Gaza, both of which lie within the biblical boundaries of the land of Israel. These territories remained under Israeli control after the 1973 'Yom Kippur' war and after the Camp David accords with Egypt under Begin and Sadat in 1978.

Since 1973 a major religious debate has centred on the question of whether the West Bank and Gaza might be voluntarily handed over to Arab control in return for peace. In 1980 a religious peace movement, Oz Veshalom, published some papers on this topic, and on the treatment of minorities according to *halakhah*, by Shilo

Refael, a *dayan* (judge) of the rabbinical court in Jerusalem. At the front of the booklet stands a summary of the halakhic rulings as agreed by Refael and the then Sefardic Chief Rabbi of Israel, Ovadiah Yosef. The summary reads as follows:

> According to the majority of early authorities[33] *they shall not dwell in your land* [Exodus 23:33] does not refer to Muslims, since they are not idolaters.
>
> All authorities agree that nowadays, when Israel does not have power to drive out nations from the land, the prohibition *they shall not dwell in your land* has no application.
>
> According to many of the greatest authorities, both early and late, the prohibition *1o tehanem* [Deuteronomy 7:27][34] applies only to idolaters.
>
> Even if it were prohibited to sell land [in Israel] to non-Israelites the possibility would remain of exchanging it.
>
> According to all authorities it is permitted to return territories of [biblical] Israel in order to remove the possibility of war, for nothing stands in the way of *piquach nefesh* [the savings of life].
>
> Even if there were disputes as to [whether this was a case of] *piquach nefesh*, wherever there is a doubt in a matter of life and death we take the more lenient view [and avoid risk].
>
> In a generation where all are righteous, and immersed in [a life of] Torah, one might trust in God even where there is risk to life, but in our generation we cannot rely on miracles, and therefore we should return the territories to remove enemies from ourselves.
>
> Even according to Nahmanides, who maintains that it is a religious duty to wage war for the conquest of the land of Israel, there is no religious duty on us today to risk our lives to hold on to the territories we have conquered against the will of the nations of the world.
>
> With the agreement of the leaders of the community not only converts but non-Jews may be appointed to any public office.

What is of interest in the above is the manner in which Ovadiah Yosef and Shilo Refael relate to the classical sources of Judaism.

In the first place, they do not go directly to biblical texts, but are rabbinic interpretations of those texts.

Secondly, they cite a principle formulated by the rabbis, that the safeguarding of life has priority over all of the commandments (except murder, idolatry, and adultery/incest) and use it in a context for which there is no clear talmudic precedent: namely, the situation where part of the historical territory of Israel is occupied by non-idolators. How is this extrapolation justified? In fact, it would seem that, engaged in a characteristic process by which theologians effect change, they have selected one value from a number of available, but conflicting, values in the tradition, and have accorded it priority. The selection of the value of *piquach nefesh* over that of settlement of the land is not dissimilar to, say, the selection of the value of human dignity over that of the ownership of slaves. Both are creative decisions, determining the direction in which the faith and law are to proceed.

Then, though the *value* priority has been established, nothing very definite follows in practice. Surely they are not suggesting that if Arabs threatened to kill just one person they would relinquish the land rather than run such a risk? Clearly, other priorities come into operation in the actual situation, for we know that Yosef and Refael both support defensive wars and even pre-emptive strikes in certain circumstances. In the end, the decision has to be made in the light of a critical assessment of all circumstances, military and political options, and the like, so, although there may be a value input from theology (based on *halakhah*), *halakhah* alone does not determine the decision. We see here another line of demarcation between theology and practical decision-making.

Finally, it should be stressed that the unequivocal rejection by Yosef and Refael of the identification of present-day Near Eastern nations with their biblical counterparts, such as Ammonites and Moabites, corresponds exactly with the second-century ruling of rabbi Joshua (see section 9.3.3) that 'Sennacherib came and mixed up all the nations', so that even if an individual today regards himself as an Ammonite we should not treat him as such to his disadvantage. As there is no halakhic disagreement with this view, it is disturbing that from time to time rhetoric apparently ignores *halakhah*.

5.6   Relating to Others: Church and State

We must proceed now to provide a broader context for the discussion of Israel in its religious dimension. Our consideration of Israel and its problems as a Jewish state highlights several general problems in the Church–state relationship. These problems are not peculiar to Judaism, though Jews have been led by the re-establishment of the Jewish state to consider them anew; they have parallel manifestations in both Judaism and Christianity as well as in other religions. Therefore they can and should be faced in dialogue. Let us list some of the major ones.

The first problem that Christians and Jews share is how to relate Church or Torah on the one hand to state on the other. The Roman Church, since Vatican II, has sought to relinquish its traditional 'confessional Church' model in favour of a 'prophetic' or 'public Church, model. Yet the Church, in those lands where it is able to do so, seeks to influence the legislature to adopt laws conforming to a Catholic standpoint, such as on abortion, birth control and divorce. Likewise, there are moves in Israel towards the adoption of traditional Jewish law, particularly in matters of personal status, and there is public concern, often led by the rabbinate, on issues such as medical experimentation and autopsies, which traditional Jewish law seeks to regulate. Both Jews and Catholics need to consider carefully how far it is right to go in urging public compliance with their religious standards. Indeed, the line between 'confessional' and 'prophetic' is not as clear as is sometimes claimed.

To what extent is a particular form of religion tied to a particular culture, time or place? At the time of the separation between Judaism and Christianity, in the first century, the impression gained ground that Christianity had seized the 'universal' initiative whereas Judaism remained tightly bound within a limited nationalistic outlook. This was never more than a parody of Judaism, for the rabbis always retained the Bible-based hope for universal salvation. Is it possible, though, that both Jews and Christians overreacted in that early period? To those familiar with the thought of religious Zionists such as Rav Kook it is clear that precisely Zionism has led to a reassessment of the Jewish position within the 'salvation history' of the world, to the hope that the 'return to Zion' would itself inspire a return to God on the part of all people.

Christian experience has moved in the opposite direction. With the discrediting of colonialism has come the profound realisation that the Church was guilty of religious imperialism, of the attempt to impose on the peoples of the world what turned out to be a culture-bound, Western version of the truths of the Bible. Hence today one recognises that the Church itself must take 'national' forms, that 'local theologies' must develop. Surely Jews and Christians have much to learn from each other in reconsidering the dialectic between the particularistic and universalistic expressions of ultimate truth.

Amongst the other problems to explore together – problems Jews have not had to face for centuries until the present time – are how to treat religious minorities including 'dissidents' of one's own faith; how to conduct external relations with countries of other faiths; how to define the nature of a 'just war'; or the form and circumstances in which to supply either arms or alms to other nations. On all these matters there is now an ample specialist literature.[35]

5.7 Normalisation

I shall now gather some of the strands of this chapter, making clear my own position on the relevance or otherwise of theology to certain problems of state and religion.

First, I reject the use of 'prooftexts' from the Bible in describing contemporary nations and events. If we are to use the Bible at all in reference to specific political issues today it can be no more than a rhetorical device; even rhetorical use, however, is fraught with the danger of stereotyping Israel and 'the nations'. I align myself with those religious Jews (see section 5.5.2) who welcome Israel as providing the opportunity to live a fulfilling Jewish life, but who relate the contemporary state to biblical prophecy only in the broad sense that in reading the Bible and reflecting on Jewish history one experiences a strong and emotionally satisfying sense of continuity with biblical Israel.

Theology affects national life – whether in Israel or elsewhere – in so far as religious institutions and values colour the life of the people. The difficult question is how far religious law, not just religious values, may become the law of the state – a problem that affects Muslim and Jewish but not Christian countries. 'Religious law' in this context is not merely law that derives from religious tradition, but law administered by the recognised authorities (rabbis, *ulema*) within that tradition. Whilst welcoming the Israeli 'Fundamentals of Law' bill discussed in section 5.4.5, and recognising the political realities which underlie the maintenance of the 'status quo', I would align myself with those who believe that ultimate responsibility for law should remain in the hands of the secular justices, and who deplore the attempts of religious parties in the Knesset (Israeli parliament) to engage in political bargaining to secure legislative backing for religious measures.

I believe that the institutions of government, whether in Israel or elsewhere, should be secular; that is, the constitution (written or otherwise) should not discriminate amongst individuals or organisations on religious grounds, though society would be open to the influence of religious values. I regard the existence of 'religious' parties within a democratic society as an anomaly. Religious people sometimes see the secularisation of government as undermining the standing of religion within society. Of course, it reduces the possibilities for religious coercion, but this is a good thing. By detaching religion from the direct exercise of power, it allows 'purer' expressions of religion to prevail, and constructive religious influence to be exercised on the basis of popular consensus rather than authoritarian demand.

Finally, I maintain that Israel, seen as a 'nation state', is nothing special; 'specialness', 'chosenness' and the like are theological concepts which have no bearing on political reality. Indeed, both the ancient Hebrews in the Bible, demanding a king from Samuel in the Bible with the words 'let us be like all the nations', and Theodor Herzl proposing to 'normalise' the Jewish people and solve their 'problem' by the creation of a Jewish state, were effectively stating the normality of statehood. Their religious critics knew that this was correct; the great fear of Samuel, as of recent religious critics of Zionism, was that Israelites (or Jews) would lapse into the normality that a king or a nation state would imply, thus disrupting the religious awareness of 'chosenness' which was the summons to national spiritual growth. But Israel's internal summons to national spiritual growth is nobody else's business, certainly not that of the international community. Hence, seen as a political structure within the community of nations, Israel must be 'normalised', that is, viewed as simply another nation state.

It is not as a nation state that the 'people of Israel' carry a mission, but as an *'edah* (see section 5.2), a people in covenantal relationship with God. Covenantal relationships with God, however, are not the subject matter of international law; the *'edah* is not the nation state. Whereas the nation state is a 'normal' component of world society, the *'edah* is a metaphysical construct. The religious state, as opposed to the state within which religion has influence, confuses politics with metaphysics, sociology with theology. This is precisely the error of nationalism as opposed to nationhood or patriotism (see section 5.3); it confuses ideology (of which religion is but one instance, and nationalism another) with socio-political reality.

6

Messiah

I was at first tempted to place this chapter at the end of the book. Is not Messiah the culmination of history, a gift to writers of perorations?

But, apart from the fact that final ringing perorations render disservice to the reader who is actually interested in what the book is about, it will emerge from this chapter that Messiah is not the total end and aim and summation; it is an ingredient, an expression of hope, in the pudding of faith, good in just measure, but poison in excess. To change metaphor, it is a finger or toe, perhaps an arm or a leg, but not heart nor head.

6.1 Bible[1]

Somewhere about the year 1500 an unknown Jewish writer composed a commentary on the Psalms in which he set out to demonstrate that every single verse of that book referred to imminent redemption, that all its lyrics were battle-songs of the final apocalyptic war.[2] This is no more extravagant than the typological exegesis by which Christians then (and some even now) read all scripture as prefiguring Jesus; and it displays the sense of urgent expectation one might expect in a survivor of the 1492 expulsion from Spain.

In the cold light of day, however, we must inquire just what the Hebrew scriptures say about the Messiah. This ought to be easy. Perhaps it is, for a Hindu, who has no preconceptions about what the Bible says. But Jews and Christians have first to set aside what they have been taught about Messiah and then to approach scripture without preconceptions; surprises are in store. Moreover, Jews and Christians understand 'Messiah' differently from each other, for the concept moved forward in the immediate post-biblical period and underwent a radical transformation in the early Church.

I cannot sit beside you, patient reader, as you work through the biblical texts. I offer just a key, and urge you to open your own eyes to the plain meaning. Will you be as astonished as I was when I first discovered not one, but three rival philosophies of history within the scriptures? Will you be disappointed that nowhere in the scriptures is there a unified portrayal of the Messiah, the anointed son of David, who will usher in the golden age[3] and restore Israel to its land? Bits are there – the son of David, the day of the Lord, the ingathering of the exiles, the unity of the peoples in the name of God, the golden age with its rule of peace – but not for centuries did these fragments coalesce into the figure of an individual.[4] The fragments are not strewn evenly through the Bible, but largely confined to sections of the prophets; and most biblical books are not prophecies.

Messiah gives hope and direction to history. But that is only one of the three biblical 'philosophies of history', which are as follows.

1   Moses: *history is cyclical*. The clearest instance of this is the 'Deuteronomic cycle', consistently applied from Deuteronomy to the end of Kings, and common elsewhere. It offers no definite end to history, but repetition of (a) people are faithless to the covenant, (b) God subjects them to the power of their enemies, (c) they turn back to God and cry out to him (d) he sends them a leader to save them. No end of such cycles is envisaged.

2   Isaiah: *history is linear*. This is the view of some prophets and all apocalyptists. There may be cycles, but they will come to an end. History moves in a line towards an end that God has defined, including 'redemption' in some sense. The many successive 'leaders' stipulated by the Deuteronomic view culminate in a final Messiah.

3   Ecclesiastes: *nothing changes*. This attitude is most common in the 'wisdom' literature, such as Job and Proverbs, addressed to the individual. It is well summed up in Ecclesiastes 1:9: 'What has happened will happen again, and what has been done will be done again, and there is nothing new under the sun.'

It is extraordinary that attention has not been given to the differences amongst these views. Traditionalists should not indeed be surprised that on this, as on so many major issues, scripture speaks not with a single voice, but rather with many, all of which have some truth to convey, and which have to be held in creative tension with one another. In stating what may strike some as a novel or even eccentric interpretation of scripture I take heart from the knowledge that the rabbis themselves noticed inconsistencies in the biblical concept of history. Rabbi José bar Hanina (*c.* 300), for instance, remarked,

> Four things that Moses decreed were annulled by the Prophets. Moses said, 'You will perish among the nations.' Isaiah came and said, 'On that day shall a great trumpet be sounded. . . .'[5]

As we might express José's insight, Isaiah rejected Moses' *cyclical* philosophy of history in favour of a *linear* one with a triumphant ending. The tension between the Deuteronomic and messianic views is a permanent feature of the dialectic of reality and vision. This political dialectic of the fate of peoples must be further complemented with the sagacity of Proverbs, Job and Ecclesiastes in aiding the individual to retain equanimity despite the apparent turbulence outside.

6.1.1   *Pseudepigrapha, Scrolls*

The apocalyptic individuals and groups who were responsible for the writings known to us as Pseudepigrapha and for the Dead Sea Scrolls seized on the linear view of history, garnered the messianic strands from scripture, and generated a composite figure of the Messiah, or rather several alternative figures, occasionally in combination – say, one each from the House of David and the House of Levi[6] – and often with transcendental overtones of a rather unbiblical kind. We cannot trace that development here, but merely note that it stimulated and was in turn fed by the apocalyptic fervour which generated messianic cults and other havoc in first-century Judaea.

6.2   Messiah Ideas in the Talmud

There is no clearly defined talmudic doctrine of the Messiah – or of anything else, for that matter. The Talmud records views expressed in many countries over several centuries, and we know of no attempt by the rabbis of that period to define orthodox belief in a rigid manner analogous to that attempted by contemporary Christians at Nicaea and Chalcedon. This is not to suggest that they were indifferent to questions of belief. Indeed, the Mishnah lists amongst 'those Jews who have no portion in the world to come' several categories of persons of erroneous beliefs, and later authorities have enlarged upon these, even to the extent of building formal creeds upon them.[7] So far as belief in a Messiah is concerned, what we find are the reactions of individual rabbis as they try to interpret the messianic tradition in accordance with the events and intuitions of their times.

Several events, or movements, provoked varying reactions as the rabbis tried to absorb them, or at least understand them, in terms of their own messianic traditions. They were as follows.

1	The rise of Christianity with its messianic pretensions.
2	The destruction of the Temple in 70 CE.
3	The failure of the Bar Kochba revolt in 135.
4	The frustrated expectations which were the fruit of the Jewish apocalyptic schools, whose activities continued at least until the early second century CE, and whose influence persisted for long afterwards, expressing itself in abortive revolts with consequent frustrations and defections.
5	The Christianisation of the Roman Empire under Constantine.

It is not to be thought that the rabbis explicitly relate their teachings to any of these events. We have only a collection of detached aphorisms and anecdotes, and it is the task of scholars to place these in their historical settings.

To assess or 'measure' some of the ideas about Messiah that the rabbis expressed, I propose a scheme of seven 'parameters'.

1	Within history / beyond history.
2	Fixed time / human effort.
3	Personal Messiah / golden age.
4	Political / spiritual.
5	National / universal.
6	Catastrophic / evolutionary.
7	Detailed / vague.

6.2.1 Within history / beyond history

Any messianic belief must be placed somewhere along a line which places it within or beyond 'normal' human history. Messiah and the messianic age may be envisaged within history and the laws of nature – perhaps as 'restoring' life as it was in the halcyon days of King David. On the other hand, the believer may anticipate a change in the order of nature, a supernatural type of life, a 'new heaven and a new earth' (Isaiah 66:22) – which may, indeed, be seen as the restoration of the state of the world in the Garden of Eden, but represents a distinct *break with history*.

These two views receive their classical expression in the words of two disciples of Judah the Patriarch, the Palestinian Yohanan bar Nappaha and the Babylonian Mar Samuel, in the first half of the third century. 'The prophets', declared Yohanan, 'spoke only of the Age of the Messiah; but as for the world to come, "No eye but thine, O God, has beheld it" [Isaiah 64:3].' Samuel, however, taught, 'The only difference between the Age of the Messiah and the present time is with regard to Israel's subjection to the nations.'[8]

Clearly, Yohanan expects the messianic age to be different *in kind* from the present; there will be new heavens and a new earth, the lamb will lie down (literally) with the wolf, and so on. Samuel understands the prophecies of the supernatural to refer not to the days of the Messiah, but to the 'world to come' – that is, the eternal life after death; redemption in this world is a political change which will enable people to live according to Torah. In reply to the question 'For whom was the world created?' Yohanan says 'for Messiah', Samuel says 'for Moses'.[9] That is, Yohanan believes that the world will culminate in its transformation to a non-material state of existence in the time of the Messiah; Samuel believes that it will culminate then in perfection in the study and observance of the Torah of Moses, but that transformation to a totally spiritual state refers only to the eternal life which is not of this world. Rabbinic tradition was flexible enough to accommodate both views, without mutual accusations of heresy.

E. E. Urbach traces the 'realist' approach, with its insistence on a 'this-worldly' fulfilment of the messianic prophecies, to Rabbi Akiva.[10] Akiva's support for the Bar Kochba revolt, he maintains, was only possible because he saw the national redemption as a process *within* the world of history; consequently he did not look to Bar Kochba for the fulfilment of any of the supernatural prophecies, but only for the fulfilment of those in Haggai 2:7 and Zechariah 8:4.[11] Surely, Akiva was reacting to the extravagant supernaturalism of the apocalyptists, and possibly to Christian claims.

6.2.2 Fixed time / human effort

Many of the apocalyptic writers, for instance the author of Jubilees, believed that God had determined a time for the coming of the Messiah; we ought always to do our best to follow the commandments, and might be saved from tribulations, but cannot alter the determined date. Some held that there was a latest possible date, but that our actions might bring it forward. At the opposite extreme, some rabbis maintained that the arrival of the Messiah was entirely contingent upon human penitence.

Rabbis Joshua and Eliezer, early in the second century, debated this against a background of Roman oppression, revolutionary ferment, and apocalyptic activity.[12] Eliezer says, 'If Israel repent they will be redeemed; if not, not'; Joshua responds, 'Will they indeed not be redeemed if they do not repent? Then God will raise over them a king whose decrees are as harsh as Haman's . . . and Israel will repent. . . .'[13]

Urbach, who has collated the extant versions of this debate,[14] concludes that these two disciples of Yohanan ben Zakkai disagree on whether any weight at all is to be attached to apocalyptic speculation. Eliezer holds that the redemption is not an apocalyptic act with an independent existence, and will not necessarily take place at all; speculation as to its appointed time is futile, therefore, for it is entirely contingent upon human effort. Joshua concedes that human effort, in the form of penitence, is necessary, but sees this as part of the apocalyptic process; he thereby leaves some room for attempts to calculate the predestined date. We are told that at the end of the debate, following a challenge by Joshua from a text in Daniel, Eliezer 'was silent'. Urbach sees in this not a concession to Joshua's views, but a refusal to debate on the premise of an openly apocalyptic text.

Remarkably, both rabbis insist on the penitence of all Israel as a precondition for redemption, and differ only as to whether this is bound to take place by a predetermined date. Clearly these rabbis differ from the apocalyptists (a) by denying that there is anything 'automatic' about the redemptive event, even if in fact its date is predetermined, and (b) by rejecting the idea, well known is apocalyptic groups such as the Essenes, that only the select few would qualify for redemption. Even Simeon bar Yohai's provocative statement that *bnei aliyah* ('those who go upwards') are very few – 'if there are only two, they are my son and I' – is understood by the Gemara as a limitation not on the number of people to enter the world to come, but on those to be specially privileged there.[15]

It may also be that the insistence on penitence as a precondition is a subtle rejection of the Christian standpoint that only the saviour's own sacrifice can suffice to atone for sin; in this context the stress on the people Israel – in its literal, historical sense – also becomes meaningful. Israel, notwithstanding appearances to the contrary, is not helpless; Israel retains the power of repentance, which alone can redeem the world. Jacob Neusner, in his prolific writings on the Tannaitic period, has emphasised and elucidated the way in which *halakhah* assigns to Israel the power to change things, to determine status. This power, arising from the inwardness of the spiritual life of Torah, is exactly analogous with that of penitence, of which we speak.

Some later rabbis 'name the day' with greater or lesser precision. For instance, Elijah – from time to time he 'reveals' himself to the devout – was reported to have taught that the Messiah would appear in the last of the 85 Jubilee cycles (i.e. from 240 CE[16]). Rav Joseph, who became principal of the Academy of Pumbeditha in 330, received a 'scroll from Rome' in which it was written that the tribulations heralding the Messiah would commence in the year 4231 after Creation – that is, 473 CE.[17]

Occasionally an event rather than a date is specified, presumably with the intention of reassuring the listener that despite the disasters currently taking place – indeed, because of them – the arrival of the Messiah is imminent. Thus the so-called 'rabbinic apocalypse' tacked on to the end of Mishnah *Sotah* was (wrongly) thought to indicate a third-century date of composition by its references to rampant inflation.[18] Likewise, Rabbi Isaac bar Joseph's claim that the Messiah cannot come 'until the whole government turns to heresy'[19] makes sense when we note that not only was Rabbi Isaac at the Academy in Galilee round about the time of the Edict of Milan in 313, when Constantine legitimated

Christianity, but he actually returned from Palestine to settle in his native Babylonia shortly afterwards, almost certainly on account of discriminatory legislation and persecution by the Christians.

THE FALSE-MESSIAH SYNDROME

What happens when the end does not come at the promised time? As we saw above, 'Elijah' promised the Messiah for the year 4000 (= 240 CE). 4000 came and went, but there was no Messiah. Messianic pretenders arose and failed to fulfil expectations, and in addition there was the constant background of Christianity with its polemical claim of 'messiahship' for Jesus, who had very obviously not initiated the era of peace which was the minimum that Jews expected of the Messiah.

Since failed revolutions and Messiahs are a common feature of human experience, we can observe chracteristic ways in which people react when confronted by such failure. Let us list some of these and investigate how the rabbis responded.

1   Like Christians after the death of Jesus, or Sabbateans after the apostasy and later the death of Sabbetai Zevi,[20] the 'faithful' might have declared that the messianic era had in fact arrived despite appearances to the contrary; the mission was to be completed at a later date. That such a reaction is nowhere indicated in the talmudic sources is a demonstration that the rabbis did not allow eschatological speculations to control their theology or disturb their realistic approach to the world's problems.

In fact, the 'mission as yet incomplete' concept does occur in later Judaism – notably in the Lurianic kabbala and in the 'commencement of redemption' philosophy of Rav Kook, which is currently fashionable in some religious circles in Israel; Rav Kook's followers use this method to explain why the return of the people of Israel to the land has not yet resulted in universal peace and redemption (see section 5.5.2).

2   The mission itself might be reinterpreted – the prophets did not mean what they plainly say. This has been a common Christian response. Instead of admitting that Jesus failed to achieve the fulfilment of Isaiah's 'nation shall no more lift sword unto nation' (2:4), they say that he did even better, fulfilling the prophet's words by bringing true, inner peace into the world. The rabbis and their successors consistently insist on the literal interpretation of

verses of this kind, not because of attachment to biblical literalism, but because they regard peace – external peace – as highly desirable, and 'inner peace' as the already available gift of the Torah.

Novel theological concepts arise in Christianity from this need for reinterpretation. Early Christians used the title 'Messiah' of Jesus, perhaps to engage in debate with Jews, but it quickly became wrapped up in incarnational theology which was at odds with Judaism, and which led to the identification of the Messiah (Jesus) with the Redeemer (God).

3 Like the prophet Malachi (3:6–12) when faced by a similar situation in the non-fulfilment of Deutero-Isaiah's glowing prophecies, the sinfulness of the people might have been blamed. Indeed, the failure of the Messiah to arrive in the year 4000 led to the admission that 'on account of our numerous sins many [of the final 2000 years] have passed [and the Messiah has still not come]'.

4 Eschatological speculation might be discouraged as likely to lead to disappointment, frustration and loss of faith. Thus the forceful protest 'May those who calculate the End of Days perish!'[21] is attributed to Jonathan ben Eleazer, who was active at Sepphoris in Galilee for some years after 240 CE. It is not clear whether the rest of the statement ('for they say since the time [designated] for the End came but he [the Messiah] did not arrive, he will never come. But wait for him . . . for though justice [i.e. punishment for our sins] delay him . . . we are rewarded for looking forward to his coming.') is attributable to Jonathan, or is a later gloss; it is at least an attempt to formulate a constructive attitude in the face of constant disappointment.

6.2.3 *Personal Messiah / golden age*

Messianic beliefs differ in the degree of emphasis they place on the personality of the Messiah. At the one extreme are those who see him as a pre-existent being, destined by God to lead Israel when redemption comes – not himself a redeemer, in the sense that he personally redeems Israel and the world, but one whom God chooses to play a leading part in the coming kingdom. Though he has an eschatological function he is no more a divine being, than Jeremiah, whose 'pre-existence' is stated in the verse 'Before I formed thee in the belly I knew thee, and before thou camest forth out of the womb I sanctified thee . . .' (1:5). The line proceeds from this extreme, through the rather more human, political warrior of the Bar Kochba type, who is to serve as God's agent in overthrowing Israel's oppressors, to the opposite extreme of no individual Messiah at all, but a golden age.

The Gemara has preserved, and not even attempted to explain away, Hillel II's affirmation 'There is no Messiah for Israel; they consumed him in the days of Hezekiah.'[22] We are apt to exclaim, as Rabbi Joseph in Pumbeditha did when he heard it, 'May God forgive him! Hezekiah lived in the days of the First Temple; Zechariah, in the Second Temple, prophesied . . . "Rejoice, O daughter of Zion . . . thy king cometh!"' Rashi understands Hillel to deny an individual human Messiah; 'but the Holy One, Blessed be He, will reign and redeem alone'.[23] If Rashi is correct, Hillel conceives the messianic era as a golden age under the direct rule of God; he is perhaps dismissing the idea of the human ruler as trivial, as something we have already had, for instance in the days of Hezekiah, but too small to figure as the glory of the new age. A similar notion is expressed in a late midrash, where Israel ask God how they can be sure that the final deliverance will be permanent, for 'have you not already delivered us by Moses, Joshua, Judges and Kings, and yet we are again enslaved and humiliated . . .?' God replies that this time they will have no human leader, but he himself will save them, and his redemption will be for ever, just as his existence is for ever.[24]

What stirred Hillel to his remarkable outburst? He became Patriarch, in succession to his father, Judah III, in 320, and remained in office until his death in 365. In 312 the Roman Emperor Constantine, through the Edict of Milan, had launched Christianity on the path to power, and Hillel must have realised, despite the short respite under Julian in the early 360s, that his task was to prepare the Jews for a long period of repression under Christian rule. His decision to fix the calendar[25] was part of this preparation, for it rendered the calendar immune from government interference. His messianic teaching had a double function. First, it restrained Jews from ill-considered revolt against Rome.[26] Secondly, it provided them with a more satisfying response to the Christian claim on behalf of their saviour. For, while Jews were previously restricted to pointing out the failures of Jesus as a purely human, political deliverer, they themselves had nothing to look forward to which could match the claims of transcendence now commonly urged on behalf of Jesus; Hillel, by denigrating the human aspect of the messianic event, and putting God in the centre of things, gave his Jews a hope which was at least equal to Christian claims. And, if anyone doubts that such defences against Christianity were needed by this time, let them reflect that Joseph the Apostate, who was zealous in disseminating Christian doctrine amongst Jews in the fourth century, had originally been an assessor at the rabbinic school of Hillel's own father, Judah III, and was now not only persecuting his former co-religionists, but spreading allegations of their secret predilection for Christianity.[27]

Whilst the overwhelming majority of rabbis accept without modification the conventional picture of the Messiah as a completely human king of the House of David with a special function in and after the redemption event, one occasionally comes across a statement which appears to convey more than this, such as a claim of the pre-existence of the Messiah, or at least of his name.[28]

6.2.4   *Political/spiritual*

And now to the fourth parameter. Is the Messiah's mission (assuming there is to be a personal Messiah) political, spiritual, or some combination of the two?

We must distinguish between (a) the personal function of the Messiah and (b) the nature of the events which take place under his rule. The material at our disposal consistently assigns political tasks, such as leadership in the final battle, or government after the dawn of the new era, to the Messiah; whereas spiritual and miraculous events, from the outcome of the battle to changes in the order of nature, are ascribed to the direct intervention of God. Redemption from sin is God's work, contingent on the penitence which, as we have explained, is a precondition. In the midrash about the slaying of the *yetzer ha-ra* (evil inclination) in the time to come, we are told unambiguously that 'the Holy One, Blessed be He, will bring the evil inclination and slay it in the presence of both the righteous and the wicked'[29] – and, although the very passage in which this quotation occurs has much to say about the Messiah (both the Messiah son of Joseph and the Messiah son of David), it is clear that it is not he, but God himself, who will finally defeat evil. The Messiah's actual task, then, is a political one; but it is seen as significant only in the context of God's redemptive acts.

6.2.5   National/universal

What relative weight is given to nationalistic and universalistic aspirations within the messianic concept? Here a similar distinction must be made to that in the preceding paragraph. The Messiah himself leads Israel, but the actual triumph, the judgement upon the wicked nations, the grace and transformation, are God's work alone. A midrash of unknown date states clearly, '"Redeemed of the Lord" – not "redeemed of Elijah" or "redeemed of the Messiah", but "redeemed of the Lord".'[30] The same midrash (on Psalm 2) does ascribe certain aspects of judgement to the Messiah personally: for instance,

> In days to come, the king Messiah will be told, 'Such-and-such a nation has rebelled against you.' He will say, 'Let locusts come and destroy it' – as it is said, 'He shall smite the land with the rod of his mouth' [Isaiah 11:4]. When the people see what great distress they are in they will come and do him homage.

But this is not a demonstration of his personal power. As the midrash itself makes clear, it is but the reflection of God's own glory: 'What is the meaning of, "His resting-place shall be glorious" [Isaiah 11:10]? He will set upon the Messiah some of the glory from above.'[31]

Another midrash[32] offers the following comment on the relationship between the Messiah and the nations:

> Israel will not need to seek instruction from the king Messiah, as it is said, 'The nations will seek unto him' [Isaiah 11:10] – the nations, not Israel. So what will be his function? He will gather the exiles of Israel, and give [the nations][33] the thirty commandments.

One version of this midrash goes on to say that the nations will fail in their undertaking to fulfil these commandments;[34] the other omits this accusation.

The presentation of the messianic idea in the writings of the talmudic period is undoubtedly ethnocentric. This is partly an overreaction to Christian universalism, partly the defensive reaction of a persecuted people. But, although the acknowledgement of the presence of at least some of the possible nations in the messianic era tends to be casual and grudging, it does not seem to be in doubt. For instance, an Amora, probably of the fourth century, discusses the possibility of the arrival of the Messiah on a Friday. Elijah would not come on a Friday, it is argued, because his arrival would distract the Jews from their Sabbath preparations. But the Messiah might arrive then, for when he arrives all the nations will immediately become subservient to Israel and complete the Sabbath preparations for them.[35] More seriously, Rabbi Joshua, early in the second century, had already asserted categorically that the righteous of the nations have a portion in the world to come.[36] A late source[37] is more explicit:

I came across an old man and he asked me, 'Will the nations be present in the days of the Messiah?' I replied, 'My son, all those nations who have humiliated and oppressed Israel will see the good that Israel enjoys, and will then revert to dust and never live again . . . but those who have not humiliated nor oppressed Israel will be present in the days of the Messiah.'

Yet another midrash asserts in God's name, 'Whosoever of the nations denies that there is another God – I shall restore him to life.'[38]

Far more striking than any of the literary sources is a passage in the New Year liturgy. This sums up admirably the hope of messianic redemption for all nations, and stands firmly in the universalistic tradition of Deutero-Isaiah:

Now, therefore, O Lord our God, impose thine awe upon all thy works, and thy dread upon all that thou hast created, that all works may fear thee and all creatures prostrate themselves before thee, that they may all form a single band to do thy will with a perfect heart. . . .

Give then glory . . . unto thy people, praise to them that fear thee, hope to them that seek thee . . . gladness to thy city, a flourishing horn unto David thy servant, and a clear shining light unto the son of Jesse. . . .

Then shall the just also see and be glad, and the upright shall exult . . . and all wickedness shall be wholly consumed like smoke, when thou makest the dominion of arrogance to pass away from the earth.

And thou, O Lord, shalt reign, thou alone over all thy works on Mount Zion, the dwelling place of thy glory. . . .[39]

It is a sobering thought for the scholar that, but for the survival of this small liturgical piece, our understanding of rabbinic teaching on the Messiah would have been wide of the mark. Yet it is the liturgy to which greater weight should be attached in assessing rabbinic attitudes; unlike the *obiter dicta* it is intended to give a balanced and authoritative picture, and is not just a pointed response to a fleeting problem. We must also remind ourselves that the main text for study in the rabbinic schools was not Mishnah or Midrash but Bible; thus the liturgical passage above – a patchwork of biblical phraseology – fits harmoniously into the rabbinic tradition.

6.2.6 Catastrophic/evolutionary

Was the rabbinic view of the actual messianic process that it would be sudden and catastrophic, or that it would be a gradual evolution? 'Rabbi Hiyya the Great said to Rabbi Simeon ben Halafta in the house of Rabbi [Judah the Prince], "The redemption of Israel commences little by little, and increases steadily".'[40] There is some evidence that some of Rabbi's students entertained hopes that he might be the Messiah.[41] Moreover, for a time the position of Jews under Roman rule in Palestine had somewhat ameliorated. Perhaps it now looked as if a new age were gradually dawning. Perhaps memories of the abortive 'catastrophic' revolts of 68, 116 and 132 were still too terrible for a repetition to be contemplated, even if the outcome this time were successful – indeed, we find several rabbis, mainly third-century, openly expressing a wish not to witness the birth pangs of the Messiah.[42] At about the same time Rabbi Yohanan taught that the son of David would come 'either to a generation that is completely righteous or to one that is completely wicked' – a view which, like that of his Babylonian contemporary, Rav, that 'the whole matter now depends entirely on penitence',[43] strongly indicates a gradualist approach. If such an approach is not the predominant one in Bible or Talmud, it is nevertheless well attested.

6.2.7   Detail

The talmudim and midrashim offer many collections of sayings replete with apocalyptic and eschatological detail, and evidently certain rabbis had a taste for this sort of thing and did not lack a public avid for authoritative expression of their dreams. On the other side, we find that Rabbi Akiva, himself implicated in the practical realisation of the messianic hope in the days of Bar Kochba, is ridiculed by his colleagues when he makes what they regarded as an uncharacteristic – and inexpert – excursion into the field of eschatological speculation.[44]

6.2.8   Possible extreme views

On the basis of the preceding analysis, we can present two possible 'extreme' rabbinic views of the Messiah and his age, as follows.

1   The events and the age are supernatural, 'not of this world'. They will come about at a predetermined time, though they must be preceded by Israel's penitence. The Messiah is a pre-existent son of David (whatever this may mean), and, though he is only a mortal, God's glory will descend upon him; it is nevertheless God, not the Messiah, who is the actual redeemer. Israel will be delivered from her enemies, and the exiles, including the Ten Tribes, will be gathered to the Holy Land. Israel will exercise dominion, particularly of a spiritual nature, over all mankind, as all come to Jerusalem to seek God. The coming of the Messiah will be a 'catastrophic' event, brought about by divine intervention in history.

2   No time is fixed, no personal Messiah will arise, no catastrophic event will take place. But, if and when Israel repents, her political independence will be restored, and Jerusalem will become a spiritual centre for mankind. The Ten Tribes will not return.[45]

One cannot be sure that any individual rabbi of talmudic times held either the 'strong' view or the 'weak' view in its entirety. But it is clear that none of the items in either view is represented as heretical, even though some of the views are regarded by some of the rabbis as erroneous.

6.3   Five Models of Messiah

Though the rabbis laid the groundwork for the Jewish concept of Messiah, philosophers and theologians developed it further in response to changing conditions and perceptions. The five whose ideas are presented below offer widely diverse models on which the contemporary theologian may draw.

6.3.1   *Moses Maimonides (1135–1204)*

Maimonides[46] states that the Messiah, a descendant of David, will

restore the Davidic dynasty to its [erstwhile] glory, rebuild the Temple, and gather the exiles. In his days all the laws [of the Torah] will again take effect as of old; sacrifices will be offered, sabbatical and Jubilee years will take effect.

No miracles will be demanded of him to confirm his mission, but,

if a king arise of the house of David, devoted to Torah and the commandments like his father David, and makes all Israel do likewise, while waging the Lord's battles, he can be assumed to be the Messiah. If he succeeds in this, and rebuilds the Temple in its place and gathers the exiles of Israel he is certainly the Messiah. And he will lead the whole world to serve God together. . . .

In those days there will be no hunger or war, no enmity nor conflict . . . but 'the whole earth will be full of the knowledge of the Lord as the waters cover the sea'   [Isaiah 11:9].

To Maimonides the prime objective of the messianic age is the fulfilment of the contemplative ideal, with the ultimate aim of perfecting souls for the eternal life in the world to come; the political aspects of the messianic age are therefore played down:

The sages and prophets did not yearn for the days of the Messiah in order that they might rule the world . . . or be exalted by the nations, or that they might eat, drink and be merry; but that they might be free of oppression and distraction, in order to [devote themselves to] the Torah and its wisdom, that they might earn [their portion in] the world to come.

Maimonides emphasises that prophecies such as that of the wolf lying down with the lamb are parables, and generally plays down the role of the supernatural in messianic prophecy, citing as authoritative the view of Samuel (reviewed in section 6.2.1) that 'the only difference between the Age of the Messiah and the present is in respect of Israel's subjection to the nations'.

With reference to such apparently specific prophecies as that concerning the war of Gog and Magog [Ezekiel 38] he states categorically,

> No one knows exactly what form these things will take, for the prophecies are obscure, and the sages have no [clear] tradition . . . such details are in any case not of fundamental religious importance, and no one should spend time on such *aggadot* and midrashim . . . for they do not lead to the fear or love of God; nor should one attempt to calculate the End. . . .

In a paragraph censored from the printed editions of the *Mishneh Torah* Maimonides rejects the truth claims of Christianity and Islam on the grounds that they fail to meet the criterion of consistency with the Torah of Moses. Despite this, he assigns to both Christianity and Islam a role in the process of world redemption:

> The teachings of him of Nazareth [Jesus] and of the man of Ishmael [Mohammed] who arose after him help to bring all mankind to perfection, so that they may serve God with one consent. For insofar as the whole world is full of talk of the Messiah, of words of Holy Writ and of the Commandments – these words have spread to the ends of the earth, even if many deny their binding character at the present time. When the Messiah comes all will return from their errors.

Maimonides' view of the Messiah's role is natural and restorative. The Messiah is 'within history'; not only will nature, including human nature, remain unchanged in his time, but the laws of Torah will remain in force and even become universally applicable, as all nations 'return to the true religion' and 'eat that which is permitted together with Israel'.

Though scathing in his denunciation of those who would calculate the time of redemption,[47] he is unclear as to its dependence on prior penitence; rather, he sees penitence as part of the pattern of events with which the Messiah is associated, and in any case he stresses penitence for its intrinsic merit at all times. He undoubtedly believes in a personal Messiah whose role is primarily spiritual, though certain political elements are present to assist the fulfilment of the spiritual purpose. He clearly holds that the Messiah's mission, though focused on Israel, is to the whole world. Whilst not explicitly rejecting the catastrophic approach – 'from a literal reading of the prophets it would appear that a war between Gog and Magog will take place at the beginning of the Messianic era' – he plays it down, and gives at least some indication of an evolutionary process, notably in the above-cited passage in which he characterises Christianity and Islam as steps towards the final redemption. He is calculatedly non-committal on all points of detail with regard to the Messiah process.

For Maimonides, the Messianic era is a means to two separate ends. One end is the achievement of individual intellectual and moral perfection on earth – beautifully expressed in the final peroration of his *Guide of the Perplexed*, significantly with no explicit mention of Messiah.[48] The second end is everlasting individual bliss, enjoyed by the soul in the radiance of God's Presence in the world to come.

Peace, in the days of the Messiah, may help one to achieve these ends, but they can be achieved even now by the righteous; hence the messianic era has no essential, indispensable function in the assurance of individual salvation.

6.3.2   Isaac Abravanel (1437–1508/9)

As a philosopher, Isaac Abravanel[49] was deeply indebted to Maimonides, though he never completed his projected commentary on the *Guide*. But on Messiah they differ radically. Whereas Maimonides minimises the supernatural element in the traditional sources, Abravanel eagerly and fervently develops it in as literal a fashion as possible. The 1483–4 commentaries on Joshua and Samuel already show his tendency, in explicit opposition to Maimonides, to revel in literal interpretation of miraculous events, thereby, as he sees it, giving greater glory to God;[50] as early as 1465, in Lisbon, he had begun to cast aside the exclusively rationalistic, philosophical approach of his youth.[51]

Abravanel's most fervently apocalyptic works, such as his Daniel commentary, were not produced until 1496, more than four years after he and his fellow Jews had been expelled from Spain. Not only the Jewish catastrophe but also the fiery apocalyptic oratory of Savonarola[52] and the general influence of Christian millenarian ideas in the later fifteenth and early sixteenth centuries[53] stimulated Abravanel to urgent eschatological specula- tion. Hints of this outlook can be discerned in his earlier works.

With consummate skill and imagination Abravanel blends together in his messianic writing apologetic, response to contem- porary events, and a philosophy of history.

Abravanel undermines Christian claims to the messiahship of Jesus by repeatedly insisting that the messianic prophecies[54] are to be understood *as a whole*; only someone who fulfils every one of them can be considered the Messiah. Since many of the prophecies are of peace in the world, of the return of the Twelve Tribes, and of other matters which have obviously not been fulfilled, it is clear that the Messiah has not yet arrived. To Abravanel's Jewish readers this meant two things: first, the claims of Christianity were unfounded, and, secondly, they were to look forward confidently to the magnificent fulfilment of all that the prophets had foretold.

A man as experienced in worldly affairs as Abravanel – by the time he composed his first apocalyptic work he had already been adviser to the monarchs of Portugal, Spain and Naples – could scarcely fail to read his Bible in terms of the stirring events of his day. The fall of Constantinople in 1453, and the defeat of the last Muslim stronghold on the Spanish mainland in 1492, followed by Charles VIII's invasion of Italy – intended as a first step to the conquest of the Holy Land – served to convince him that the great messianic wars would arise out of the conflict between Muslim and Christian; Spanish and Portuguese sailors returning from Africa with reports of the Ten Lost Tribes of Israel enabled him to envision the tribes emerging from long exile to come to the aid of their oppressed brethren of the House of Judah and to defeat the might of both Turk and Christian, wreaking vengeance on the wicked and re-establishing Jewish control of the land of Israel, with the Messiah ruling the whole world through the spirit of God. His awareness of the passion, crime and violence of the age, and his somewhat reactionary attitude to humanism and to technologi- cal advance and scientific discovery, together with his deep identi- fication with the apparently unmerited and seemingly unending sufferings of his people, predisposed him to a conviction that the End was imminent. A complex broth of biblical, talmudic and astrological argument actually led him to publish a date for the arrival of the Messiah – the year 1503. When 1503 came and Messiah did not, he resiliently amended the date to 1531 – a possibility built into the original calculations, which related the date of arrival to the 'variable' of penitence.[55]

He expounds his philosophy of history in his commentary on Genesis 11. Adam, Cain and the 'generation of the division' (who built the Tower of Babel) all erred in the same way. They ought to have been satisfied with the bounty granted them by God through nature, and to have devoted their entire energies to spiritual perfection. But instead they developed in three ways which disrupted their erstwhile perfect relationship with God through harmony with nature. They 'improved' on nature by developing the sciences of agriculture and medicine; they developed technologies 'strange' to nature, such as the manufacture of clothing, the building of houses, and the construction of ships; worst of all they opposed nature by 'casting stones upwards and fire downwards' (the arts of warfare?) and by the imposition of human government, which, by granting authority to some men over others, directly opposes nature, which has made men free and equal. Abravanel's debts to Seneca[56] for his idealisation of the state of nature, and to Augustine[57] for his political concept of the basic equality of man, impaired through sin, are clear. Our present-day institutions of government, even those proposed by the Torah, are compromises, for only when sin is removed can the ideal state of life come about; the Israelite monarchy itself was a compromise to the needs of a sinful people – that is why Samuel rejected it.[58] But from this point of view it follows that the final redemption is a return of the original order of things before the sin of Adam, when people were directly dependent on the bounty of God and pursued no material aims. Penitence is thus of the essence of Abravanel's messianic theory, and so is the 'new order', i.e. the return to the mythological past, outside of history.

Abravanel's commentaries brought hope and comfort to the Jews of his day, and stimulated the development of mysticism in a tragic age when more rationalistic philosophies could not grip the soul of an oppressed people. His concept of Messiah is utopian, and accepts within narrow limits the predetermination of history. The Messiah is a person, his mission at first political – he fights wars and executes vengeance, gathers the exiles and liberates the land – but ultimately transcends politics, as the need for government disappears when all are equal and just, and becomes an entirely spiritual mission. Although Abravanel does not think that the remnant of the nations will match Israel spiritually, he allows them a place in the messianic era, and thus preserves universalism. The events at the time of the advent are undoubtedly catastrophic, and are described by him in awesome detail.

6.3.3 Isaac Luria (1532–72)

Late in the sixteenth century the Galilean town of Safed was a focus of intense Jewish spirituality in both *halakhah* and mysticism; amongst its leading saints and scholars were Spanish refugees and their descendants, drawn to the Holy Land in the expectation of imminent redemption. Yet they had not really escaped *galut* (exile, displacement), and, though on holy soil, felt and shared the sufferings of their people.

Rabbi Isaac Luria, the most influential of the Safed mystics, saw the *galut* not only 'as a terrible and pitiless state permeating and embittering all of Jewish life, but . . . [as] the condition of the universe as a whole, even of the deity'.[59] Not only Israel, but cosmos and, indeed, Creator, were 'in exile' – a concept derived from early rabbinic passages which speak of God as being in exile with Israel.[60] The rabbinic passages recognised the divine pathos[61] – God's 'fellow feeling' with Israel – but did not take Luria's further step of *universalising* the concept of exile; for them *galut* was essentially the experience of Israel at the hand of the Gentiles, and certainly not an experience of which the Gentiles were part. Luria was enabled to take this further step only in consequence of his extraordinary theory of creation, according to which God creates by simultaneously (a) limiting himself, so as to 'make room' for something other than himself, and (b) emanating 'light' into the 'empty space'. The 'vessels' into which God, in the process of creation, emanated light, were not strong enough to contain it. As the vessels shattered, some of the light returned to its origin, but the rest, consisting of 'sparks', was scattered in confusion, thus putting *galut* at the very heart of things. Some of the light even fell into the 'husks', 'shells', which inhabit the abyss of evil, the 'empty space' from which God withdrew himself, and aspire to rise from the darkness and return to their source, but cannot do so without help. Thus God himself, so to speak, has partly 'fallen' into exile.[62]

Within a generation or so, the imaginative qualities of this bizarre cosmogony had captured the hearts and minds of the Jewish masses over much of Europe, and within two centuries it had spawned the Sabbatean and Hasidic movements. It was quickly perceived as a robust and fertile expression of the experiences and hopes of sixteenth-century Jewry. Life, with all its suffering and disappointment, became at once comprehensible and acceptable; *galut* was the embodiment of the 'fallen sparks' of creation captured in the 'husks' of impurity, the divine light within us striving to return God-wards. With the assurance that every time they performed a *mitzvah* they restored some of this light to its place of origin, Jews experienced redemption as having commenced; it was indeed a continuous process, in which every Jew not only could but had to participate. Thus the everyday minutiae of Jewish life, its festivals, its dietary laws, the study of Torah – matters perhaps irksome to downtrodden Jews and ridiculed by their detractors – became the actual vehicle of cosmic redemption. To tie on one's *tefillin* (phylacteries) correctly, to pray with full devotion and in carefully formulated words – these were no longer merely (as if it would not be enough) a means to private salvation; the whole world stood or fell by Israel's performance of the commandments. Indeed, if Israel played her part well enough, it would even be possible to escape the 'birth pangs of the Messiah'; he would come merely to 'round off' the redemption process, as the symbol of what had been accomplished: the Lurianic concept of the Messiah does not necessarily involve a 'catastrophic' scenario.

6.3.4   *Elijah of Vilna (1720–97)*

Though Rabbi Elijah, the 'Gaon' of Vilna, Lithuania, did not succeed in his own attempt to reach the Holy Land, many of his disciples settled there, forming one of the cornerstones of the *yishuv* (settlement) in the nineteenth century. But not until 1968, when M. M. Kasher published *Qol ha-Tor* ('The Voice of the Turtle–Dove') by the Gaon's nephew and disciple, Hillel ben Benjamin of Shklov, was there a coherent account Elijah's views on the Messiah and land.[63] Rabbi Kasher informs us that the Gaon characterised the years 5500–600 (1740–1840) as *saf ha-atchalta* (threshold of the commencement of redemption) and the years 5600–5750 (1840–1990) as the actual *atchalta*, or commencement of redemption, thus foretelling the course of events for almost two centuries after his death; and that 'details', such as the Holocaust, or the opposition of the United Nations to Israeli rule in Jerusalem, are predicted by him. Unless Kasher has deliberately withheld from publication just that part of the manuscript which might have substantiated his claim, we must assume that he has let his imagination run away with him, and has read into the text things which are not there.[64]

The little book nevertheless contains much material which is hardly less astonishing and certainly of greater significance than the fortune-telling which Kasher seems to regard as its principal selling point. I shall now review some of this material, though it should be noted that (a) the full kabbalistic setting is too complex to be reproduced here, and (b) we do not know when we are dealing with authentic views of the Gaon, and when Rabbi Hillel's own thoughts intrude. Reluctantly, I abandon Hillel's 'Seven basic principles of redemption', 'Seven practical aspects of the commencement of redemption', '156 facets of the Messiah son of Joseph', and other lists, in favour of an ordering of material more convenable to our purposes.

The Gaon, it seems, became convinced that he was 'called' to initiate the resettlement of Israel in preparation for the advent of the Messiah son of David; but his attempts to journey there himself in 1780 were unsuccessful, perhaps because he learned that the land was desolate, ill-governed, disease-ridden and desperately poor. In 1782 he experienced a vision[65] confirming his mission, and spelling out the possibilities of its fulfilment. How much of the following doctrine was 'revealed' at that time it is impossible to say; but the event was of far-reaching importance, and it is by no means absurd to see that vision of 1782 as the point of origin of modern Zionism, in the sense of a recognition of the need for a practical programme of regeneration of the land in its physical as well as spiritual aspects.

The present age, in which 'the voice of the turtle-dove is heard in our land' (Song of Solomon 1:12), is already the 'commencement of redemption'. As we have not shown ourselves worthy of the immediate appearance of the Messiah son of David, leader of the final redemption, we undergo this preparatory period of the commencement under the guidance of the Messiah son of Joseph. Since his mission is to achieve the 'awakening from below' (the 'left side', 'the attribute of judgement'), he works in a natural fashion, without 'open' miracles. His task is threefold. He will (1) reveal the mysteries of the Torah, (2) gather the exiles to the Holy Land, and (3) remove the 'unclean spirit' which at present contaminates the land, by cultivating it and thus enabling the *mitzvot* relating to it to be fulfilled.[66] The process will be a gradual, quiet[67] one, the length of which relates to the effort we put into it; there will be troubles and economic hardships, but these, through God's compassion, will lead on to redemption.[68] A prerequisite for redemption is the presence of Jews in Jerusalem, which should become a centre for the propagation of Torah. These new settlers should be men of honesty and integrity; special attention should be given to the accuracy of weights and measures and to the practice of social justice and charity.[69]

Rabbi Hillel constantly stresses in the name of the Gaon that Jerusalem must be rebuilt and the land cultivated. This refutes the allegation made by generations of Zionist historians that the early religious settlers were devoid of interest in worldly matters, but content to live on the *haluqah* remitted from abroad and to await the miraculous advent of the Messiah. 'Our master's greatest desire', writes Rabbi Hillel, 'was [to fulfil the verse] "But ye, O mountains of Israel, ye shall shoot forth your branches, and yield your fruit to my people Israel" [Ezekiel 36:8].'[70] The Gaon's intentions were perfectly clear, but it would seem that they were largely frustrated. Rabbi Hillel tells of a typical situation in which he found himself, as leader of the Jerusalem Kolel in the early 1800s.[71] One of his emissaries had preached, on the Gaon's *Jahrzeit*, in a certain town in Lithuania, and had appealed for funds to assist the rebuilding of Jerusalem. He was immediately followed in the pulpit by a leader of the local community, who castigated him for not being satisfied with money to buy bread for the poor, and for his 'impertinence' in soliciting money for such 'dreams' as the rebuilding of Jerusalem and the purchase of fields. Surely, argued this ignoramus, if God wanted to bring about the redemption, he would not expect us to purchase fields ourselves? Rabbi Hillel bitterly compares this attitude with that of the Twelve Spies in the days of Moses, and explains that their sin is still upon us, and can only be expiated by our commitment to developing the land.

The present age is compared to that of Cyrus; like Ezra and Nehemiah, we must concentrate our efforts on building up the land. But it is also compared with that of Joshua, the conqueror: not that there is any suggestion of taking possession of the land by force, but that we should be steadfast in holding on to that which comes into our possession – '. . . and settle in the towns of which you have taken hold' (Jeremiah 40:10).[72]

Hillel refers to his master, the Gaon of Vilna, as 'a light of the Messiah son of Joseph'. He does not mean that the Gaon was *the* Messiah ben Joseph, as some have erroneously inferred. What has happened is that the concept of Messiah ben Joseph has been 'smeared out' in his kabbalistic system in such a way that it is no longer possible to think of Messiah as one individual man to the exclusion of all others. There are three planes on which Messiah ben Joseph exists.[73] On the highest plane, he is identical with Metatron, the Angel of the Presence. On a lower plane, he is to be identified with the righteous leader of each generation – from Joshua in his generation to the Vilna Gaon in his – who labours for the salvation of Israel. On the third plane, each individual Jew who takes part in the gathering of the exiles and the other work of Messiah ben Joseph is himself a 'remnant of Joseph', a part of Messiah ben Joseph. Messiah ben Joseph is thus eternally present, though mostly unrecognised. Elsewhere[74] Messiah ben Joseph is defined as the supernatural power that ensures the physical survival of Israel and gives her strength; the Messiah ben David is the supernatural power that maintains and strengthens Israel's spiritual being. Both exist and react with each other eternally.

The Gaon's attitude to the role of the nations in the redemption may be gleaned from the following scheme of events for the last days.[75]

1 Ingathering of the exiles.
2 Rebuilding of Jerusalem.
3 Removal of the 'unclean spirit' from the land by planting it and observing the special commandments relating to it.
4 'Redemption of Truth' – i.e. the growth of a society consisting of men of honesty and integrity.
5 The resulting Sanctification of God's Name amongst the nations.
6 Revelation of the mysteries of Torah.
7 The whole world established as the Kingdom of God.

Major wars and international conflicts do not figure in this scheme. The Gaon sees the predicted wars, such as the war of Gog and Magog, or the war against Armilius, not so much as actual physical wars, but as symbols of the triumph of Truth over Error and

Darkness.[76] The purpose of the redemption is unequivocally defined by him as 'The Redemption of Truth and the Sanctification of the Divine Name',[77] and this is conceived as a process, led by Israel, but ultimately involving all mankind.

Looking at all this in terms of the parameters we have set, we find that the Gaon's view of the messianic era is restorative.[78] The time of its coming depends greatly on our efforts. The balance between the political (physical) and spiritual elements is maintained by the relationship between the twin concepts of Messiah ben David and Messiah ben Joseph. The ultimate hope is universalist, though its achievement rests upon Israel, and includes Israel's national restoration in her own land. The process by which it is achieved is evolutionary rather than catastrophic.

Shorn of its kabbalistic integuments this view is remarkably similar to Hermann Cohen's, to which we turn next. Both see the ethical attainment of Israel as the springboard to universal redemption. Whereas the Gaon attaches great importance to the actual physical restoration of a spiritually regenerated Israel to the land, Cohen dismisses this as obsolete tribalism. Why, having transcendentalised the concepts of the Messiahs and of the wars of the End in such a way that they no longer refer to specific human individuals or situations, does the Gaon not do the same with the concept of the land? The difference arises from his experience and understanding of contemporary life. Whereas Cohen thought he could find the embodiment of high spiritual and ethical ideals around him, in 'civilised' German society, the Gaon, to whom ethical behaviour and spirituality were rooted in the deep mysteries of Torah, could not conceive of the burgeoning of the new era in his native Lithuania, surrounded by 'the abominations of the nations'. The literal fulfilment of the promise of national restoration provided the only setting within which redemption could be envisaged.

6.3.5   *Hermann Cohen (1842–1918)*

Hermann Cohen brought to its culmination the liberal–rationalistic approach to the interpretation of Judaism which was first clearly and effectively formulated by Moses Mendelssohn in the eighteenth century. Cohen spent most of his working career as professor of philosophy at Marburg, and was regarded as the leader of the Marburg school of neo-Kantian philosophy. After his retirement he was persuaded to lecture, for the last three years of his life, at the Berlin Hochschule für die Wissenschaft des Judentums, and this commitment, as well as a journey to Eastern Europe, led him to modify some of his earlier views on Judaism and religious philosophy, and to produce a full-length study of Judaism, in which Judaism was presented as the religion of reason *par excellence*;[79] nevertheless, the main outlines of his understanding of Judaism were already apparent in the numerous articles and papers published throughout his career at Marburg.

Cohen expressed his ideas on Messiah in an essay first published around 1893.[80] Hope, which is the central idea of messianism, distinguishes monotheism from paganism.

> Hope is the product and expression of belief in one divine providence . . . [which] relates not primarily to the individual, and not exclusively to a special people, but to all mankind, the children of God.[81]

Israel's faith is a belief in Man – i.e. in the progress and perfectibility of Man – and its hope for the future of Man is the essence of the messianic idea and the high-point of Israelite prophecy. Even the most profound and general ideas which have taken hold of the world, claims Cohen, have grown up in particular national contexts or individual circumstances. The messianic idea indeed first appeared in a strictly national context, manifesting characteristics that were incompatible with what it was later to become; but it is essentially a historical rather than a political concept, and cannot be confined within the national limitations of its origin. Cohen cites a number of prophetic passages, attempting to demonstrate that the later ones emphasise 'the day of the Lord' – that is, the period in which justice will prevail on earth – rather than the personality of the Messiah. In similar vein, he cites the Talmud in such a way as to show how the rabbis stressed the ethical implications of the messianic era rather than the personality of the Messiah. He concludes that, difficult as it is to transcend the narrowly nationalistic outlook, the prophets of Israel in fact achieved this through the messianic idea – the idea of Man – for, though indeed not all of them grasped the idea clearly themselves, their teachings pointed unequivocally towards universalism. This was not incompatible with the idea of the chosen people, for, says Cohen,

Election, in the religious sense, simply means historical vocation. . . . Rarely has any nation kept itself free from the darkness of nationalism. . . . There is only one way to do so and the prophets, founders of our religion, discovered it, and for this discovery suffered prison and exile. But through it they made known the God of Israel. This discovery, with which they fought against nationalistic egoism, and through which they, and they alone, revealed the idea of Man – this is the messianic idea.[82]

The tragedies of the twentieth century have shaken our faith in human progress and rationality. Moreover, Cohen's readings of biblical and talmudic texts frequently fail to meet the demands of more recent scholarship. But let us at least recognise the nobility of his conception, and the deep yearning it expresses for peace, brotherhood and justice amongst people.

6.4   Assessment of Messiah

We must now assess the value of the messianic idea in today's society. But let us not be trivial. Of course, there are wars and disturbances and our lives are insecure, and so 'we want Moshiach [Messiah] now'.[83] But to state that the world is in a mess and needs clearing up is a very different thing from stating just what we envisage as a solution to the world's problems. As we learned in Chapter 4 when considering proposals to change the economic 'system', an emotional response without a constructive alternative merely distracts people from the effective ways in which progress could be made, and leads to frustration when that in which they pin their hopes fails, or even makes things worse. In that context we spoke of 'false utopianism', and now we are scouting out the very realm of utopia we must not forget the earlier lesson.

The world in which we live is so different from that in which messianic ideas developed that it is hard to extrapolate from the traditional sources to our own situation. Before we even attempt to do so, let us enumerate the changed insights arising from, or reinforced by, modern learning and experience, insights which provide the context for our own expression of messianism.

1   Most messianic theories in earlier times were put forward on the assumption that the world we know has a total existence of

some thousands of years only, from start to finish. Typical of this is the 6000-year scheme to which reference was made in section 6.2.2. It is indeed interesting that those biblical books, such as Job and Ecclesiastes, which seem to assume a different time scale, a very much longer one, are markedly non-apocalyptic in tone.[84] But nowadays it is clear not only that people have been on earth for some millions of years, but also that in all probability earth, and people with it, will continue to exist for hundreds or even thousands more millions of years.

2   Modern communications and the better understanding of languages and history have led us to revise our attitude towards other peoples and their cultures. The naïve concept of the conflict between Israel and the nations as the equivalent of the struggle between Good and Evil has become merely ridiculous when regarded as a theory of world history, though it may still function as a prototype or symbol of processes observed in many societies and at many periods of history. Ethnocentricity has become not just distasteful but implausible; we have learned to recognise the revelation of God's will in many times, places and societies.

3   Our attitude towards sacred texts, in particular the Bible and the Talmud, has changed under the impact of modern scholarship. We have learned to see them as the record of the Israelite and Jewish response to God over a period of some thousands of years, and in varying cultural environments. We therefore try to relate statements to their social–historical contexts, and we recognise the views which then emerge as attempts, not always perfectly executed and by no means always mutually consistent, to grapple with major issues. Bible and Talmud are not 'proof texts' but guides to life, aids to our rediscovery and reformulation of the teachings and insights they enshrine.

4   The concept of organic evolution, as well as evolutionary models of society, make it difficult to accept any doctrine about a final end, in the sense of a final and permanent state of society which will be brought into existence at a particular point in time.

We are now ready to answer, within the framework of our set parameters, seven questions which might be propounded today concerning the Messiah.

6.4.1   What is the age that he will usher in?

For the following reasons I reject all theories that offer to cure the
world's ills by bringing about some undefined 'new order'.

1   If the 'new order' is one in which the substance and laws of
nature are to be different from the present, and it is clearly discon-
tinuous with history and natural science, I do not understand what
it is, and certainly do not understand how it can be relevant to
justice and peace on this earth.

2   If the 'new order' is one in which people's nature will change,
and they will all be good, the problems which exist in our present
'order' would not have been solved, only evaded. An anonymous
talmudic report does tell us that in the messianic days the 'evil
impulse' will be slain;[85] probably this means that the basic psychological structure of human beings will be changed, so that people
will have no tendency to do evil. If so, we have not learned how
humans, creatures of free will and conflicting impulses, are to be
redeemed, but only that they are to be replaced with some newly
designed creature, some new-fangled humanoid which has no
conflicting impulses, and presumably therefore no free will. But
such a creature is not human, so our problem has not been solved.

Are we any better served by 'restorative' utopias, which seek the
solution to the world's problems 'on the stage of history', *within*
the present order of nature?

Plato, in his *Republic*, outlines an ideal city state whose constitution is the embodiment of Justice; this is truly a utopia within
history. Likewise, Karl Marx wants us to believe that, once a
classless society is attained, and certain economic requirements
fulfilled, exploitation will cease and there will be no strife amongst
people.

But there is an astonishing difference between these two 'enemies of the open society'.[86] Marx proclaimed that the millennium
would be final and permanent; post-rabbinic and pre-Freudian, he
overlooked human nature. Plato, a percipient psychologist, allowed for the constant of human nature; in books VIII and IX of *The
Republic* he traces the degeneration of society from his own ideal of
rule by philosopher kings to tyranny, thereby demonstrating that
even the best-planned and most virtuous of societies retains within

itself the seeds of destruction which arise from the multiple impulses within the individual human psyche. Plato had not read the Bible; still, he knew that every Eden has its serpent.

Milovan Djilas has adeptly dispatched the illusion that there is some form of society which is intrinsically perfect, and in which the normal strains and stresses of human relationships will not arise:

> I need perhaps to explain here my use of the word 'unperfect', with which I seek to make a semantic distinction from the more common 'imperfect'. As the chapters that follow will illustrate, it is my belief that society cannot be perfect. Men must hold both ideas and ideals, but they should not regard these as being wholly realisable. We need to comprehend the nature of utopianism. Utopianism, once it achieves power, becomes dogmatic, and it can quite readily create human suffering in the name and in the cause of its own scientism and idealism. To speak of society as imperfect may seem to imply that it can be perfect, which in truth it cannot. The task for contemporary man is to accept the reality that society is unperfect, but also to understand that humanist and humanitarian dreams and visions are necessary in order to reform society, in order to improve and advance it.[87]

Contrast this with Karl Marx in 1844:

> Communism as a complete naturalism is humanism, and as a complete humanism is naturalism. It is the *definitive* resolution of the antagonism between man and Nature, and between man and man. It is the true solution of the conflict between existence and essence, between objectification and self-affirmation, between freedom and necessity, between individual and species. It is the solution of the riddle of history and knows itself to be this solution.[88]

There is no 'solution of the riddle of history'. There is no 'riddle', but there is a permanent need to strive to understand human nature, to conceive ideals towards which we should labour, and to develop our technology, resources and social organisation, without dogmatism and violence, towards the creation of an environment which will ease the attainment of these ideals; to the religious, this will appear as an influx of spirituality and holiness in life, as 'the wolf will dwell with the lamb' and 'the name of God will be one'. We have already spoken, in earlier chapters, of ways in which some of this might be accomplished. As Djilas reminds us, we cannot expect a perfect society; we an nevertheless realistically hope to make improvements, and keep the ideal before us.

Such is the age to which we must look forward, but we must know that, however close we get to it, we are still human beings with mixed impulses, with a complex psychology, and can easily falter and forfeit what has been attained. This is why Deuteronomy, in contrast to the messianic prophets, knows of no final end, but simply of an indefinite number of repetitions of the cycle to and from harmony with God. As remarked in section 6.1, the tension between the Deuteronomic and messianic views is a permanent feature of the dialectic of reality and vision.

6.4.2   *How long, O Lord, how long?*

At first sight, one thing is certain. All the predictions made so far as to the time or year of the Messiah's arrival – at least, those which relate to years that have already past – were false. He has not come.

But how certain can we be that the predictions were false? In actual fact the people who make this type of prediction, or believe in it, never allow themselves to be proved wrong. Somebody assured me the Messiah was coming in or about 1968. 'He would have come,' they now tell me, 'but the generation was unworthy.' Evidently it's my fault! The predictions, even in the eyes of the 'true believer', are thus conditional. Since no one can be sure the conditions have been fulfilled, the predictions are unfalsifiable. Hence the condemnation of 'calculations of the End' we spoke of in section 6.2.2 (under 'The false-Messiah syndrome').

Mention of 'falsifiability' leads us to think of Karl Popper. Popper criticises that modern analogue of the apocalyptic predetermined world programme, the Hegelian–Marxist idea that there are fixed historical laws governing social development, and that these laws can be discovered by philosophers or scientists. He rightly argues that there can be no such thing as a 'law of history' – at any rate, in the sense in which there are laws of physics or mechanics. We may indeed legitimately attempt to establish laws governing certain aspects of human or social behaviour in definable, repeatable situations. But history as a whole is a unique process, and *ipso facto* not amenable to generalisation – as Popper graphically put it, 'The most careful observation of *one* developing caterpillar will not help us to predict its transformation into a butterfly.'[89]

Popper does not intend to deny that 'history may repeat itself in certain respects', or that there can be significant parallels between events far apart in time and space, but he warns sharply against ignoring the dissimilarities.

IS A THEOLOGICAL ACCOUNT OF HISTORY POSSIBLE?

We ignore those, such as Sir Isaac Newton, who frustrate themselves 'working out' the prophecies of Daniel. But even a sophisticated theologian might be tempted to invoke 'revelation' as a source of our knowledge of some sort of historical 'law' – for instance, the Deuteronomic doctrine that the prosperity and well-being of a nation, at least of Israel, depends on keeping the covenant with God; indeed, a great deal of theology has been devoted to defending this doctrine from its *prima facie* lack of correspondence with the facts of life.

Since the eighteenth-century Enlightenment it has been common to identify the messianic idea with belief in human progress towards an undefined ideal, as Mendelssohn and Hermann Cohen did. Reinhold Niebuhr was at the forefront of theologians who challenged 'the idea that history is itself Christ, which is to say that historical development is redemptive'.[90] From the secular Marxist standpoint of the Frankfurt School, Adorno and Horkheimer, in a work written in 1944 'when the end of the Nazi terror was in sight',[91] likewise undermined the Enlightenment belief in progress by demonstrating that all progress in civilisation so far has involved some limitation of people's capacity to lead free and whole lives. I believe that the shock waves of the Shoah have traumatised many thinkers into too radical a rejection of the evolutionary optimism of the nineteenth century. Certainly, there can no longer be any easy optimism, and on Popperian grounds I would reject any doctrine of historical inevitability, but at the same time an attempt such as that of Alain Finkielkraut[92] to 'rescue' the values of liberal enlightenment is strongly to be commended.

Putting together the three biblical 'philosophies of history' I sketched in section 6.1, I conclude that theology can help us to respond constructively to the specific historical events with which we become involved. Learning from Moses, Isaiah and Ecclesiastes respectively, we can

(1) note and encourage justice in the affairs of nations;
(2) without assuming that it is constant and inevitable, discern moral and spiritual progress in the world, distinguishing it carefully from mere technological advance, and encourage its development – this is where the values of liberal enlightenment, carefully interpreted, should be espoused;
(3) reconcile our individual personal lives 'under the sun' to the 'incessant round of toil', as a framework within which we must 'work out our own salvation'.

There *must* be a balance amongst these three. Scripture does not choose between Moses, Isaiah and Ecclesiastes, but leaves them in dynamic tension. This is what we must do, and not commit the post-biblical writers' error of making Messiah an idol.

But as to whether there is some theology of history which would enable us to discern an objective pattern in past events, and from them predict the future – No! We have had enough of abortive revolts against Rome, of Sabbetai Zevi and messianic pretenders, of pseudo-messianism in Israel today, of escapism and frustrations. The pursuit of the millennium, as Norman Cohn has shown in his powerful study of revolutionary millenarians and mystical anarchists in mediaeval Europe, is a fraught and terrifying enterprise.[93]

6.4.3   Who steps across the hills?

Are we to expect an individual – perhaps, as Maimonides imagines, to rule over us, and to be succeeded by his son and his grandson and so on for the limited remainder of the earth's existence?[94] Or are we to expect a golden age?

It is far easier to be moved (if anyone wants to be moved) by a person than by an abstract idea; that is how dictators whip up mass followings, and why people derive satisfaction and sense of stability from a personalised if powerless institution such as the British monarchy. So one can instruct the young and delight the wise by talking about Messiah as a person even if, as an academic theologian, one inclines to a 'golden age' model.

But 'golden age' is no more than a model. It signifies an ideal at which to aim, not a clearly defined period of history. When the possibility of millions of years of human life on this planet looms before us, we cannot confine our ideas in the same way as we could when we thought in terms of a mere 'millennium', a thousand years. The 'end of days' has receded too far. Commitment to a 'golden age' is an aspect of present existence, an expression of determination to live, and to move events, in the direction of what we understand as a higher moral plane.

The value of belief in a golden age is that it offers hope and consolation in times of distress and gives a sense of purpose and direction to one's life; it makes existence meaningful. The danger of literal belief in such an age is that one may come to believe in a particular structure for the perfect society. Once again, balance is needed.

6.4.4 *Politician or prophet?*

We saw in section 6.2.4 that the Messiah's task, as conceived both by both Bible and rabbis, is essentially political, though it is seen as significant only in the context of God's redemptive acts.

The kabbalists indeed tended to spiritualise his mission, though not to the point where he himself usurped God's prerogative of, for example, the forgiveness of sin. The Vilna Gaon, as we saw in section 6.3.4, achieved a balance between the political and spiritual elements in the messianic work by apportioning the political tasks to Messiah ben Joseph and the spiritual tasks to Messiah ben David. 'Both exist and react with each other eternally.' The Gaon is calling for a permanent balance between political and spiritual activity; spiritual growth presupposes the context of a society which is governed by laws which are just and therefore conducive to the expression of spiritual values – that is, for the Gaon, the laws of Torah as codified by the rabbis.

Prophet or politician? Both. But first his political work must be completed – society and its institutions are the first object for improvement; the just society is the vehicle of spirituality.

6.4.5 *Jew or Gentile?*

It is absurd to view the world and all its problems as centred wholly for all time on one group of people and on one little parcel of land on the shores of the eastern Mediterranean; to regard one people and land as the central problem in the historical process for all time is only possible if one's horizons remain as narrow as those of an ancient Israelite who thought that the Indus and Ethiopia were the ends of the world (cf. Esther 1:1), who knew little of the culture of either, and whose awareness of time did not extend far from the present. Very few people have such an attitude; what sometimes looks like it is rather a sense of alienation arising from bitter experience of the world, as in the Shoah, breeding indifference to the 'world outside'.

If the messianic idea is to be taken seriously, it must be universal. Yet universality does not imply the abandonment of individuality or nationality. Those movements which have been avowedly universalistic, such as Christianity and socialism, have ultimately had to allow for variations of expression along national as well as individual lines, and have found the process of adjustment difficult. Judaism has had the opposite problem, especially since the break with Christianity, and has been reluctant to transcend the bounds of 'peoplehood'. I follow Hermann Cohen in maintaining that the messianic idea is the transcendence of the national bounds of early Israelite religion, but I do not think that he grasped the fact that this transcendence is compatible with the retention of nation-oriented forms of Judaism.

I see Zionism and its 'fruit', the establishment of Israel, as an important component in the expression of messianism on the national level; to be a complete expression on this level it requires a national self-awareness of rebirth as a people in a covenantal relationship with God.

Yet it would be absurd to describe it as the only possible expression of messianism by Jews, let alone the only possible or viable form of Judaism in the present world. Zionism, mission and universalism are discussed more fully in Chapters 5 and 9, to which reference should be made. On the diaspora level, Jewish messianism is expressed through the Jewish mission, which might be described as the self-awareness of diaspora Jews as a faith community, their fellowship arising from a covenant relationship with God, and involving a special responsibility towards the people amongst whom they live, and whose nationality they may well share.

Both levels of messianism should be understood as paradigms for all people and creeds. On the national level, any nation whose self-awareness involves a relationship with God is to the extent that it does so an embodiment of the messianic idea – it is an 'Israel'. Most nations, at some time or other, have accepted a particular faith or creed and made it part of their 'personality'; on the level of faith or creed, it is the society of the faithful which is the expression of messianism, in so far as its self-awareness incorporates a sense of responsibility to the world beyond.

Is the Messiah Jew or Gentile? I may imagine Messiah as a Jew whose mission extends to all mankind; others may imagine him, or her, in some other guise. It does not really matter, so long as the job is done, and so long as people keep their eyes on the job rather than on the personality.

6.4.6   In war or in peace?

If wars and human suffering are the price we must pay for the coming of the Messiah, we have surely paid ten times over.

There is a certain apocalyptic mentality characterised by the graphic Dead Sea Scroll title *The War of the Sons of Light and the Sons of Darkness*. People who possess this mentality divide the world into the Good (the tiny number of the 'elect', including themselves) and the Bad (countless millions, generally including you, gentle reader, and me), with whom they unwillingly share the planet. It is a small thing to them to call down divine wrath on their enemies, to conjure lurid scenes of the slaughter and the battles which will rid the earth of the pollution of the non-elect. They regard it as treason to the cause to talk with the Other, to attempt mutual understanding. Continuous revolution, destruction, *jihad*, the day of the Lord – these are their catch-words. Even the possibility of their own death deters them not a whit, for they have fled reality, shed their own personalities, become actors in a fearful scene, to whom the Enemy is no more than a shadow, an idea, certainly not a sibling.

Though the rabbis were realistic enough not to rule out the possibility of future wars and tribulations, they also indicated (section 6.2.6) that another path is possible, a peaceful, evolutionary path, in the footsteps of the Messiah. Personally, I should prefer that the good Lord delay the Messiah for a thousand years rather than bring another world war or another Shoah.

6.4.7   *In conclusion: what car will he drive?*

But surely the prophet declares he will ride upon a white ass (Zechariah 9:9)?

No, we do not know the details of Messiah, nor of the age to follow. But, whereas the details of Messiah are trivial, those of the age to follow are not. In imagining the age to follow Messiah, we are designing the ideal society, fashioning the way forward from our own imperfect one.

This is important, but impossible to achieve with finality. That is why so many vision of Messiah are rich in detail of miracles and battles and victories but poor on what comes next, when Messiah is in place, and why science-fiction writers fail, even with the most extravagant technological assumptions, to create a blueprint of an everlastingly happy new world. It is also the reason why some theologians, both Jewish and Christian – for they all agree that the 'kingdom of God on earth' is still awaited – insist that the 'kingdom' must come from God; it cannot be designed and brought about by people.

We have glanced at Bible and Pseudepigrapha and considered more carefully the profound teachings of rabbis, philosophers and mystics, and constructed a framework, and delineated a theory and two theories and half a theory (cf. Daniel 12:7).

So what of the details?

Fortified with the caution born of philosophy, with the skill to distinguish between poetry and prose, it is permissible to go back to the rabbis and cull from their legends and fancies and speculations what you will. Unfortified, it is far too dangerous, and one risks arousing the ire of Maimonides (section 6.3.1).

God, we learn from Bible and Talmud, has a sense of humour. He laughs, not only with scorn but also with delight. I cannot recall any passage in any holy book where the Messiah is said to laugh; perhaps it is simply taken for granted that he does. We, at any rate, should laugh, else we court the greatest of idolatries, that of becoming worshippers of our own beliefs, of taking too seriously our own pretentious theories.

And, if, for fear of undermining simple faith, we dare not laugh at that which people hold sacred, we can still smile gently, with the great bard, at the inadequacy of human designs 't'excel the golden age':

Had I plantation of this isle, my lord . . .
I' the commonwealth I would by contraries
Execute all things; for no kind of traffic
Would I admit, no name of magistrate;
Letters should not be known; riches, poverty,
And use of service, none; contract, succession,
Bourn, bound of land, tilth, vineyard, none;
No use of metal, corn, wine or oil,
No occupation; all men idle, all;
And women too, – but innocent and pure;
No sovereignty. . . .
All things in common nature should produce
Without sweat or endeavour; treason, felony,
Sword, pike, knife, gun, or need of any engine,
Would I not have; but nature should bring forth,
Of its own kind, all foison, all abundance,
To feed my innocent people.[95]

'Fair is the prize and great the hope . . .', says Socrates, getting round to the subject of the immortality of the soul.[96] That is indeed the greatest of possible themes, but the muse has not carried me so far.

I have spoken only of the things of *this* world, and have not yet learned to reach beyond, to grasp eternity.

But, as for this world, I know that we must be genial, patient and humble. Pragmatic as well, and level-headed. Even when talking about Messiah. *Especially* when talking about Messiah.

Part III
Philosophy

7

Shoah and Theology of Suffering[1]

Theodor Adorno observed that after Auschwitz the metaphysical capacity is paralysed.[2] However, the present chapter is written in the conviction that some sort of talk is possible about the Shoah[3] (Holocaust), that it is the duty of theologians and philosophers of religion to engage in such talk, and that at least part of this talk may be shared by Jews, Christians, and even by those, such as Adorno, who accept no traditional religious commitment; after all, notwithstanding his remark, Adorno himself reflected voluminously and productively on the Shoah.

We are still so close to the Shoah that if we are to talk about human suffering the Shoah must be our focus. We cannot talk of an abstract theological 'problem of evil' when real evil confronts us.

7.1 Uniqueness of the Shoah

I like the dedication of Julie Heifetz's *Oral History and the Holocaust*:[4] 'With love and gratitude for my Grandfather, Joe Waltuch, whose parents died in the Holocaust, yet who maintained his faith in Man and God throughout his lifetime.' It reminds me of a couple of German origin who were members of a Synagogue I served as rabbi over twenty years ago. They aroused my sympathy when they confided that they had lost their faith on learning of the suffering of their parents in the concentration camps. Only some time later did they reveal that their parents had actually survived, were alive and well in another country, and after their dreadful experience had become deeply religious. Those who had actually suffered, who had burned in the fire and could give authentic witness, had deepened their faith; those who had 'heard only with the ear but seen not with the eyes'[5] had lost theirs. Certainly, faith can be stronger than Shoah. But it is not necessarily so. Even when it endures the fire, it may be hardened rather than changed; only

173

rarely is it transformed into a profounder sense of the sadness and yet the beauty and redeemability of the world.

Was the Shoah unique? If we look at books of logic, we find discussions not of 'uniqueness', but rather of 'similarity', of which 'truthlikeness' is a special case.[6] It is easy to say 'The Shoah is unique' without realising the consequences or range of possible meanings of such a statement; if one rephrases this as 'The Shoah is in no way similar to any other event' it is immediately apparent that one has made a statement in need of modification.

There is a *trivial* sense in which every event is unique, tied to a singularity of time and place. However, communication amongst people demands that events be classified, by considering their similarities, into general groups, for otherwise we could have no common language to talk about them. One may classify the Shoah as 'an act of mass murder', indicating its similarities with innumerable human atrocities of past and present; however, this broad category fails to draw attention to the most distinctive features of the Shoah. One may narrow the field by classifying it as 'an attempted genocide';[7] there have been other attempted genocides (of the Armenians, for instance) and also actual genocides (for instance, of the indigenous population of Tasmania by the hand of the European settlers). Vahakn N. Dadrian has recently[8] made an impressive attempt to sketch a theory of genocide which would incorporate the Holocaust, but it is doubtful whether even this grim classification captures the distinctive horror of the Shoah. Yehuda Bauer[9] distinguishes between 'genocide', as 'the forcible denationalization of a people, accompanied by selective mass murder of the victim people . . . the destruction of the educational, economic and religious systems of the conquered people, and their ultimate enslavement' and the special case of 'holocaust', which is 'the planned total annihilation of a whole people . . . [perhaps] for ideological reasons'.

Emil Fackenheim offers the following preliminary list of 'basic facts' about the Shoah which, though some may have occurred elsewhere, are in their combination unique:

> Fully one-third of the Jewish people was murdered; and as this included the most Jewish of Jews – East European Jewry – Jewish survival as a whole is gravely in doubt.
>
> This murder was quite literally 'extermination'; not a single Jewish man, woman or child was to survive, or – except for a few

that were well-hidden or overlooked – would have survived had Hitler won the war.

This was because Jewish birth was sufficient cause to merit torture and death; whereas the 'crime' of Poles and Russians was that there were too many of them, with the possible exception of Gypsies only Jews had committed the 'crime' of existing at all.

The 'Final Solution' was not a pragmatic project serving such ends as political power or economic greed. Nor was it the negative side of a positive religious or political fanaticism. It was an end in itself. And, at least in the final stage of the dominion of the Third Reich (when Eichmann diverted trains to Auschwitz from the Russian front), it was the only such end that remained.

Only a minority of the perpetrators were sadists or perverts. For the most part, they were ordinary jobholders with an extra-ordinary job. And the tone-setters were ordinary idealists, except that the ideals were torture and murder.[10]

To this list Fackenheim might well have added a sixth factor, over which he agonises at length later in his book:[11] the studied and perverse manner in which the Nazis and those under their direction sought to humiliate, dehumanise and induce self-disgust in the Jews even before killing them.

Yet another factor compounds the horror and uniqueness of the Shoah. The attitudes which enabled the Nazis to 'demonise' the Jews and thus carry out their programme were already deeply embedded in the popular cultures of the nations amongst whom they operated. For so long had Christians taught that Jews were a despised people, the rejecters and killers of Christ, obdurate in their adherence to a superseded faith, that European culture was saturated with this image of the Jew. It is surely unique that for little short of 2000 years one people has been singled out for constant and *religiously sanctioned* vilification through much of the 'civilised' world, Muslim as well as Christian.

Jews have suffered major tragedies before – the destruction of the Temple in 70 CE, the expulsion from Spain in 1492 – and these were accompanied by horrendous sufferings. Fackenheim writes,

> The earlier catastrophes were great but not beyond belief, and thus lived on in the memory of the generations until the time was ripe for a response. Our catastrophe, in contrast, is beyond belief and becomes ever more so with the passage of time.[12]

Well, this is not quite true. It happened; it must and can be reflected upon. Fackenheim himself reflects upon it volubly. But the tendency to deny is strong, and manifests itself not only in the fringe phenomenon of outright denial by 'revisionist' historians,[13] but in the tendency to assimilate the Shoah to general categories of tragedy and cruelty, 'losing' it as 'just an example' of something or other, denying its special character.

7.2   The Main Types of Jewish Holocaust Theology

7.2.1   *Traditional responses: halakhic*

The most characteristic expression of traditional Judaism is the *halakhah*, or law. God, in his gracious compassion, granted us the Torah with its many commandments (*mitzvot*) so that we might learn from it to live according to his will.

The *halakhah* of *qiddush ha-Shem* (sanctifying the Name, i.e. God) is specially relevant to the problems faced by victims of the Shoah. Let us listen to the measured words of Maimonides on this subject in his great code, the *Mishneh Torah*[14] – bearing in mind that he is merely codifying a long process of halakhic development[15] reaching back to biblical times:

All the House of Israel are commanded to sanctify this Great Name [i.e. God], as it is written, 'I shall be sanctified amongst the people of Israel' [Leviticus 22:32]. Likewise, they are commanded not to profane it, as it is written, 'Do not profane my holy name'[22:32]. How is this fulfilled? If an idolater arises and forces a Jew to transgress any of the commandments of Torah under pain of death, he should transgress rather than be killed, for it is written of the commandments 'that a man shall do and live by them' [18:5] – *live* by them, not *die* by them – if he die rather than transgress he is guilty of taking his own life.

In what circumstances does this apply? With regard to any of the commandments other than three: idolatry, adultery/incest and the shedding of blood. With regard to these three, should he [the Jew] be ordered to commit them or face death he should die rather than transgress. . . .

If the idolaters said to a group of women, 'Hand over one of you and we will defile her or else we will defile all of you', they must not hand over even one Jewish soul. Similarly, if the idolaters said [to a group of Jews], 'Hand over one of you and we will kill him, or else we will kill all of you', they must not hand over even one Jewish soul. . . .

It would be a romantic reconstruction of Shoah history to claim that all victims followed the ruling of Maimonides in these matters.[16] Most were plain victims, not martyrs. Jews were not murdered because, refusing to abjure their faith, they gave witness to it, but simply on account of their 'race'; they had no option. It would be a singular lack of compassion to condemn those who, contrary to Jewish teaching, did in fact save their skins at the expense of others. The remarkable thing is not that some failed, whether out of weakness or ignorance or self-interest, but rather that so many succeeded in maintaining a high standard of moral integrity – in 'giving witness to God', as the religious express it – in these appalling circumstances.

In this sense, the *halakhah* of *qiddush ha-Shem* was the everyday law of the Shoah. Sadly, confessing Christians acted the part of the 'idolaters' of whom that law speaks.

But it was not the only *halakhah* that was applied in facing the horrors. The rabbinic responsum is the genre which over the centuries has been the crucible within which the practical expression of Judaism has been forged. *She'elot u-teshuvot* (questions and answers) afford us an intimate window into the concerns of ordinary Jewish men and women as they turned for guidance to their spiritual leaders. The process of composing them did not stop in the Shoah – indeed, the careful application of *halakhah* in the most extreme circumstances is a supreme expression of Torah; somehow, where theology was inadequate, *halakhah* survived and made survival possible.

> If emotion is evident in a responsum, it is rarely overt. The rabbi's juristic function imposed upon him the discipline of composure and reason. To have yielded entirely to emotion would have been to forfeit the crucial responsibility entrusted to him by his people.[17]

Rabbi Ephraim Oshry survived the Holocaust in the ghetto of Kovno, Lithuania. There, people approached him with their questions. He committed the questions and answers to writing on

paper torn surreptitiously from cement sacks, and hid the writing
in cans which miraculously survived the war.

> The daily life of the ghetto, the food we ate, the crowded
> quarters we shared, the rags on our feet, the lice in our skin, the
> relationships between men and women – all this was contained
> within the specifics of the questions. . . .[18]

A glance at the range of subjects bears out how ordinary people in
the ghetto, with the deep strength born of faith in God, were
concerned quietly to walk in the precepts of God: 'Jews Forced to
Shred a Torah Scroll', 'Sabbath Torah Reading for Slave Labourers',
'The Blessing for Martyrdom', 'Saving Oneself with a Baptismal
Certificate', 'Contraceptives in the Ghetto', 'The Repentant Kapo' –
such headings rend the heart of the reader as the answers gave
sacred meaning to the lives and deaths of the victims.

> We Jews of the ghetto of Kovno . . . were enslaved by the
> Germans; were worked to the bone night and day without rest;
> were starved and were paid nothing. The German enemy de-
> creed our total annihilation. We were completely dispensable.
> Most would die.

So was it proper to recite the customary blessing in the morning
prayers thanking God 'who has not made me a slave'?
Oshry's brief answer encapsulates the spirit of this work:

> One of the earliest commentators on the prayers points out that
> this blessing was not formulated in order to praise God for our
> physical liberty but rather for our spiritual liberty. I therefore
> ruled that we might not skip or alter this blessing under any
> circumstances. On the contrary, despite our physical captivity,
> we were more obligated than ever to recite the blessing to show
> our enemies that as a people we were spiritually free.[19]

Yet of all the questions submitted by quite 'ordinary' people to
Oshry and thousands of other rabbis of the Shoah period, none are
so agonising as those involving harm to the life of other victims.
The Nazis did their utmost to degrade and dehumanise Jews by
forcing them to destroy each other. In substantial measure they

failed. And that they failed is due in large part to the spirit engendered by the *halakhah* on the sanctity of life.

7.2.2 *Traditional responses: theological*

Much of the serious Jewish theological writing which has seen the light of day in various European languages in the last two decades has been marked by its outspoken rejection of traditional answers to the 'problem of evil'. It is asserted that such answers are inadequate to explain the special suffering that accompanied the Holocaust. Not only, it is said, are they inadequate, but they are misleading and harmful. For instance, to 'explain' the Holocaust as God's punishment for Jewish sins insults the memory of the martyrs who perished, for amongst the 6 million there must surely have been many, let alone young children, who had not sinned in such measure as to warrant the horrors and humiliations of this terrible destruction. No one is denying that people have sinned – such a denial would be totally contrary to Jewish principles – but there is a strong sense that, if the Shoah was the punishment for Israel's sins, the punishment was out of all proportion to the guilt.

The quality and accessibility of these writings, many of which will be referred to in succeeding sections, obscures the fact that a large number of Jews, particularly amongst the orthodox, continue to express the traditional responses, with greater or lesser conviction.

It has to be stressed that the traditional interpretations of suffering depend heavily for such cogency as they may have not only on a strong sense of guilt (see below, subsection B) but also on the belief in life after death. This belief, whether expressed as bodily resurrection, eternal life of the spirit, or some combination, remains central in orthodox teaching.[20] Some of the orthodox, under the influence of Kabbala, have adopted in addition the concept of the transmigration of souls.[21] Such beliefs simplify the theology of suffering, for (a) they diminish the significance of the vicissitudes of 'this world', and (b) they provide an opportunity for 'compensation' for the evils of this world in the next. The transmigration of souls easily explains the suffering of innocent children – either they are being punished now for sins committed in a previous incarnation, or else they will get compensation for their present sufferings in a later one.

A. PROVIDENCE: INDIVIDUAL AND GENERAL

Fundamental to the traditional Jewish understanding of suffering is the distinction between *hashgacha peratit* and *hashgacha kelalit* – individual and general (collective) Providence. In terms of general Providence the Shoah can be 'understood', for it is not hard to rationalise the destruction of part of the people of Israel as part of God's redemptive process, leading ultimately to Israel's restoration, whether or not in terms of the land. It is the individual Providence which is most problematic. Since everything is subject to God's will, it is legitimate to ask not just why the people of Israel suffered, but why each individual suffered. Maimonides, it is true, denied that God extended Providence to individuals in the sublunar sphere other than to those whose spiritual excellence raised them above sublunar materiality.[22] But, if spiritual excellence is something we can recognise at all, it certainly characterised many of those who perished.

Unfortunately, the statements we report briefly below do not always distinguish clearly between the individual and general aspects of God's Providence.

B. GOD'S JUDGEMENT

Elchanan Wasserman (1875–1941)[23] was one of the leading rabbis of the pre-war generation. His writings, speeches, life and martyrdom offer a paradigm of the orthodox theology of suffering. Wasserman visited the United States in 1938, and was there when the news of *Kristallnacht* arrived. He was dismayed by the lack of Torah learning and observance amongst the Jews he met in America, and there he completed his pamphlet *Iqvata di-Meshicha*,[24] in which he predicts that dire destruction will come upon the Jewish people on account of its lack of faith and its laxity in the observance of God's commandments. Gershon Greenberg, in a perceptive paper on Wasserman and his brother-in-law, Chayyim Ozar Grodzinski of Vilna, has summed up their views as follows:

> for Achiezer [Grodzinski], Reform is responsible. It, along with the suffering it evokes, is now pressing eastward. The response must be education to engender faith and Torah. Wasserman blames religious and cultural assimilation; nationalism as an act of normalization and defiance of religion and God; and denunciation of Torah. The response called for is the same for both leaders. For Achiezer, Torah and faith are means to endure the

suffering, to turn the catastrophe back, and to bring redemption. Wasserman believes the catastrophe is the birth pain of the Messiah . . . man's role is to turn to God through Torah.[25]

Similar views are nowadays commonplace in orthodox writing, and have even received popular expression.[26] The most sophisticated sources are the introductions to the Hebrew volumes of *halakhah*, commentary and *derashot* (sermons) which issue from the orthodox rabbinate; however, I know of no comprehensive review of this material.

Wasserman was martyred (here we use the word advisedly – not that he chose to die, but that in dying he consciously dedicated his life to God: see subsection C) on 6 July 1941 -- *before* the actual *Endlösung* (Final Solution) was put into operation. Many of us today who write with some knowledge of the actual horrors of the Shoah tend angrily to dismiss all talk of 'punishment for sin' in this context as gratuitously insulting to those who perished and as demanding an image of God as unforgiving, intolerant of even the smallest lapses, and unready when punishment is unleashed to distinguish between the innocent and the guilty. To understand the rabbis who spoke and even now speak in this way it is necessary to know how deeply they felt the gulf between the ideal demanded by Torah and the reality of modern secular civilisation. It was for them, in their piety and faithfulness, as if the modern way of life, adopted by many Jews through assimilation to 'the ways of the nations round about', had totally destroyed the holy world of the Jew nurtured over the centuries; not unnaturally they feared, and believed they witnessed, the prophesied chastisement of Israel with but a small and faithful remnant escaping.

C. 'QIDDUSH HA-SHEM'

Earlier (section 7.2.1) we learned of *qiddush ha-Shem* in its halakhic setting. What did it mean in terms of religious faith?

'It is clear beyond all doubt that the blessed Holy One is the ruler of the universe, and we must accept the judgement with love. . . .' These words of the Hungarian rabbi Shmuel David Ungar[27] exactly express the simple faith of those who entered the gas chambers with *Ani Maamin*[28] or *Shema Israel*[29] on their lips. What was happening defied their understanding, but their faith triumphed over evil and they were ready, in the traditional phrase, to 'sanctify the name of God' – *qiddush ha-Shem*. Hence it is normal amongst Jews to refer to those who perished under the Nazis as *qedoshim*, 'holy ones, saints'.

The concept of 'dying for *qiddush ha-Shem*' is analogous to, some would say identical with, that of martyrdom. Although normally one would use the term only of those who voluntarily give up their life in a situation of choice between sin and death, from mediaeval times onwards it has been applied to those killed because of their faith even where they had no choice. It is still a moot point whether it is justified to extend its use to those killed not because of their faith but, as in the Shoah, because of their 'race'. In practice, we do make this extension, erecting memorials to the '6 million martyrs'; but although the emotion is understandable the theology is precarious. We shall return to this topic in subsection F.

D. GOD'S LOVE

Has not God acted *un*justly towards Israel? Israel has indeed sinned, but surely others, not least Israel's oppressors, have sinned more? The traditional reply to this is that of Amos, that it is precisely God's love for Israel that leads him to chastise them more than any other nation: 'For you alone have I cared among all the nations of the world; therefore will I punish you for all your iniquities' (Amos 3:2).

Suffering is thus received as a token of God's special concern for Israel.

Note Amos's standpoint, though. Amos was an Israelite preaching to his fellow Israelites. He could tell them about God's love and chastisement and call his people to a greater sense of responsibility. Any non-Israelite talking in that manner to Israelites, or any Israelite talking in that manner to non-Israelites, would be acting improperly, demanding a 'double standard'. So, for instance, should there still be Christians who presumptuously regard themselves as *verus Israel*, their only appropriate application of such a verse would be to Christians, not to the Jewish people.

E. BIRTH PANGS OF THE MESSIAH

The title of Wasserman's pamphlet *Iqvata di-Meshicha* ('In the Footsteps of the Messiah') is taken from a well-known Mishnah passage, sometimes referred to as the 'rabbinic apocalypse'. It is a passage all the more remarkable in the light of the general rabbinic tendency to play down apocalyptic. This passage, in the commonly used versions, reads (in part),

To whom can we turn for support? [Only] to our Father in Heaven. In the footsteps of the Messiah insolence will increase, respect will diminish . . . the wisdom of the sages will decay, sin-fearers will be despised, truth concealed, the young will shame the old, the old will stand in the presence of children . . . the daughter will rise against her mother . . . a man's own household will be his enemies, the faces of the generation will be as the faces of dogs. To whom can we turn for support? [Only] to our Father in Heaven.[30]

The sense of apocalyptic, of being part of the events heralding the Messiah and the final redemption of Israel and the world, was strong amongst the orthodox victims of the Shoah, and if anything has become stronger since. It was already part of Jewish tradition, receiving its most potent expression in the Lurianic Kabbala, according to which every *mitzvah* performed by a Jew is part of the cosmic process of *tiqqun* (repair), part of the messianic work of redemption. Indeed, precisely the same concept was being developed, before and independently of the Holocaust, by Rav Kook, the first Chief Rabbi of Palestine in modern times, for he understood the Return to Zion as *atchalta di-geulta*, the commencement of redemption.[31] The further step, taken by many religious Zionists, has been to interpret both the Shoah and the strife surrounding the emergence of the State of Israel as 'birth pangs' of the Messiah.

F. SACRIFICE AND ATONEMENT

In subsection C we drew the analogy between *qiddush ha-Shem* and martyrdom. *Qiddush ha-Shem* is a demonstration of faith which leads those who witness or hear about it towards God. This shades into redemptive suffering and the vicarious atonement for sin.

Rabbi Israel Shapiro of Grodisk and his Hasidim were herded into box cars and transported from Warsaw to Treblinka. When they arrived he told his Hasidim that these were at last the *real* birth pangs of the Messiah, and that he and they were blessed, for their ashes would help purify Israel and thus hasten the end.[32]

The matter was expressed even more powerfully by Wasserman just before his own martyrdom, and for this we have the graphic eyewitness account by Rabbi L. Oshry of Wasserman's response as he was seized to be taken to his death:

Reb Elchonon spoke in a quiet and relaxed manner as

always . . . the same earnest expression on his face . . . he addressed all Jews:

'It seems that in Heaven we are regarded as *tzadikkim* [righteous],[33] for we are being asked to atone with our own bodies for the sins of Israel. Now we really must do *teshuvah* [repent] in such a manner – for the time is short and we are not far from the ninth fort[34] – we must have in mind that we will be better sacrifices if we do *teshuvah*, and we may [?save] our American brothers and sisters.

'God forbid that anyone should allow any improper thought to enter his head, for the *qorban* [sacrifice] is invalidated by improper thought. We are about to fulfil the greatest *mitzvah* of all – "with fire You destroyed it, with fire You will rebuild it"[35] – the fire which destroys our bodies is the selfsame fire which will restore the Jewish people.'[36]

Implicit in Oshry's account is the notion of vicarious atonement. Although Jewish apologetics has tended to minimise the role of vicarious atonement in Jewish theology, Wasserman was perfectly in accord with a continuous tradition running from the biblical understanding of animal sacrifice through such rabbinic concepts as the death of the righteous atoning for the 'sin of the generation' to the hyperbole attributed to the second-century Simon bar Yohai that 'I could exempt the whole world from judgement since the time I was born, and were my son Eleazar to join with me, from the day the world was created until now.'[37] The theme is widely echoed in mediaeval Hebrew liturgical poetry.[38]

Ignaz Maybaum, a non-orthodox rabbi and a survivor, openly expressed the concept of vicarious suffering at Auschwitz and included in it atonement for non-Jews:

In Auschwitz, I say in my sermons – and only in sermons is it appropriate to make such a statement – Jews suffered vicarious death for the sins of mankind. . . . Can any martyr be a more innocent sin-offering than those murdered in Auschwitz?[39]

G. THE 'HIDDEN GOD' AND THE NEGATION OF EVIL

The idea of God being 'hidden' features strongly, perhaps because of its full development by the mystics (kabbalists). It links with the common midrashic idea of God, or the *Shekhinah* (divine presence), being 'in exile' with Israel, for 'I am with him in his distress' (Psalm 91:15).[40] Martin Buber asks, 'How is a life with God still possible in a time in which there is an Auschwitz? The estrangement has become too cruel, the *hiddenness* too deep' (emphasis added).[41] Eliezer Berkovitz seems to go further than anyone else in his attachment to the notion of the 'hidden face of God',[42] but he is in accord with tradition when he not merely finds the hiddenness of God compatible with God's existence, but discovers God's actual presence within his silence.

On the other hand, there seems little echo of the idea espoused by Maimonides[43] that evil is merely the absence of good. This may be because the Holocaust gives such a strong sense of the *reality* of evil that any doctrine asserting its non-reality is self-evidently false.

Curiously Hannah Arendt, by no means a traditional Jewess, comes close to the doctrine of *privatio boni*, for to her only the good has depth, whereas even the most extreme evil is superficial and banal.[44] Barry Clarke has rightly rejected Arendt's characterisation of Eichmann's activities in organising transport to the gas chambers as 'banal'. Organising transportation may indeed be 'banal', as compared with 'radical evil' as understood by Kant. However, the concept of freedom of the will means that

> Eichmann surrendered only his autonomy and not his spontaneity and at each moment of time he could presumably have resumed exercising his judgment and reason and used his freedom of will to recommence choosing for himself.

As Clarke concludes,

> The foundation of the greatest political evils is not to be found in the few who deliberately choose to inflict evil on the world but in the heteronomous evil of those who elect to defer to evil persons, practices or policies.[45]

7.2.3 *The critique of traditional responses*

Many people are shocked, as we have seen, at the application to the Shoah of the traditional view of suffering as a punishment for sin (see section 7.2.2, introduction and subsection B). We now chart some further general objections to the orthodox approach.

A. A NEW POINT OF DEPARTURE?

The philosopher W. V. O. Quine has argued that the totality of our beliefs is 'a man-made fabric which impinges on experience only along the edges'.[46] Beliefs in the centre are less amenable to modification or refutation than those on the periphery. Indeed, a central belief may sometimes be maintained despite a considerable body of *prima facie* evidence against it; it may become virtually immune to refutation.

Emil Fackenheim[47] in like vein argues that normative Judaism and Christianity act as if they were immune to all future events except messianic ones, as if there could be no epoch-making event between Sinai and Messiah. He rejects traditional responses as underestimating the radical challenge of the Shoah, equal in its significance to a new revelation. He cites approvingly Kierkegaard's remark that a single event of inexplicable horror 'has the power to make everything inexplicable, including the most explicable events',[48] and in the light of it condemns Heidegger, Barth, Tillich and others for continuing to teach after the Holocaust 'as though nothing had happened'. This is a puzzling use of Kierkegaard's remark. Surely there were 'single events of inexplicable horror' before the Shoah, and far more horrendous than the crucifixion, the event to which Kierkegaard refers. If so, the Shoah itself would not demand a new way of thinking; the demand for such a way was already there (see section 7.3).

B. EVADING THE ISSUE

Lionel Kochan, drawing on Hermann Cohen, deplores the intense focus on the Shoah and the tendency to isolate 'holocaust Studies' from the disciplines, such as history and sociology, in the general context of which it should be treated. He regards 'explanation' in terms of life after death as a particular evasion of the historical reality of the Shoah and, in terms reminiscent of Plato carping at the tragedians, decries the artistic representation of suffering.

> The problems of history – suffering for example – are not to be overcome through the representation of its relief in another world. This must indeed be a source of positive harm for it produces the illusion of a solution and thereby derogates from a genuine solution. . . .
>
> The work of art, like the idol, must therefore at best be indifferent, at worst harmful, to human interest by reason of

the fact that, because they introduce man to fiction, they offer no purchase to that process whereby suffering may be relieved. . . .[49]

Gershom Scholem likewise stressed the flight from reality which has been the price paid for messianism throughout the ages. I am not so sure of his assessment that this was the only way to furnish consolation and hope in the years of powerlessness, but he correctly diagnoses recent messianism as 'born out of the horror and destruction that was Jewish history in our generation'.[50]

C. THE QUESTIONING OF GOD

Judaism and its Christian and Muslim offshoots all teach their faithful that God shapes history, on occasion actually intervening even for the sake of individuals. But, as Irving Greenberg has put it,

> The Holocaust poses the most radical counter-testimony to both Judaism and Christianity. . . . The cruelty and the killing raise the question whether even those who believe after such an event dare to talk about God who loves and cares without making a mockery of those who suffered.[51]

Richard Rubenstein[52] is driven by reflection on the Shoah to reject the traditional idea of God as the 'Lord of history'. God simply failed to intervene to save his faithful. Though denying atheism, he urges both Christians and Jews to adopt non-theistic forms of religion, based on pagan or Asian models, and finds deep spiritual resources within the symbolism of Temple sacrifice. The Reconstructionist rabbi Harold S. Kushner, addressing the general problem of suffering rather than specifically the Shoah, has written a popular book in which he explores the concept of the non-interventionist God.[53]

Rubenstein and others of similar outlook are determined to maintain Jewish identity – in his case a *religious* identity – even if not based, as it was in the past, on theistic faith. Other Jews would express their identity in secular terms, including the secular forms of Zionism, or simply in social terms.

One should also note that in his later writings Rubenstein adopts a more theistic outlook than when in the depths of his spiritual struggle with the Shoah.

7.2.4   Narrative exegesis: liturgy

I am not sure that Elie Wiesel would care to be described as doin
'narrative exegesis', or indeed any kind of theology. Yet Wiesel
achievement is to have enabled people to talk about the Shoah,
enter, so to speak, into its 'social and cultural context'.[54]   I
imposes no systematic structure or interpretation on the reality h
places before us, but rather creates a new myth (in the mo
constructive sense of that term), through which the reader
hearer absorbs the meaning that cannot be said. His stories a
indeed a 'narrative exegesis' of the Shoah.

Theologians will see in many of Wiesel's stories paradigms
suffering leading to salvation. This is a common-enough Jewi
concept from Exodus onwards, but Wiesel's closeness to Christi
expressions of the theology of suffering verges on the substitutio
of the 6 million for Christ on the cross.[55]

It is not far from story-telling to formal liturgy, which, ul
mately, is the religious means of conveying that for which wor
are insufficient. Marcia Littell[56] is amongst those responsible f
the development of Holocaust liturgies for use by Christians, Jew
or both together, and these have achieved widespread use pa
ticularly in North America. Yom ha-Shoah (Holocaust Day), whi
often attracts joint Christian and Jewish participation, is so
observed by only a minority of Jews, as some prefer to assimila
remembrance of the Holocaust to the existing fast of 9 Ab.[57]

7.2.5   The assertion of meaning and value

The psychiatrist Viktor Frankl developed his 'logotheraphy' as
victim in Auschwitz and Dachau, and has left us a profound
moving account of how he discovered meaning and 'sup
meaning' precisely there, where the oppressor aimed to depri
the life of the Jew of all meaning and value. Those who we
unable to achieve the 'will to meaning' soon perished, observ
Frankl; those who could somehow find meaning survived whe
ever survival was physically possible.[58]

Likewise, in religious terms, Rabbi Isaac Nissenbaum declared
the Warsaw Ghetto at the time of the uprising,

This is a time for *kiddush ha-hayyim*, the sanctification of life, a
not for *kiddush ha-Shem*, the holiness of martyrdom. Previous

the Jew's enemy sought his soul and the Jew sanctified his body in martyrdom [i.e. he made a point of preserving what the enemy wished to take from him]; now the oppressor demands the Jew's body, and the Jew is obliged therefore to defend it, to preserve his life.[59]

There is an aesthetic version of *qiddush ha-hayyim* also. Much of the visual art produced in the appalling hell of the concentration camps has been rescued, exhibited, published. But what of music? Could the 'songs of the Lord' be sung in that dark land (cf. Psalm 137)? In 1979 Joza Karas, in Hartford, Connecticut, formed the Karas String Quartet for the express purpose of performing music written in Terezin (Theresienstadt), where Jews of Czechoslovakia were interned prior to being exterminated in Auschwitz. These good Jews – amongst them some of the cream of Central European artists and intelligentsia, their only 'offence' the racial one of being Jews – did not despair when confined to ghettoes, intimidated, persecuted, deprived of all rights and provided with only those modest necessities which would enable the Nazis to present Terezin as a 'model' camp. No, this was when they asserted the beauty (for this is an aspect of holiness) of life with ever-greater courage and determination. Orchestras[60] were formed, operas staged, the composers wrote and the singers sang. Even Verdi's *Requiem* received a performance; the nuances of meaning attached to the Catholic words by these Jewish artists defying their Nazi captors have been well brought out in Josef Bor's little novel.[61] Indeed, this was *qiddush ha-hayyim*; as a survivor, the singer Greta Hoffmeister (at the age of twelve, in Terezin, she sang Annette in *The Bartered Bride*) exclaimed, 'Music! Music *was* life!'[62]

7.2.6   *The imperative of survival: 'tiqqun'*

Fackenheim grounds his own Holocaust theology in the actual resistance of Shoah victims to whom no realistic hope remained.[63] 'A philosophical *Tikkun*[64] is possible after the Holocaust because a philosophical *Tikkun already* took place, however, fragmentarily, during the Holocaust itself.'[65] Before writing *To Mend the World* Fackenheim had achieved note for his statement that there should be a 614th commandment – to survive as Jews, to remember, never to despair of God, lest we hand Hitler a posthumous victory.[66] What one discerns in his evolving position is, at least, an affirmation of life and of God, and a challenge to Christian, Jew and all humankind to 'mend the world'. For Fackenheim, the State of Israel is the central affirmation of Jewish survival, central in the world process of *tiqqun*; hence, he has now made his home there.[67]

7.2.7 Beyond survival

The Talmud cites the remark of a 'sectarian' that the Jews are an impatient people, for how otherwise would they have been so eager to declare 'All that God says we will do and we will hear' (Exodus 24:7) before they had heard in full what that implied?[68] Maybe there is an element of impatience in those who, before we have had a chance to develop a Holocaust theology, are already concerned with *post*-Holocaust theologies, i.e. with the 'next stage'. On the other hand, the eminent Jewish philosopher Emmanuel Lévinas is not alone in demanding that we go beyond the Holocaust,[69] that we do not allow ourselves to be permanently imprisoned in it.

The phrase 'beyond survival' is the title of an important book by Dow Marmur,[70] who expresses the feeling not only of Reform Jews such as himself but of many others that the 'imperative to survival' which is the end result of Holocaust theology such as that of Fackenheim is a hollow call. Survival is not an end in itself, nor is the proving wrong of Hitler an adequate goal for life in general. One has to ask, 'Survival for what?' Marmur answers in terms of his own vision of Judaism and what it means in the context of world development. Though many would dispute Marmur's precise account of the Jewish mission, his point that we are not to allow ourselves to be so tied to the Shoah that we cannot look forward would be widely accepted.

A similar view, refusing to allow Jews to be imprisoned by the Shoah in the Holocaust alternative of 'a cruel God or none', and instead concentrating on the development of Torah in ethics, with special application to ecology and world peace, emerges from Robert Gordis's fine religio-ethical work.[71]

Irving Greenberg divides the history of Judaism into three eras.[72] The first extended from Sinai to the destruction of the Second Temple. The second, the rabbinic period, characterised by powerlessness and by the 'hiddenness' of God but at the same time by a deep faith in the covenant of redemption, extended from 70 CE until the Shoah. The Shoah shattered the naïve faith in the covenant of redemption, inaugurating a third era the shape of which is determined by our response to the crisis of faith. Greenberg insists that this response must involve *all* Jews, not merely those who share his orthodox commitment. Auschwitz was

> a call to humans to stop the Holocaust, a call to the people of Israel to rise to a new, unprecedented level of covenantal responsibility. . . . Even as God was in Treblinka, so God went up with Israel to Jerusalem.

Jews today, in Israel and elsewhere, have a special responsibility, in fidelity to those who perished, to work for the abolition of that matrix of values that supported genocide.

So, for Greenberg, post-Holocaust Jewish philosophy has to be formulated in terms of empowerment: now that Jews have 'taken on power and responsibility to act', how will they use that power? It is but a small step from this (a step Greenberg has resisted) to espousing some form of Jewish 'liberation theology', and the step has been taken by Dan Cohn-Sherbok[73] and Marc Ellis.[74]

7.2.8   *The imperative to dialogue*

Dr Gerhart Riegner, in the office of the World Jewish Congress in Geneva in 1942, had the task of relaying to a disbelieving world the news of the 'Final Solution'. Since then, he has devoted his life to the furtherance of international Jewish–Christian dialogue. I once asked him how it was that his experience in 1942 had not embittered him, had not made him turn away from the 'nations of the world' who had been unwilling to help Israel in her hour of need. His answer was illuminating. 'It was then that I decided that my task in life was to end the isolation of the Jewish people.' Though the response of many – Berkovitz for example – has been to declare that dialogue with a church which failed to warn its followers away from Hitler is simply not possible, Riegner and others have determined otherwise.

A. ATTITUDES TO CHRISTIANITY

The Roman Catholic Church at the present time seems intent on creating an image of itself as victim of the Holocaust, if not to the same extent as the Jews. The beatifications of Maximilian Kolbe and Edith Stein are symptomatic of this trend. In Poland the process is a natural-enough one. Auschwitz has become, to Poles, a national symbol of suffering under the Nazis, and Polish Catholics now come there to pray and to seek atonement and reconciliation. After all, Auschwitz was set up as a concentration camp for the Polish intelligentsia, mainly (though not entirely) Catholic, and hundreds of thousands of them perished there.

One asks, therefore, why Jews reacted so strongly to the siting of a Carmelite convent in the 'Old Theatre' on the perimeter of the Auschwitz site. Why did they see the Catholic presence at Auschwitz as the appropriation of a uniquely Jewish symbol – worse, as the oppressor donning the garb of the victim? Why do Jews find it so hard to recognise Christians in general (they are very ready to note the exceptions) as their brothers and sisters in suffering?

The fact is, that Jews tend to view the Shoah as the culmination of their degradation and persecution at the hand of Christians. They see Christians by and large as persecutors, with a relatively small number as victims and even smaller number showing the least concern for Jewish victims. Since the Holocaust, Jews have ceased to take the moral credibility of the Church seriously.

The voice of the Shoah was the voice of the pagan Hitler, but the hands that implemented it were the hands of ordinary Christians.

They see the same pope, Pius XII, whose concern to save many individual Jewish lives is now the boast of his Church, and which has been warmly recognised by many Jews[75] – they see this same man as Vatican Secretary of State Pacelli, architect of the 1933 concordat between Hitler and the Vatican, a document which restrained the representatives of the Church from speaking out as they ought to have done. Had Church leaders spoken out in time and with forthrightness, they might have prevented the Shoah and even the war – but, even had they not been heeded, they would at least have preserved the Church's integrity and moral credibility.

Both Pius XI and Pius XII did indeed speak specifically against antisemitism. 'Antisemitism is inadmissible; spiritually, we are all Semites', wept Pius XI on 6 September 1938 – but only *in a private audience* to a group of Belgian pilgrims, in a statement unreported even in the faithful *Osservatore romano*.[76] After the infamous *Kristallnacht* of 9–10 November 1938 the Pope, *with difficulty*, prevailed upon Cardinal Faulhaber to condemn, half-heartedly, the desecration of prayerhouses, and to provide a truck for the Chief Rabbi of Munich to save the Torah Scrolls before his synagogue was thoroughly vandalised. So the desecration was condemned, the scrolls might be saved, but not the people. The few statements made aloud had little effect on German and other local bishops, and none at all on the Nazis. When the Nazis needed officers and men to do their foul work for them, the sons of the Church were to hand; no one excommunicated them – even Hitler, Himmler and Eichmann, all baptised Christians, were not formally cut off or condemned by their churches.

The voice was the voice of Hitler, but the hands were the hands of ordinary Christians.

It was not even a matter of the Nazis having to seek officers and men to do their work. Kovno, in Lithuania, where Jews had lived peacefully side by side with Catholics for generations, is surely no exception, though it happens to be well documented.[77] In the summer of 1941 the Nazis conquered Lithuania.

> After a few weeks they set up the ghettoes which were dedicated to destruction, and after their fashion commenced the slow murder of their sacrifices. Hell at once opened under the feet of the Jews of Kovno, and even beyond what the accursed German soldiers did to them was inflicted on them by their uncircumcised neighbours of the local population, fanatical Lithuanian Christians, who stormed against the unprotected Jews like vicious wild dogs, wreaking slaughter amongst them until the cry ascended to Heaven.[78]

As against this, we have seen, the Pope had privately wept to a handful of Belgian pilgrims that spiritually we are all Semites, and so antisemitism is inadmissible. The remedy was hardly sufficient to the disease. Anyway, that pope was already dead.

Was the Shoah, then, a Christian product? Was it not rather the work of the anti-Christian Hitler, with Christians next in the firing line after the Jews?

If the Shoah was a non-Christian, even an anti-Christian, enterprise, where were the Christians? 90 per cent of Germans before the war, and in all probability an even larger proportion of Poles, attended Church weekly. Did the sermons they heard outspokenly condemn the demonic anti-Christ Hitler? By no means. First of all, in his early writings and speeches Hitler, seeking the support of the masses, spoke overtly Christian language:

Hence I believe that I am acting in accordance with the will of the Almighty Creator: *by defending myself against the Jew, I am fighting for the word of the Lord.*[79]

His attacks on Jews and Judaism were consciously expressed in the language of traditional Christian antisemitism, and the infamous laws of Nuremberg consciously modelled on the legislation of the mediaeval Church. It *was* the Church that had instigated trade restrictions against the Jew (a direct model for the Nazi boycott of 1 April 1933), and the ghetto and the yellow badge; it *was* Christians who first utilised the blood libel as an excuse to murder Jews.[80] It was the Church that sewed into the fabric of Western culture the images and stereotypes of the Jew that allowed so many of its faithful sons to accept without demur the alienation and vilification of the Jew preached by Hitler. For it was the Church whose gospel concerning the Jews was, as Jules Isaac called it, *l'enseignement du mépris*, the teaching of contempt. Hitler's hatred of the Jews was not significantly greater than that of Luther – and it has taken all the courage of the post-Holocaust Lutheran Church to repudiate that aspect of the 'Great Reformer's' teaching.[81]

Too often, Christian opposition to Hitler was explicitly *not* opposition to his antisemitism. The foremost leader of Church opposition to Nazism in pre-war Germany was Pastor Martin Niemoeller. Yet Niemoeller – at that stage – did not oppose antisemitism. Robert Michael has written,

Christian antisemitism was a key element in Niemoeller's attitude toward the Jews and a factor whose profound implications fatally damaged his moral leadership and the will of the Confessing Church and the German anti-Nazi movement in general to resist National Socialism on the Jewish question.[82]

The question of whether Christianity is or need be antisemitic is seriously debated by Christian theologians at the present time.[83] But there is no shadow of doubt that in the past the expression of Christianity has normally been antisemitic, sometimes vigorously so. Jews in Christian Europe have seen Christians as people who despised and tormented them, marginalised their position in society, accused them of being 'Christ-killers'. It need occasion no surprise, therefore, that Jews tend to see Christians collectively as involved in the Shoah in the role of persecutors rather than victims; what is more surprising is the readiness of Jews to recognise the numerous Christian exceptions to the rule and to build a new and constructive relationship with contemporary Christians.

B. DIALOGUE WITH CHRISTIANITY

Notwithstanding the above, Jews have responded positively to post-Holocaust opportunities for dialogue with Christians, and often taken the initiative.

To a considerable extent the contemporary dialogue is a vehicle for the joint assertion of ethical spiritual values in today's society, and involves at the least a mutual recognition of each other's integrity and an acceptance of the idea that God (or the 'holy spirit') continues to speak through people of different faiths. Dialogue, after all, commenced before the Shoah.

However, as Fackenheim has eloquently put it,

> Christianity is ruptured by the Holocaust and stands in need of a *Tikkun*. . . . Surely the Christian Good News that God saves in Christ is itself broken by *this* news.[84]

The repentance required of Christians in order that authentic dialogue may take place is not, Fackenheim avers, merely a repentance of the open antisemitism which led to Auschwitz, but something far more radical. It is a 'repentance of supersessionism vis-à-vis Judaism and the Jewish people'.[85] As A. Roy Eckardt, a Christian, puts it,

> Decisively, Christians view the witness of the New Testament as pointing to the historical–divine consummation of the expectations of the so-called old Testament (Hebrew Scripture, the *Tanak*) and hence as a fulfilment of, and judgment upon, Judaism and Jewishness.[86]

It is this element of 'judgement' which fed the antisemitism of Christendom over the ages, and which, notwithstanding its manifest irrelevance to Jews beyond the New Testament narrative, persists in many Christian theologies today. Eckardt discusses five Christological models offered by theologians whom he praises for their vigorous opposition to the 'teaching of contempt', and finds them all wanting; for, in his view, they fail to overcome the supersessionism which is the generating force of antisemitism.[87] Paradoxically, it may be that a new and adequate Christology can only be created, if at all, together with Jews.

Yet, on the other hand, Jews must beware of imposing a particular Christology on Christians with whom they engage in dialogue. It is ultimately up to Christians to define themselves, and to decide to what extent some form of 'supersessionism' is unavoidable. Cardinal Willebrands, clarifying an article by Cardinal Ratzinger[88] which had caused much offence to Jews, stated, 'We acknowledge and respect the Jewish people in its own faith and expectation' and 'Through dialogue we hope to overcome misunderstandings, the teaching of contempt in order to develop true knowledge, respect and love.' It would be wrong for Jews to ask more than this. Indeed, so long as we Jews believe in the ultimate theological superiority of our own faith and expect Christians to engage in dialogue with us on the basis that we so believe, we cannot expect them to abandon their own beliefs in the interest of the dialogue. Of course, there are many Jews and Christians who in any case take a 'relativist' position, denying that any theology is ultimately superior to any other; but for such people dialogue is in any case not problematic.

7.3 Does the Shoah Require a Radically New Theology?

We are now in a position to address the question of whether, as so many of those whose views have been cited claim, a 'new theology' is demanded of Jews (we do not speak here of the special problems for Christians) as a result of the Shoah.

Let us concede that the Shoah is *historically* unique. Is it *theologically* unique?

Consider Irving Greenberg's striking statement that after the Shoah 'no statement theological or otherwise should be made that could not be made in the presence of burning children'[89] – or Kierkegaard's remark, cited in section 7.2.3A, that a single event of inexplicable horror 'has the power to make everything inexplicable, including the most explicable events'. Then reflect sombrely that children were burned long before the Shoah and continue to be burned, and people, many of them undoubtedly innocent, were crucified long before Jesus and frequently afterwards (not that one crucifixion is an impressive matter where we are talking of the systematic humiliation and extermination of millions).

Both Judaism and Christianity developed at least partly in response to horrible experiences, and in the awareness that such horrible experiences were likely to be the lot of mankind until some transforming event (Messiah, Kingdom of God on earth) came about. Therefore, they both have a 'theology of suffering', an attempt to 'assert Eternal Providence, and justify the ways of God to men'.[90] Whereas Deuteronomy presupposes a direct relationship between sin and suffering, obedience and prosperity, Psalms, Job and Ecclesiastes in their different ways try to come to terms with the presence of suffering and injustice in the world. The biblical seeds bear fruit in the writings of theologians, both Jewish and Christian, to the present day.

Holocaust theologians insist that the Shoah was not only quantitatively but also qualitatively different from previous suffering. It introduced a *novum* (Fackenheim[91]), a *tremendum* (Arthur A Cohen[92]), which invalidates previous responses to suffering.

Certainly, it is more horrible for a million to perish than for one to perish, and it is more horrible to be subjected to humiliation and killed than to be killed without humiliation. Also, some of the traditional 'answers' are harder to apply to large numbers than to small; for instance, if a mere handful of righteous people suffer apparent injustice we can easily convince ourselves that, despite all appearances, they were not really righteous, whereas if millions suffer it becomes much less reasonable to suggest that *all* of them were really evil. But this is an effect of quantity, not of quality. *If* we could know that an individual was really righteous (as, for instance, scripture assures us in the case of Job), then the dodge of saying 'perhaps appearances were deceptive' cannot be used, any more than it can where the numbers involved are so great that it would be absurd to maintain that none of the sufferers was righteous.

So, even though the Shoah was in significant ways dissimilar from other historical events, it does not appear to have posed radically new questions for theology. The questions were there all the time. The Shoah has focused our attention on them as never before, but they are the same questions.

To a surprising degree the answers given by the Holocaust theologians are *the same answers* as those to be found in earlier traditional sources. Many of them – those we have described under the headings of narrative exegesis, liturgy, the assertion of meaning and value, the imperative of survival, and *tiqqun* (sections 7.2.4–6) – are varieties of one of those answers, that of redemption through suffering, worked out with new insights arising from modern psychological and sociological perspectives and applied, often with great sensitivity, to the present situation of the Jewish people. But they are not radically new answers. Even those responses (section 7.2.3C) which demand a revision of the traditional concept of God follow in a modern, but certainly pre-Shoah, theological trend which, in Jewish terms, is specially associated with Kaplan's 'Reconstructionism', and in general terms with the 'death of God' movement sparked off by Nietzsche.

Occasionally there is a glimmer of something new. Irving Greenberg, for instance, has devoted much of his life to espousing a new unity of the Jewish people, which is not limited by the old insistence on traditional practice and doctrines; he feels that this is called for in the 'third era', following the Shoah, since Hitler made no distinction between religious and non-religious Jews. It is certainly a novelty for an orthodox Jew such as Greenberg to embrace this attitude. However, it seems to me that, if greater mutual understanding and tolerance are now demanded of Jews, this is something intrinsically desirable, and would have been desirable irrespective of the Shoah. Moreover (and Greenberg has shown himself aware of this), this extension of tolerance and understanding to non-orthodox Jews has to be part of a general call for tolerance and understanding among all people.

If the Shoah does not of itself demand a new theology, and the demands for new theologies made by post-Shoah theologians do not result in anything really new, why have so many of them felt impelled to distance themselves from traditional Jewish theologies of suffering?

There are two reasons.

First, the traditional theologies of suffering *never were satisfactory*. In the words of the second-century rabbi Yannai, 'It is not in our power to explain either the prosperity of the wicked or the afflictions of the righteous.'[93] Yannai's words did not stop rabbis in his own or later generations speculating on the problem of evil. Indeed, though none of the answers is satisfactory, they may all *contribute*, if only a little, to the upholding of faith in the face of evil.

Second, the reason why non-orthodox Holocaust theologians

reject 'traditional' answers may be something quite other than the intrinsic inadequacy of those answers. In section 7.2.2 it was stressed that the traditional interpretations of suffering depend heavily for such cogency as they may have on the belief in life after death and/or the transmigration of souls. Equally, they depend upon a belief in the inerrancy of scripture and in the authenticity of its rabbinic interpretation. These beliefs have been under attack in modern times for reasons which have *nothing to do with* the Shoah. Jews, like Christians, have been challenged by, for instance, modern biblical studies, which tend to undermine the traditional type of scriptural belief and demand a new kind of attitude to the authority of the Bible. Likewise, modern intellectual developments, such as the radical questioning of Cartesian dualism, have placed new strains on the concept of life after death. These changes have so weakened the traditional arguments justifying the ways of God with humankind that the Shoah has provided the *coup de grâce* to lead the modernist wing of Judaism to abandon traditional theodicy altogether.

Thus it is not that the Shoah poses a new challenge to theology, but rather that the Shoah came at a time when theology was already in a greater ferment than ever before in its history, a ferment occasioned by the intellectual movements of the modern world. This explain why earlier tragedies, such as the expulsion from Spain, occasioned not the abandonment but the development of traditional modes of response to suffering.

It is dangerously misleading for Holocaust theologians to base their challenge to traditional beliefs on the fact of the Shoah. The serious intellectual issues of faith in the modern world thereby become submerged in a deep emotional trauma which prevents them from being directly faced. The agenda for Jewish theologians ought to comprise not only the broad social issues which confront theologians of all faiths in contemporary society, but also the intellectual problems which lie at the root of theistic, revelation-based faith. It would be superficial to ignore the Shoah in these contexts, but to centralise it distorts the very framework of the Jewish faith.

It is a remarkable fact that, notwithstanding a long and continuous tradition, from the Bible onwards, of theology of suffering, and notwithstanding a history of martyrdom second to none, suffering has not in the past been the focus of Jewish theology. In rabbinic Judaism, certainly, the focus has consistently been God and his commandments. I submit that there is no reason for this to change even after the Shoah.

Is it otherwise for the historian, or for the politician whose first concern is 'to work for the abolition of that matrix of values that supported genocide'? Even for them it is salutary to remain aware of similarities as well as dissimilarities between the Shoah and other events, for to ignore the similarities would be to fail to encompass the Shoah in human terms at all, to remove it from history and transform it into a supernatural event.

7.3.1 On the challenge of the Shoah to Christianity

We may likewise ask whether there is a new and radical challenge to Christianity arising from the Shoah. Of course, there is the same challenge, on the level of 'explanation of suffering', as arises in Judaism – and for the same reason: the radical change of perspective of modern thought. But what of the special challenge (see section 7.2.8A) posed to Christians in view of their complicity in the Shoah, whether by preparation of the anti-Jewish ideology or by actually doing the work of the Nazis? Here, likewise – and this, if properly understood, is a terrifying thought – there is not a *new* problem for the Christian theologian. Those elements in traditional Christology which lie at the heart of this particular Christian failure have been there since New Testament times. The implications of supersessionism were *always* there to be faced. The Shoah may have concentrated the mind, but that is all. Yet this is a 'problem' which *can* be solved by people, for people formulate creeds and liturgies. And – again for reasons which have less to do with the Shoah than with the ability for self-criticism achieved by the Church in modern times, and by the Roman Catholic Church notably since Vatican II – it has at last become possible for the Church to face up to this inglorious aspect of its heritage.

A church which has the courage to question its own past is one with which it is a privilege to engage in dialogue. But only time and consistency will alleviate the age-old fears and mistrust which culminated in the terrifying eruption of the Shoah into history.

8

Language and Dialogue[1]

8.1 Dialogue within the Modern World View

I recall a conference, held under the auspices of the World Congress of Faiths, at which representatives of several of the world's major religious communities addressed the audience on the 'problems, possibilities and challenges encountered through the use of language and symbolism in dialogue between the great religions of the world'. I presented the viewpoint of the 'committed, orthodox Jew'. All of us who participated drew on the traditional sources of our faiths – in my case the Bible, the Talmud and the writings of the rabbis – and with diligence and ingenuity cited apt texts in support of our views. Yet we soon discovered that the language we were using was only *in part* the language of our traditions. If we had not also been articulate in modern English (certainly *not* the principal language of any of our traditions) we should not have been able to communicate with our audience or with one another. Evidently, the organisers had invited only fluent English-speakers to lecture. Had they realised the full implications of this practical necessity?

It was not merely that we lecturers all spoke the same natural language, English. If we had not utilised certain concepts of modern scholarship and science, particularly those of history, linguistics, sociology and anthropology, we should have lacked any conceptual framework within which to place our observations about religions in general.

Indeed, such a dialogue about dialogue could not have arisen within the confines of any one faith nor even within the limited horizons of the interrelationships between any group of faiths, but sprang from the broader dialogue between religions and the modern world. If one calls this activity 'theology' rather than 'philosophy of religion', it is, in Wilfrid Cantwell Smith's powerful phrase, 'global theology'.

201

8.2   The Nature and Use of Language

8.2.1   *Ways of using language*

Let us consider the nature of language and its use. The rabbis,
possibly as early as the second century, discussed whether someone who causes something to happen simply by the power of
speech can be held to have 'acted', in a legal sense, and therefore
be liable to punishment by a court for his misdeed; they agreed
than an oath, which is certainly no more than speech, should be
considered an 'act', with full legal consequences. Eighteen centuries later, in 1923, the pioneer anthropologist Bronisław Mali-
nowski (1884–1942) wrote that 'language functions as a link in
concerted human activity, as a piece of human behaviour. It is a
mode of action and not an instrument of reflection.'[2] As William
Downes succinctly puts it, 'Utterances are actions.'[3] We might add
that in the light of modern studies of animal behaviour and communication it is no longer possible to regard language as such as
the unique, distinguishing feature of *Homo sapiens*; it is seen as
continuous with the non-speech actions by which animals, as well
as humans, achieve the communication necessary for their survival.

So what we are talking about is not *words*, but *speech acts* – acts
that may speak *without* words. In religion there are many categories of such acts. All religious ritual functions as 'speech acts', for it
is through ritual, which may not involve words, that the faithful
communicate with one another and with God. A sacrament in
Christianity, a *mitzvah* in Judaism, is such a 'speech act', part of the
broader 'vocabulary' of the religion.

Let us follow the convenient scheme of D. Hymes[4] to show what
characterises speech acts. He lists the following components of
speaking, to which I have added 'religious' instances.

Component	*Explanation*	*Religious instance*
SITUATION	Setting, locale, scene, e.g. committee meeting, [*Example*: criticism of the Bishop of Durham arose not so much from the substance of what he said, as from the	Sermon

Component	Explanation	Religious instance
	situation – what was acceptable as a lecture to students at a university was not acceptable as a bishop's sermon.]	
PARTICIPANTS	Speaker, addresser, hearer(s), addressee, e.g. 'chairman' – affects *communication rules*	Bishop
ENDS	Purpose, goal, outcome, e.g. verdict, diagnosis	Conversion Subversion
ACT SEQUENCES	Message form/content, e.g. 'interview'	Service, liturgy
KEY	Tone, manner, e.g. mocking or serious	Sanctimonious
INSTRUMENTALITIES	Mode, form of speech – spoken, written, dialect	Prophetic inspiration
NORMS	of interpretation or interaction – normal expectation, turn-taking, etc.	
GENRES	Categories, e.g. poem, myth, lecture, commercial	Creed

How could one apply the above categories to, for instance, the common biblical verse 'The Lord spoke to Moses' – a verse which started to worry me a lot as a small child, when I would sit in the synagogue puzzling out what it actually meant? What did Moses feel like when it happened? What would I have seen had I been there watching? What would it have felt like if God had spoken to me? Did the experience have any empirical content? Do the words in which it is described have any reference? Are they, rather, perhaps a sign or symbol for something which cannot be properly articulated? And, whatever the answer to any of these questions, what are the 'social' rules for such a conversation between God and man, and how do such rules guide us in interpreting the actual speech attributed to God? How do we graft 'thought'– or 'intentionality', as philosophers from G. E. M. Anscombe[5] onwards would prefer to call it – on to 'act' and 'speech' as described above? Do God's 'words' have intentionality?

8.2.2 Locutionary, illocutionary and perlocutionary (Austin)

The uses of speech acts have been divided by the philosopher J. L. Austin[6] as follows.

LOCUTIONARY: actual utterance of the sentence.
ILLOCUTIONARY: intended effect at which the speech act (not necessarily the literal meaning of the words) is directed (e.g. talk about the weather is intended not to *inform* the hearer but to put him at ease).
PERLOCUTIONARY: unintended consequences of speech act (addressee becomes evasive, apologetic).

Illocutionary and perlocutionary effects can encompass social bonding (cf. point 5 in section 8.3.5B), hostile or friendly intent, and so on. If, for instance, meeting an old friend, I were to say 'You look younger than ever', the *locutionary* aspect of my utterance is the actual sentence; the *illocutionary* aspect, which is not contained in the literal meaning of the words, is something like 'I want to be nice to you and make you feel good' (I am certainly not saying 'You look thirty-four rather than thirty-five'); the *perlocutionary* aspect, if any, would vary according to the circumstances, and might include such reactions as confusion about who I really am or annoyance at some wrongly perceived intention.

In interfaith dialogue one *illocutionary* aspect of whatever we are saying is that it also carries the message 'Let's be friends!' *There is perhaps no more important practical step in dialogue than that all utterances should carry this simple message.*

8.2.3 Indeterminacy and non-translatability of natural language

Central to the whole question of dialogue is the problem of whether, even in principle, it is possible to communicate across the boundaries between languages. W. V. O. Quine raised the question of whether words, or even whole statements, have determinate meanings. Can a word or statement be detached from its context, which in most cases is that of a fully developed natural language? He writes,

> it is misleading to speak of the empirical content of an individual statement – especially if it is a statement at all remote from the experiential periphery of the field. . . . Any statement can be held true come what may, if we make drastic enough adjustments elsewhere in the system.[7]

A clear consequence of the indeterminacy of natural languages is their mutual non-translatability. It would thus seem that the enterprise of using the language of any one religion to talk at all adequately about others is doomed to failure. Such a theoretical conclusion is borne out by the actual failure of religions to talk about each other in a manner which those being described would find adequate.

It also underlies the failure, or at least unexpectedly long delay, in engineering a broadly based 'artificial intelligence' or a machine with conversational powers matching those of human beings. Some time in 1987 I heard a man from Marconi being interviewed on the radio. He was excited about the computer he was marketing, which would accept spoken instructions in natural language, rather than the normal keyboard entry. His machine would learn the vocabulary and voice inflections of its human operator and respond appropriately. 'How many words does it understand?', asked the interviewer. 'About 160', came the reply, 'with an enhanced version capable of about 400.' Indeed, our fifth-generation computers do no more than tickle at the complexity of natural language; even the trifling vocabulary of a mere 400 words exaggerates the program's power, for it certainly could not handle those words with anything approaching the subtlety of a human speaker. H. Dreyfus's attacks on the 'articial-intelligence brigade' are truly perceptive of the extreme difficulty if not impossibility of programming 'meanings' into machines.[8] Recently, there has been renewed debate on the 'thinking' capabilities of computers, with John Searle leading those who argue that computers cannot have 'intentionality' and can therefore never be described as 'thinking' in the same sense as humans; they manipulate symbols, thus handle syntax, but do not attach meanings to them, hence have no semantics.[9]

8.3   The Nature of Religious Language

We now turn to the specific problems of religious language, or, rather, of the multiplicity of religious languages used within the different faith traditions.

8.3.1   The framework problem

We shall first consider the 'framework problem'. There is a danger, when discovering somebody else's religion, of using the wrong key words, or of attaching the wrong weight within the system to words which actually are used; but in using an unsuitable or an incorrectly weighted vocabulary one misrepresents the religion one is trying to present. Using English to describe the Muslim or Sikh religious cultures instead of presenting them in their Arabic or Punjabi words and contexts inevitably leads to a measure of mis-understanding and wrong emphasis.

Consider the following wordlists. The first list was produced at a teacher training college by a class of first-year Christian students whom I had asked to provide me with what they considered would be the key words if they were asked to explain what Christianity was about. Here it is:

> God the Father, Son and Holy Spirit; resurrection; salvation; baptism; forgiveness; crucifixion; conversion; confirmation; ascension; justification; scriptures; faith; love; nativity; holy communion; prayer; trust; fellowship; 'born again'; obedience; eternal life; discipleship.

I leave it to the reader to speculate what sort of Christian background these students came from; certainly, one would not anticipate the same lists from Eastern and Western Christians, or from conservative evangelicals and liberal churchpeople. Moreover, though such a list appropriately charts a certain type of Christianity, and is at least relevant to other forms of Christianity, it is totally inapt for Judaism and Islam, let alone for Buddhism and other religions. One cannot define Jews, for instance, as unthinking Christians still tend to do, in terms of what they have to say about Jesus or the Trinity or about justification by grace or works, any more than can understand Christians in terms of their opinions on Muhammad or on reincarnation; to attempt that would be no more sensible than defining the political stance of the Swiss in terms of their maritime policy or lack of it – you won't comprehend a land-bound people if your whole conception of politics is tied to questions about the sea.

My second list is one which I have presented to students as an initial framework for the understanding of Judaism. Note that I not only have to resort to Hebrew terms, but need to gloss even those terms which are familiar to English-speaking Christians. Here is the list.

God	Personal, historical, protean relationship
Torah	The way, instruction, teaching (*not* law!) *Restricted senses*: first five books of Bible (*sefer Torah*); instruction in specific subject
Mitzvah	'Commandment': the practical unit of Torah – the good deed; *opposed to*
Averah	Transgression, sin
Free will	
Teshuvah	Penitence: 'returning' (to God)
Tefillah	Prayer
Tzedakah	'Fairness, correctness' = charity
Hesed	Love, compassion, kindness
Yetzer tov	'Good impulse': the innate (psychological) tendency to do good, *contrasted with*
Yetzer ha-ra	The impulse to do evil (*the cause and the remedy for man's unfaithfulness to God lie within him*)
Israel	People, land, covenant

We see that a major difficulty in the dialogue amongst people of different faiths lies in the different choice and weighting of the words or concepts they use to define themselves. However, the moment we step outside our own pattern of definition we enter 'global theology', the philosophy of religion, or some other discipline which is equipped to talk about religions in general, and to handle a multiplicity of thought systems within itself.

8.3.2 *Same words, different meanings*

Yet it is not just the weighting and choice of words that constitutes a pitfall. Even more subversive to mutual understanding, because it so easily escapes notice, is the habit of religions in a historical and therefore linguistic relationship with one another to use the same words in quite different senses. In 1984 Leon Klenicki and Geoffrey Wigoder edited a *Dictionary of the Jewish–Christian Dialogue*,[10] which contains Jewish and Christian essays on thirty-four important words, many of them shared by Jews and Christians. Examples are: Covenant, Election, God, Holiness, Israel, Justice, Law, Love, Messiah, Mission, Repentance, Salvation.[11] Of these thirty-four words, not one is used in exactly the same way by Jews and Christians – nor, one might add, by all Jews or by all Christians.

Worse than all the foregoing is the extreme difficulty of knowing what even the most fundamental religious words stand for. Much of the *Guide of the Perplexed*,[12] by the great mediaeval Jewish thinker Moses Maimonides, is devoted to rebutting the views of those who interpret literally the anthropomorphic expressions applied to God in the Bible. Maimonides himself follows the *via negativa*: one cannot affirm anything of the transcendent God, only deny attributes – a doctrine which can be traced back to Pseudo-Dionysius in the fifth century, and has had many Christian and Muslim as well as Jewish adherents. But what of the simple believer who actually conceives of God as possessing positive attributes? What such a man believes in, says Maimonides, is not God at all, and therefore he is in effect an atheist.

> I shall not say that he who affirms that God, may He be exalted, has positive attributes either falls short of apprehending Him or is an associator or has an apprehension of Him that is different from what He really is, but I shall say that he has abolished his belief in the existence of the deity without being aware of it.[13]

One is reminded of the debate as to whether Spinoza was an atheist or, as Novalis would have had it, 'a man intoxicated by God'. Or of the debate as to whether Theravada Buddhists can, for all their denial (no stronger than that of Maimonides) of the existence of a personal deity, be regarded as believers. Such is the problem of discerning what, if anything, one is talking about even at the very heart of the rarefied discourse of theology.

8.3.3 *Talking within one faith about others*

Is it possible to find within the language of any one religion or denomination adequate resources to talk intelligently and perceptively about any other? We can refer to this as the problem of the creation of 'theological space' for other religions, and indeed many modern theologians have tried hard to demonstrate the possibility, with varying results.

This is achieved within Judaism in terms of the 'seven *mitzvot* of the children of Noah'; this, together with the affirmation that 'the righteous of all nations have a share in the world to come', ensures that Judaism allows 'theological space' for other faiths. These matters will be fully explained in Chapter 9. For now it is sufficient to note that there is no basis, from a Jewish perspective, to deny the acceptability to God of non-Jews; indeed, since from the Middle Ages onwards it has been normal for Jewish teachers, such as Halevi and Maimonides, to affirm the value of other faiths, whilst continuing to regard the truths of their own faith as superior to those of all others and as objectively correct.

Christians have had greater difficulty than Jews or Muslims in finding 'theological space' for other faiths. Paul F. Knitter notes that,

> Against Barth and many contemporary conservative Evangelicals, mainline Protestants argue that Christians not only can but must recognize that the God revealed in Jesus is truly speaking through voices other than that of Jesus.[14]

So far the position would appear to be analogous with that in traditional Judaism. However, the Christian cannot stop at that point. Much Christian talk concerns 'salvation', with the very special meaning attached to that term within the belief context of Christianity. The whole human race, irrespective of the deeds of the individual, is somehow flawed, and the flaw can only be removed by 'plugging into', or appropriating, Jesus's cosmic act of redemption and atonement. How can one handle Christian language to encompass salvation as well as revelation for non-Christians? 'Revelation – Yes! Salvation – No!' are Knitter's graphic headings for the mainline, Christocentric Protestant model – which he does not endorse.

That the problem has strong linguistic overtones may be seen in the way that some Protestant theologians, notwithstanding their intensive study of other religions, are led to describe them in terms which enable them to deny or at least limit their salvific aspects, but would be regarded by adherents of those religions as tendentious misrepresentations. Brunner for instance asserts that 'in all non-Biblical religions, no matter how deeply mystical or highly ethical, " . . . man seeks himself, his own salvation; even in his surrender to the Deity he wants to find his own security"'.[15] Such religions, Brunner claims, are therefore egocentric and cannot effect salvation. This, of course, is doublespeak; it does not proceed from objective assessment of other religions, for the evidence is quite otherwise. It is a way of talking about other religions designed to enable Brunner to continue talking conventional Christian language whilst ignoring the realities of the faiths he disparages. The same group of theologians allege also that religions other than Christianity, in trying to achieve their own salvation, attempt to 'capture' God – for instance, by somehow manipulating him with 'good works'. What a travesty! For a non-Christian it really is ironic to hear the Christian Paul Tillich accusing others of 'absolutizing their mediating symbols' – an aberration which, to the outsider, would appear to be the most distinctive feature of Christianity itself, in which Jesus, the 'mediating symbol', is absolutised into the very incarnation of God! Against this absolutisation Jews and Muslims have been the contant witnesses.

The failing of such an approach, which attempts to account for all religions from within the narrow perspective of one, is that it makes a specific interpretation of one religion the criterion for judgement of all. Where a global theology is called for, it provides only a restricted one. Its exponents have failed to generate a language which can encompass other faiths without distortion.

8.3.4 *Using an 'outside' (independent, impartial, scientific) language to talk about religions*

If, as the foregoing suggests, the internal resources of a religious tradition are inadequate to handle other faiths without distortion, is there perhaps some external discipline which can afford appropriate resources?

Attempts, such as Jung's, to use common symbolism to establish similarity of religious experience across faith (doctrinal) boundaries are helpful, but leave out of each religion much that its adherents consider essential. Jung's approach has the further weakness that the whole scheme is dependent on his concepts of individuation and of the archetypes of the unconscious. As these cannot be objectively established (there are many equally workable alternative hypotheses) he is providing an arbitrary framework with which to assess the various religions.

Much the same is true of other methods – for instance, anthropological accounts of innate structure or common forms of religious ideas (Lévi-Strauss, Mircea Eliade).

Sociological descriptions (such as Weber's) of the structure and dynamics of the faith community/society are useful, and explain much about the 'cumulative tradition'. However, they do no address themselves to the experiential questions which are important to believers.

Psychological accounts of religion, especially reductionist ones, such as Freud's, certainly reveal some of the self-deception that is common amongst the religious with regard to their motivation; but they leave untouched major aspects of religious attitudes and behaviour.

Is there a 'common essence', or an experience common to religions, as Toynbee suggested? He seems to think[16] that all religions share the following insights.

1   The universe is mysterious, not contained in itself or in humanity.
2   The meaning of the universe is found in an Absolute Reality.
3   This presence contains not only truth but also good; people should strive to experience it and be in harmony with it.
4   To achieve this harmony people must cease being self-centred.

The approach fails because it ignores real differences between the religions on precisely these points, and because it makes an arbitrary distinction between essentials and inessentials, often very different from that made by authentic representatives of the religions.

Wilfred Cantwell Smith (he prefers 'faith' and 'cumulative tradition' to 'religion') is sounder historically. For him 'faith' is the unifying concept; it is 'what one feels and the way one lives when one encounters what Smith calls "transcendence"'.[17] History thus becomes the discipline within which religions are studied.

The problem with these approaches seems to lie in the difficulty of coming up with any description of the transcendent ('faith') experience which is not completely vacuous and which can distinguish it from states definable (at least in principle) in non-transcendent psychological or physiological terms.

Exactly the same difficulty confronts the attempts of Husserl and others to define religious experience in phenomenological terms. Is phenomenology of religion possible? The description of the 'phenomenon' usually demands stripping so much away from the reality that one wonders whether anything at all is left. It is rather like (to use a metaphor employed earlier) tightening one's grip on a handful of sand, and in the process losing most of what one is trying to grasp. António Barbosa da Silva has argued, on a phenomenological basis, in favour of the widely held theocentric hypothesis – that there is a common, describable, irreducible element in all mystical experience; but he acknowledges that this must be complemented by an ontology which would allow one to discriminate between conflicting truth claims.[18] At best, however, this sort of approach can never give a satisfactory account of religion as a full cultural–historical phenomenon.

With the possible exception of the phenomenological, these approaches all leave the epistemological questions concerning religion untouched.

8.3.5   *The language of belief systems*

The whole issue of the relationship between belief and cognition (faith and knowledge) floats in a quagmire of linguistic confusion. We must therefore give some consideration to the nature of a belief system.

A. BIOLOGY OF BELIEF SYSTEMS

K. M. Colby has the distinction of being the first person to create a paranoid computer: that is, to implement a program which interacted with humans in a manner actually diagnosed as paranoid by psychiatrists who read transcripts of the 'dialogue' without being informed that 'Parry' was a machine.[19] Conversely, studies of human and animal behaviour reveal the function of belief systems as the operating systems of the individuals concerned. There are thus today both a biology and a mechanics of belief systems.

The physiology of mind, primitive as it still is, offers several insights into the functioning and interactions of the several systems within the human brain. Jerry Fodor summarises the vertical and modular psychological organisation underlying biologically coherent behaviours. He distinguishes[20] between two major types of system that we possess.

1   *Input and language systems*

Domain-specific
Operation is mandatory
Limited central access
Fast
Informationally encapsulated

2   *Central processing systems*

These lack the above characteristics and are in general far less well understood physiologically. However, it is precisely here that we may think of a 'belief system' as being 'located'.

B. SYNTAX, SEMANTICS AND CREEDS

This view of mind as a hierarchy of interacting systems, taken together with some of our earlier observations on the use of language, has several consequences of great significance for theologians. The following are some ideas which need to be explored.

1   What is the relationship between the formal 'creed' to which a believer assents and the *actual* 'beliefs' which consciously or otherwise control his nervous system?

2   To what extent are beliefs affected by input (feedback) from the outside world (how do we modify doctrine in the light of experience)? Quine distinguishes between central beliefs, which are scarcely affected by input, and peripheral (in the sense of non-central to the system, rather than not intrinsically important) beliefs, which are more responsive. Speaking of scientific rather than theological beliefs he says,

total science is like a field of force whose boundary conditions are experience . . . but the total field is so underdetermined by its boundary conditions . . . that there is much latitude of choice as to what to reëvaluate in the light of any single contrary experience.[21]

3   To what extent are beliefs, or groups of beliefs, affected by each other? How do parts of the belief system interrelate? Is an individual belief only testable/meaningful within the system?

4   S. Stich[22] distinguishes beliefs from 'subdoxastic states', which are typically both unconscious and inferentially unintegrated. But the distinction is by no means clear. The 'faithful', in assenting to a creed, may indeed articulate words, but it has often to be asked whether and to what extent these correspond to conscious beliefs or are 'inferentially integrated' with other beliefs held by the individual. A formal creed in any case never represents the whole 'belief complex' of an individual.

5   Particularly in the light of what is said above on the social aspects of language use, one has to ask whether credal summaries do more than instruct the faithful on how to use words in a conversation which associates them with other 'faithful'. A creed necessarily has syntax; it has rules about how to use words. But it need not have any semantics, it need not actually refer to anything in the outside world. (In practice, of course, it is unlikely to be totally lacking in semantics, but the semantics are a good deal more flexible and negotiable than theologians tend to suppose.) Commitment to a creed means at least the determination to use a particular form of words in a particular context because it is convenient, habitual, and a means of social identification. The very fact that the words are used variously by different people and on different occasions aids this.

8.4   Conclusions: Language, Dialogue and Continuity

1   Dialogue cannot rely on the internal sources of specific religious traditions. Some sort of 'global theology' (philosophy of religion) is necessary to enable people to progress from using their own terms to talk about and judge the other to using frameworks appropriate

to a dialogue of equals. But, in setting up such a philosophical framework within which to communicate, one transcends the bounds of what is possible within any one, defined faith. Here, then, is a clear line of demarcation between theology and the other disciplines we have invoked, in particular philosophy, anthropology and social and computer sciences.

2   External ('objective') languages for talking about religions are provided by disciplines such as history, anthropology, sociology and psychology; one is reluctant to rate phenomenology a 'science'. But, useful as these disciplines are in refining our understanding of the phenomena of religion and religious communities, none of them gives a complete account. The religious person tends to see their concerns as peripheral to his commitment.

3   Linguistics and the philosophy of language constitute an essential critique of talk about religions, particularly about beliefs and belief systems. Computational modelling of 'belief systems', as well as neurological studies of the brain, throw further light on the function of belief within the individual.

4   It will be evident from what has been said about the function of speech acts that creeds have many functions other than truth claims, and, indeed, it is unclear that they carry truth claims at all. The question arises, what is the point of carrying on with the same credal language in changing circumstances, if words do not mean the same thing, or at least do not carry the same, identifiable truth claims? The answer to this is in terms of the non-truth-claim aspect of creeds, and I would suggest that the prime function of creeds is not their truth claims at all, but their social function as binding together the members of a faith community by common language; this is independent of truth claims, and quite consistent with members of the society using the same credal formulations in mutually incompatible ways.

Despite these complexities, from a practical point of view the most important factor in dialogue is also the simplest: a readiness to talk as one friend to another (section 8.2.2).

9

The Plurality of Faiths[1]

9.1 On the Plurality of Faiths

We saw in Chapter 8 that religion involves very much more than formal creeds. In so far as a religion binds people together in a society, purges emotions, teaches morals, comforts the lonely or heals the sick, there is no necessary contradiction between religions, no puzzle as to why God has 'permitted' or even inspired different religions in different societies, no damper or restraint on a relativist view of religion according to which each religion harmonises with a particular time, place, individual or society. Of course, there would still be the possibility of conflict between religious people, because people are quarrelsome; but there would be no logic in the quarrel.

Logic enters when religions make truth claims. As we saw in the previous chapter, there is often little reason to believe religions are making truth claims even when they appear to state propositions about the world, for the uses of language are many, and the staking of truth claims only one, and not the most frequent, use. We even questioned whether creeds are really sets of truth claims.

Still, if religions really are making truth claims, even if such claims are neither as clear nor as extensive as believers think, the possibility arises of logical contradiction between those claims. We may then ask, is it reasonable to suppose that God would inspire understandings of the world which contradict each other? Would he not inspire truth only, and in that case is it not evident that no more than one of several mutually contradictory religions can be true (though maybe none is), and therefore that no more than one can have been inspired by God?

Such a question ignores several factors. It may well be that each of several religious creeds contains, say, exactly 80 per cent of completely true statements, or 100 per cent of statements which are partly true, for the nature of religious language is such that credal statements, owing to the indefinability of their meaning, may be true only in part, or in some way. God may have inspired the total truth, but, accidental inaccuracies apart, it may simply be impossible to convey 'total truth' in human language. God may not himself be constrained by human language in communicating with his prophets, but the prophets are constrained when they use language to communicate with the people.

In the light of our consideration of religious language, the logical problem of the exclusivity of religious truth claims may lose much of its sting. However, it has greatly troubled modern theologians, and must be addressed, bearing in mind the reservations we have already expressed.

9.1.1   Is the plurality of faiths a problem?

Keith Ward, following John Hick,[2] formulates the 'problem' of plurality as follows:

> The problem is this: many religions claim to state truths about the nature of the universe and human destiny which are important or even necessary for human salvation and ultimate well-being. Many of these truths seem to be incompatible; yet there is no agreed method for deciding which are to be accepted; and equally intelligent, informed, virtuous and holy people belong to different faiths. It seems, therefore, that a believing member of any one tradition is compelled to regard all other traditions as holding false beliefs and therefore as not leading to salvation.[3]

Besides the assumption that religious belief involves truth claims ('claim to state truths about the nature of the universe and human destiny'), two additional assumptions underlie this formulation. Since these added assumptions are not the inevitable starting point for non-Christians, we must make them explicit.

First, it is assumed that somehow there is a radical disorder, even malignancy, in the human situation, from which we need to be 'saved'. This malignancy is not simply natural disorder, such as disease or poverty or accident, which one might hope would eventually be overcome through natural means, including progress in science and economics. Indeed, there is no sort of 'natural' knowledge which could overcome it, even if people were all of mind to do so. Of course, varied interpretations of 'original sin' have been adopted by Christians, and the Augustinian interpretation which used to be taken for granted in the Western churches is often questioned; nevertheless, without the premise of radical evil in the world it is difficult to make any sense at all of the Christian 'economy', for the prime function of Christ is said to be the redemption of people from precisely this radical evil.

The second assumption is that some sort of esoteric knowledge, or gnosis, inaccessible other than by initiation (baptism, faith), or by special revelation, constitutes the only path by which we can be 'saved' out of the mess. Of course, this assumption also has been called into question by modern Christians of pluralistic leanings, but it remains the normal Christian starting point when considering the function of faiths. Moreover, it is entirely dependent on the first assumption, for, unless one assumes that there is a radically corrupt predicament from which to be redeemed, the question of what special mysterious knowledge is necessary to achieve this redemption does not arise.

If these twin assumptions were correct it would indeed be important to each individual to do his or her utmost to acquire this knowledge, or gnosis, especially if people live for a long time after their 'natural' death, let alone if they live for eternity. It is on this basis that 'Christian love' has from time to time led to hideous abominations, such as the methods of torture employed on behalf of the Inquisition to ensure that people would acquire true faith and hence escape eternal damnation.

But is not the problem contrived? Is there any justification for the belief that the various messes in which people find themselves are not in principle amenable to 'natural' solutions, or at least to solutions which do not depend on precise formulations of the nature of the Godhead? Certainly, no esoteric, 'revealed' knowledge has helped the sick as much as modern, exoteric medical science, even though there have been many claims of esoteric healing knowledge. Nor has gnosis helped create wealth or distribute it to the needy as well as exoteric industry and economics do. Indeed, those who emphasise theological mysteries as solutions to human problems often distract people from the effective solutions.

So obvious is this that Christian theologians do not usually make such claims for 'faith'. They do not even dare to claim that their distinctive piece of knowledge has withheld societies from conflict and war, or the individual from sinning. The standard claim for 'faith in Jesus Christ' is that it 'saves from sin', but from all the preceding reservations it is evident that this 'saving' is itself a metaphysical process related to radical evil, and with no definite, observable consequences in the world.

Returning now to Professor Ward's formulation of the 'problem' of the plurality of faiths, we may accept that many religions do indeed 'claim to state truths about the nature of the universe and human destiny'. Certainly, they would claim that such truths are *valuable* for human well-being. But they would not necessarily claim that such truths are 'necessary for human salvation', and indeed they may well not share the concept of 'salvation' which underlies the question; further, there is no reason why they should be 'compelled to regard all other traditions as holding false beliefs and therefore as not leading to salvation'.

So far as Judaism is concerned, it will be shown that right and attainable behaviour rather than assent to metaphysical propositions constitutes the standard for a 'portion in the world to come', at least for Gentiles. Within the terms of the Torah, there is no sharp question as to why God has allowed different belief systems to develop, even if only one is totally true; one is not excluded from 'the world to come' on the grounds of incorrect metaphysical beliefs, hence it is no more surprising that God has refrained from 'informing' everyone about metaphysics than that he has refrained from revealing physics or biology or economics – all useful subjects indeed, but not indispensable to preparation for 'the world to come'.

9.1.2 *Scripture and mystery*

When we look at the Hebrew scriptures and the sort of knowledge revealed through the prophets we find, with small exceptions, that it consists not of deep or mysterious propositions about the nature of the universe, but of exhortations to justice and virtue and compassion, and of down-to-earth legislation. Moses, for instance, tells Israel that the wisdom revealed to them, and for which the nations will esteem them, is a system of wise and just *laws*:

> I have taught you statutes and laws, as the Lord my God commanded me; these you must duly keep when you enter the land and occupy it. You must observe them carefully, and thereby you will display your wisdom and understanding to other peoples. (Deuteronomy 4:5–6)

And later in the same book:

> What then, O Israel, does the Lord your God ask of you? Only to
> fear the Lord your God, to conform to all his ways, to love him
> and to serve him with all your heart and all your soul.   (10:12)

Likewise, it would be crass to suggest that Jeremiah had in mind
esoteric knowledge when he contended that God wanted people to
understand and know him:

> These are the words of the Lord:
>   Let not the wise man boast of his wisdom
>   nor the valiant of his valour;
>   let not the rich man boast of his riches;
>   but if any man would boast, let him boast of this,
>   that he understands and knows me.
> For I am the Lord, I show unfailing love
>   I do justice and right upon the earth;
>   for on these I have set my heart.
> This is the very word of the Lord.
>
> (Jeremiah 9:23)

Or that Micah of Moreshet was hinting at secrets and mysteries
when he declared,

> and what is it that the Lord asks of you?
> Only to act justly, to love kindness,
> to walk humbly before your God?
>
> (Micah 6:8[4])

Even Wisdom personified, as in Proverbs 8, offers no 'mysteries',
but a pattern for the just society:

> Pride, presumption, evil courses,
> subversive talk, all these I hate.
> I have strength, I also have ability;
> understanding and power are mine.
> Through me kings rule and governors make just laws. . . .
>
> (Proverbs 8:13–15, NEB modified)

Mysteries have been read into Ezekiel 1 and are clearly present in Daniel 12:4. Ezekiel's vision offers inspiration, and Daniel's secret brings reassurance, but there is no suggestion that one needs such knowledge in order to be 'saved'. Apart from Daniel and a few traces in other books, apocalyptic literature was excluded from the Jewish canon; this exclusion, probably in the first century, was in part at least a process by which the rabbis attempted to free Judaism from gnostic as well as apocalyptic accretions. Of course, they did not entirely succeed, nor is it clear just what they intended. Recently scholars have demonstrated the existence of a flourishing Jewish gnosticism at least as early as the first century, and flowing into the mainstream of Jewish mysticism; there are traces in the Talmud itself.[5] The exact nature of this early gnosticism is in dispute; indeed, since scholars identify the writings as Jewish on the basis of their strict monotheism and their conformity with *halakhah*, it may be misleading to refer to them as gnostic; perhaps it would be safer to use a more specific term, such as 'merkabah mysticism'.

Whereas some of the writings are concerned with descriptions of the ascent and heavenly peregrinations of the ecstatic, undertaken in holiness and purity, others aim to aid him to acquire a perfect knowledge of Torah, including its mysteries. But is this ecstatic 'journey' merely joyful and enlightening, or is it also salvific? If salvific, is it a necessary or merely a specially privileged path to salvation? One version of the *Lesser Hekhalot* speaks of an angelic figure whose function is 'to arrange the throne . . . and to open the Gates of Salvation',[6] but it would be erroneous to conclude from this one passage that salvation, in some deep sense, was the object of the journey. We are on much surer ground taking the texts at their face value, as being concerned with enlightenment, not salvation. And it is even more certain that the vast majority of people, who could not aspire to the heavenly journey, were not excluded from salvation simply because this privileged enlightenment was beyond their grasp.

9.1.3   *Knowledge and salvation*

In its early struggle with the dualist gnostic doctrine of this world as inherently evil, the Church reached a sort of halfway point at which this world is seen not as inherently evil but as redeemably evil. Evil arose not from the nature of the world as created, but from the Fall, however that was explained. Christian 'redemption' differs from gnostic 'escape' for the individual in that it allows for the world itself to be redeemed. Still, the world needs redemption – 'salvation' – and it is the function of the saviour to achieve this cosmic redemption.

But, even if, which there is no reason to assume, the world needed 'salvation' in the melodramatic Christian sense, and if esoteric knowledge were available about the nature of the universe, why should one assume that salvation depends upon knowledge? *Prima facie* it would be a very strange God indeed who was unable or unwilling to accept good and holy people who, in good faith, refused to assent to some set of metaphysical propositions about his nature and his created universe. The special knowledge might be interesting, or marginally useful, or perhaps even inspiring; if that was so, it might well be regarded by those who believe they possess it as a gracious and blessed gift. They must not be surprised if others regard ethics, law, technology, economics and other 'natural' subjects as more relevant to improving the human situation than their metaphysics.

In sum, there is little reason to suppose that the difficulty experienced by sensitive Christians in reconciling their traditional teachings on salvation with the conviction that God must surely take pleasure in good and holy people of all faiths arises within Judaism. I am far from stating that it cannot or does not arise indeed, as we shall see in section 9.3.1A, Moses Mendelssohn raised something very like this point in his correspondence with Jacob Emden in 1773 in the light of Maimonides' introduction of belief into the Noahide criteria. The question I shall address is not whether, in fact, Jewish theologians have involved themselves with arbitrary belief criteria in saying what God wants of the 'Gentiles', or even whether they have developed concepts of radical evil or of esoteric ways of salvation. They have done all these things. What I wish to demonstrate is that (a) there is no inner logic within rabbinic Judaism which leads to such a position and (b) there are ample resources within Judaism to construct theories of the plurality of religions free from the problems arising from the assumptions I have called into question.

9.2 Bible

We build upon traditional foundations, else there would be no continuity. Yet in the interest of coherence and relevance we must be selective in our use of sources. The questions we ask are not those our predecessors asked; though we draw on tradition there are no ready-made, 'off the shelf', traditional answers; some creative effort is demanded.

Four periods span Hebrew/Israelite/Jewish history to the present, and in each the Jewish faith has been tested in its relation to those of the surrounding peoples. The period of the Hebrew scriptures was one of polemic against idolatry; the talmudic–rabbinic period was one of adaptation to a defensive role in a hostile, largely pagan society; the Middle Ages witnessed a struggle to survive under the missionising power and zeal of Christianity and Islam; and the modern era has seen Jews, like others, strive for continuity of their faith within the new world view brought to birth by the scientific discoveries and technological advances of the last few centuries.

There is striking continuity between biblical and later Judaism in the matters with which we are concerned here. Three leading concepts on 'other people' underlie much of the Hebrew scriptures.

1 *Universality*: the certainty that God's concern is for all people.

2 *Openness of the knowledge of God*: such knowledge is not exclusive to Israel, nor is it esoteric, limited to initiates.

3 *Boundaries*: there is a strong line of demarcation between right and wrong, true and false, holy and profane, those who follow God and idolaters. These distinctions tend to be confused with that between Israel and the nations.

Let us examine these aspects more closely.

9.2.1 Universality

Genesis not only stresses the unity of mankind: it shows God first, through Adam, trying to relate to mankind as a whole. Abortive

attempts with Adam and Noah leave him with Abram, an individual, the only one in his time strong enough in faith to enter into a
covenant with God. Through Abram/Abraham God eventually
relates to a family (Genesis 18:19). In bonds in Egypt the family
becomes a nation, a people. But the people itself is chosen not for
its own sake but for God's mission, and he never, so to speak,
loses sight of the fact that Israel is his means for impressing the
nations. When God threatens to destroy Israel and to make Moses
into 'a great nation', Moses dares to invoke God's concern for
public relations (cf. Exodus 32:12). What impression would such a
deed make on the Egyptians, whom, surely, God wants to win
over by demonstrating his care and power? When Solomon dedi-
cates the Temple he sees it as a religious centre for all humankind;
the nations will look to Jerusalem not (let it be stressed) as a seat of
imperial power but as a source of spiritual inspiration (1 Kings 8).
The shortest Psalm (117) crystallises this thought:

> Praise the Lord, all Nations,
>   extol him all you peoples;
> for his love protecting us is strong,
>   the Lord's constancy is everlasting.

The *goyim* – 'nations', 'Gentiles' – should learn about God not
through conquest by Israel but through grateful and admiring
acknowledgement of what God has done for Israel. 'You are my
witnesses', says Isaiah (43:10) – meaning not your suffering, not
even your virtuous life, but the great things God is seen to do for
you. It is perhaps naïve to expect one nation to feel gratitude for
the mighty saving acts God has done for another, yet such is the
cornerstone of the Hebrew scriptures' concept of Israel's mission to
the nations. Once the conquest of the promised land is completed
there is to be no empire-building for the sake of spreading God's
word.

9.2.2   Openness

Scripture does not lack the recognition and appreciation that God
is 'known' by people other than Israel. These may be independent
individuals, such as Melchizedek (Genesis 14:18), or individuals
impressed by particular acts of God (Jethro in Exodus 18; Naaman

in 2 Kings 5). In later times there is a glowing satisfaction that the nations are getting to know God: 'From the rising of the sun to its setting the name of the Lord is to be praised' (Psalm 113:3 – other interpretations are possible).

An individual may, of course, like Ruth, be adopted into Israel; but this is neither required nor expected. The fulfilment of Israel's mission is not that all other people become Israel, but that each nation, remaining what it is – Egyptian, Assyrian or whatever – pays homage to God and is guided by his will. The nations are expected to remain ethnically and culturally distinct, whilst cleansing themselves of idolatry.

The Hebrew scriptures lend no support to the notion that the spread of God's word is to be accomplished through political imperialism.

9.2.3 Boundaries

The acceptance of the idea that other nations, too, are cared for by God (Amos 9:7, *contra* Amos 3:2) and are part of his ultimate plan for the world does not carry the corollary that idolatry, their normal form of worship, is acceptable. True, Yehezkel Kaufmann, in his monumental study,[7] contends that according to the Bible only Israel was forbidden to worship idols. Philo[8] and Josephus[9] as well as more recent Jewish apologists[10] have argued on this basis for tolerance of 'pagan' religions, even though the alleged destruction of temples in Cyrene during the revolt under Trajan suggests that some Jews took an opposite view, and undoubtedly the rabbis distinguished in this respect between the land of Israel, where no idolatry was to be tolerated, and the lands outside, where Gentiles should not be disturbed in their worship.[11] But, even if Kaufmann is right, this would merely show that God was prepared to put up with idolaters for a bit longer, not that his ultimate design was that all people should continue to worship idols.

Kaufmann points out that the Hebrew scriptures are to a very considerable extent polemic against idolatry; scripture shows neither interest in nor understanding of a 'deeper level' in what it castigates as mere 'worship of sticks and stones'. This does pose a problem today for the biblical monotheist who seeks an understanding relationship with Buddhists or Hindus. Is it honest to represent such religions as 'worship of sticks and stones', especially where such a characterisation is categorically rejected by Hindus and Buddhists themselves? We may not feel comfortable with worship directed to or through images, but neither can we any longer feel comfortable with the biblical equation 'idolatry = immorality'. We shall return to this question in section 9.6.3.

Still, scripture does draw boundaries – emphatically so; for instance,

> You shall not make yourselves vile through beast of bird or anything that creeps on the ground, for I have made a clear separation between them and you, declaring them unclean. You shall be holy to me, because I the Lord am holy. I have made a clear separation between you and the heathen, that you may belong to me.   (Leviticus 20:25–7)

How do we interpret those boundaries? Are they just those between Israel and the nations? Evidently not, for Israel is not perfect, and the separation between Israel and the nations is secondary to the higher boundary between sacred and profane. Is it between those who worship through images and those who do not? Much of the Bible reads as if this were so, yet the boundary before idolatry is always justified by scripture itself in terms of either (a) a further ethical or moral boundary, or (b) a rejection of the literal belief that the image worshipped has power to 'save'. Neither of these arguments supports a wholesale rejection of Hinduism or Buddhism, the former because many Hindus and Buddhists are people of high ethical and moral standards, and the latter because the simplistic type of belief in idols portrayed in scripture does not correspond with the reality of Hindu and Buddhist teaching (which is not to deny that some Hindus, as some simple Christians, may fall into the error of ascribing power to images).

9.3   Talmud

9.3.1   'Sheva mitzvot'

Rabbinic Judaism divides the Word of God, for practical purposes, into units called *mitzvot*, each derived from some phrase or verse in the Pentateuch, and ranging from 'Thou shalt love the Lord thy

God with all thy heart, soul and strength' (Deuteronomy 6:5) and 'Thou shalt love thy neighbour as thy self' (Leviticus 19:18) to minutiae of civil and Temple legislation and religious ritual. The *mitzvot* are a God-given privilege:

> The precepts of the Lord are right and rejoice the heart.
>   The commandment [*mitzvah*] of the Lord shines clear
>   and gives light to the eyes.
> The fear of the Lord is pure and abides for ever.
> The Lord's decrees are righteous and true every one,
> more to be desired than gold, pure gold in plenty,
>   sweeter than syrup or honey from the comb.
>
> (Psalm 19:8–10)

Rabbi Simlai, a third-century rabbi who used to commute between Palestine and Babylonia, declared that there were 613 *mitzvot* in all, 365 negative and 248 positive.[12] Though the number was chosen for homiletic purposes rather than derived empirically, it captured the Jewish imagination, defying the ingenuity of scholars to specify precisely which were the 613.[13]

Some unknown rabbis, at about the same time, attempted to list the *mitzvot* incumbent upon the 'children of Noah' – that is, that part of the human race that had not identified itself with the Jewish people by committing itself to the Sinai covenant. Notwithstanding other proposals, the number that caught the imagination was seven. The earliest list we have is incorporated in the following text, formulated perhaps in the late second or early third century:

> The children of Noah were given seven commandments [*sheva mitzvot*]: Laws [i.e. to establish courts of justice], [the prohibitions of] Idolatry, Blasphemy, Sexual Immorality, Bloodshed, Theft, and the Limb from a Living Animal [certain types of cruelty to animals?].[14]

Tosefta interprets each of these 'commandments' in some detail, and the discussion is taken still further in the Gemara and other rabbinic writings, where serious attempts are made to anchor the whole system in scripture, particularly Genesis 9.

What is the origin or purpose of such a selection of laws? In a recent study,[15] David Novak summarises five ways in which scholars have approached this question.

1   The traditional view, most clearly expressed by Biberfeld,[16] taking the scriptural references at their face value, and seeing in this set of laws given by God to Noah as the terms of the post-diluvial covenant the prototype of all legal systems.

2   Tchernowitz's theory,[17] according to which the rabbis were simply acknowledging the existence of an actual ancient non-Jewish law code, the Hittite, seen by them as a version of the laws of Noah.

3   Finkelstein's[18] theory that the Noahide laws are a *ius gentium* devised in the Maccabean period to provide a constitutional status for non-Jews in the Jewish state.

4   The talmudic approach, not dissimilar from Finkelstein's, according to which the Noahide laws define the status of the *ger toshav*, or resident alien.[19]

5   The theory, founded in the rabbinic sources themselves and elaborated by scholars such as Guttman[20] and Agus,[21] that the Noahide laws describe a halfway house, a 'quasi-Judaism', through which a pagan proselyte might move towards full Jewish status. This would equate those who chose to keep Noahide law with *sebomenoi*, *phoboumenoi*, or *yirei ha-Shem*.[22]

To these discrete theories must be added the question of the relationship of Noahide law, or some part of it, to 'natural law'.[23]

While the last two theories provide us with some clues as to the development of rabbinic concepts, particularly in the first two centuries CE, all five fail the simple chronological test of establishing when, in fact, the idea of the Noahide commandments was formulated by the rabbis. Finkelstein, for instance, commits a double historical blunder in reading back to the second century BCE, the Maccabean period, both the later Roman concept of *ius gentium* and a rabbinic concept of at the earliest the late second century CE. I have no hesitation, therefore, in endorsing Novak's own hypothesis[24] that the seven laws constitute a 'theological–juridical theory rather than a functioning body of laws administered by Jews for gentiles actually living under their suzerainty at any time in history'. They are presented by the rabbis as 'pre-Sinaitic law perpetually binding on gentiles', and their precise formulation reflects 'a period in Jewish history when the line of demarcation between Jews and gentiles was fully drawn, and when Jews were required to determine those moral standards which were inherently right'. This would have happened when the split between

Judaism and Christianity was forcing strong lines of demarcation to be drawn.

A. DO NOAHIDES HAVE TO BE BELIEVERS?

Occasionally scholars, summarising the *sheva mitzvot*, include 'belief in God'; this is careless representation of either the prohibition of idolatry or that of blasphemy. I have examined several early versions of the *sheva mitzvot* and have not found one which expressly demands belief in God. Why is this? I suggest that it is careful and deliberate. The rabbis were far more concerned with the rejection of idolatry than with the formulation of 'definitions' of God. An express demand for belief in God would have required some understanding, some definition, of God, and this was precisely the area into which the rabbis did not wish to enter. They asked only that the worship of idols cease and that the worship of God be taken seriously and treated with respect; there was to be no emphasis on the substantive content of belief in God. Assertions about God did not matter, holiness of life did. In complete conformity with this view the third-century Palestinian rabbi Yohanan declared, 'Whoever denies idolatry is called *yehudi* [a Jew].'[25] For this reason it appears to me that Novak is mistaken when he claims that Rabbi Isaac, who places the prohibition of idolatry first in his list, holds that 'God's absolute authority over man is the beginning of the Noahide law and its foundation'.[26] It is the rejection of idolatry, and the respect for God-talk and worship, not the recognition of a defined divine authority, which is the foundation of Noahide law as conceived by the rabbis.

Maimonides indeed held that a Gentile ought to observe the Noahide laws not merely out of reason but through acceptance of the fact that God commanded them in scripture.[27] It may well be, as Novak argues, that Maimonides' philosophy of law leads him to this, for there is certainly no talmudic basis for such an opinion. But then Maimonides, unlike our contemporary philosophers and theologians, had no doubt that the human intellect, used with integrity, would lead one to belief in the authenticity of the biblical text and tradition, hence his assumption that correct belief would accompany moral virtue.

On 26 October 1773 Moses Mendelssohn initiated a correspondence on this theme with Jacob Emden, in terms prescient of Keith Ward's formulation of the 'problem of plurality' cited in section 9.1.1:

And to me these matters are difficult . . . that all the inhabitants
of the earth from the rising to the setting of the sun are doomed,
except us . . . unless they believe in the Torah which was given
to us an inheritance to the congregation of Jacob alone, especially concerning a matter not at all explicit in the Torah . . .
what will those nations do upon whom the light of the Torah has
not shone at all?[28]

It cannot be said that Emden's reply grasped the epistemological
problem that worried Mendelssohn; indeed, the correspondence
between the two on this and other problems resembles an abortive
attempt at communication between the Middle Ages and modern
times.

B. NOAHIDE LAWS AND JEWISH MISSION

It would seem natural that Jewish mission towards the Gentiles
should centre on the Noahide laws, for these laws were designed
to express the Torah's minimum standards for non-Jews. However, the date of their formulation in the third century coincided,
as we shall see in section 9.3.3, with an increase in 'straight'
proselytising by Jews, and by the time proselytising had been
made virtually impossible under Christian rule it was no longer
realistic to proselytise even on a Noahide basis.

In modern times, however, there have been attempts to revive
the concept. The best known of these was that of the kabbalist
rabbi Elia Benamozegh (1823–1900) of Leghorn, who persuaded a
Catholic would-be convert to Judaism, Aimé Pallière, to adopt
Noahism rather than full-blown Judaism. Pallière championed
Noahism until the end of his life in 1949; he attracted interest
rather than followers.[29]

Aaron Lichtenstein has attempted to document more recent
Noahism. He rightly observes that 'the worst hardship borne by
practising Noahites is the lack of fellowship'. The Centre for
Transpersonal Studies in Los Angeles has a *knesset bnei Noach*,
described by its director, Dr Lawrence Corney, as a collective of
Jews and Gentiles 'who jointly participate in the study and practice
of Noahism'. The Revd Vendyl M. Jones, director of the Institute of
Judaic–Christian Research of Arlington, Texas, reported contact
with some 2000 'committed Noahites'. No one can tell whether all
this is mere 'straws in the wind' or the tentative first steps of a
major new religious initiative.[30]

Closer to the mainstream of Jewish religious activity is the impetus the *sheva mitzvot* concept gives to Jews to accept moral responsibility in society in general, for it demands that support and encouragement be given to 'the nations' to uphold at least this standard. A notable instance of this has been a series of public addresses and interventions through which the Hasidic leader Menahem Mendel Schneersohn (the 'Lubavitcher Rebbe') of New York has expounded the Noahide laws in relation to the needs of contemporary society. This initiative included an exchange of letters with President Reagan in 1986 in which Schneersohn commended the President for 'giving valuable support to the dissemination of the Seven Noahide Laws, so basic to any society worthy of its name'.[31]

C. THE 'RIGHTEOUS GENTILES'

Some two or three generations before the formulation of the Noahide laws, rabbis Joshua and Gamaliel II had debated whether Gentiles 'have a portion in the world to come' (i.e. without conversion to Judaism – it goes without saying that converts irrespective of ethnic origin have such a 'portion'), and the debate was resolved in accordance with Joshua's view that 'the righteous of all nations have a share in the world to come'.[32] It is testimony to the irrepressible universalism of Judaism that, at a time when it faced Gentile, including Christian, hostility, the Jewish teachers not only refused to write non-Jews off from God's ultimate promise, but positively asserted the worth of each good person, even *unconverted*, in the eyes of God, and formulated a fresh and original doctrine outlining the responsibilities of all humankind within the 'covenant of Noah'. Judaism does not have an equivalent to *extra ecclesiam nulla salus* (outside the Church no salvation).[33]

The reports of this debate between Joshua and Gamaliel do not use the term 'saved', but rather the relatively cumbersome expression 'have a portion in the world to come'. Quite possibly this reflects a reaction to Christian use of 'save', a rejection of the central Christian presupposition that people are somehow 'condemned' until 'saved' by a special act of cosmic redemption which must be believed in to be efficacious.

The notoriously unreliable second-century-CE biographer Diogenes Laertius attributes to both Socrates and Thales the following saying: 'I thank Tyche that I was born a human being and not an animal, a man and not a woman, a Greek and not a barbarian.'[34] In some curious way this striking utterance rebounded across cultural barriers, modifying its meaning, and illuminating thereby the differences between the cultures.

Paul, for instance, had already said, 'There is no such thing as Jew and Greek, slave and freeman, male and female; for you are all one person in Christ Jesus' (Galatians 3:28). Scholars differ radically in their interpretations of Paul's words. Still, the context of 'faith versus law' in which the remark is set means that it is and was popularly understood as meaning that faith, or belief (whether or not that means propositional belief), in Christ Jesus was that which saved – belief, not deeds. Belief, according to Paul, is the criterion of God's favour, and it is the line of demarcation between the issue of Abraham and other people.

A rabbinic variation of the saying runs, 'I call to witness heaven and earth, that whether *goy* [Gentile] or Jew, whether man or woman, whether manservant or maidservant, it is entirely according to the deeds of the individual that the heavenly spirit rests upon him.'[35] It is not possible to date this sentence, versions of which appear in several midrashim. However, there is no version of it which would lead us to believe that it is earlier than the third century. It can not have been the model for Galatians 3:28. Rather, it is a comment, a reaction. Whilst it is not likely that any of the rabbis actually read the Epistle to the Galatians, they may well have heard the saying, interpreted it at face value, and countered with the statement that 'all is in accordance with the deeds of the individual' – a point of view in which they would have been firmly in accord with Ezekiel 18, for Ezekiel graphically stresses the concept of individual responsibility and, like the Hebrew scriptures generally, does not seek assent to statements of belief as a condition for finding favour in the eyes of God.[36]

9.3.2 *Discriminatory and anti-social legislation*

The 'demarcation' aspect of rabbinic Judaism is most clearly evidenced by the lengthy history of rules, particularly regarding food, idolatry and ritual purity, which were devised by the rabbis and their predecessors with the aim of separating Jews from the heathen environment, and occasionally even from their less devout brethren.[37] This is paralleled by developments within the early Church.[38] Rabbinic hermeneutic, moreover, not infrequently

The Plurality of Faiths 233

restricts the operation of some biblical rules to the faithful among
the people of Israel. This restrictive interpretation leaves the rabbis
with the problem of how to apply such basic ideas as respect for
proprietary rights and regard for human dignity to non-Israelites.
Their solution (it has not commanded sufficient attention from
scholars) is masterly. Side by side with the restrictive interpretation of the Bible there emerged a series of broad principles such as
tiqqun olam ('establishing the world aright'), *darkhei shalom* ('the
ways of peace') and *qiddush ha-Shem* ('sanctifying God's name', i.e.
behaving in such a manner as to bring credit to God) which are
used *inter alia* to govern the relationships of Jews to those outside
the bond of faith or peoplehood.[39]

9.3.3 Conversion to Judaism

The pride and relish with which Josephus regales his readers with
tales of converts to Judaism, such as the royal house of Adiabene,[40]
is complemented by the welcoming attitude to proselytes common
in the Talmud and early rabbinic literature. As S. J. Bamberger and
W. G. Braude showed,[41] converts of all nations were welcomed by
Jews throughout the early centuries of this era.

The destruction of the Temple in 70 CE might have been expected to diminish fervour, but it did not. It must have been very
soon after 70 that Yohanan ben Zakkai waived the requirement for
a convert to bring sacrifice in the Temple, thus enabling conversion
to take place independently of the sacrificial system,[42] and it was
only a generation later that Joshua ben Hananiah, 'at a stroke',
enabled so-called Ammonites and Moabites not only to convert to
Judaism (that was not in question) but to marry within the community.[43]

Welcoming proselytes, however, is by no means the same as
going out purposely to seek them. As Martin Goodman puts it,

Jews were often eager to change the general attitudes of gentiles
both to God and to each other; they liked non-Jews to admire
and respect Jewish customs; they encouraged the spread of
monotheism; and they speculated with some interest on the
eventual status of gentiles in the last days. But a mission to gain
converts, a phenomenon most familiar from the history of Christianity, requires an attitude rather different from any of these.[44]

Goodman goes on adduce a great deal of evidence that a more positive attitude to proselytisation came to be regarded by many rabbis of the second to fourth centuries as desirable – for instance, several stories from that period depict Abraham, Jethro and others as missionaries – though none produced a coherent strategy for active proselytisation. But why should such a change have taken place precisely in the years after the fall of the Temple and the failure of the Bar Kochba revolt? Goodman thinks it unlikely that Christian proselytising activities prior to the third century were significant enough to have induced a Jewish response along similar lines, and hazards the idea that the new emphasis on clear definition of who was or was not Jewish and hence on the religious responsibilities of those who were not Jewish resulted from the imposition of the *fiscus judaicus* on all Jews outside Judaea after 70. Under Nerva, in 96, the tax was reformed so as to recognise the existence of both defectors from and proselytes to Judaism, and made it impossible to leave the status of Gentile sympathisers with Judaism ambiguous. Perhaps the title 'God-fearers' found in third-century inscriptions in the Aphrodisias Synagogue was a way of indicating Jewish sympathies whilst evading fiscal obligations!

Ultimately, one cannot expect to discover in 'normative' Jewish sources the reality of Jewish life of those periods. Indirect evidence of what must have taking place in those early centuries is exemplified by the Ethiopian Jews whose flight to Israel stole the headlines a few years ago. In pre-Islamic times there were numerous Jewish tribes right across North Africa. Some doubtless converted voluntarily to the new religions, some were forcibly converted, many murdered. In later centuries those who retained Jewish identity were put under enormous pressure, moral and physical, to convert to the dominant faith; few showed the tenacity of the Falashas, whose conversion predated the conversion of the Axum dynasty to Christianity in the fourth century and who survived as a Jewish tribe for almost 2000 years.[45] As few such tribes were ethnically Jewish, one must assume that they had become Jewish by conversion. Who converted them, and how? We await hard evidence.

9.4   From Mission to Survival

How did it come about then that Jews changed from an outgoing though not aggressive attitude on proselytism to first a more cautious, then a defensive, inward-looking, nervous attitude?

9.4.1 The rise of Christendom

It used to be thought that the first change took place after the abortive Bar Kochba revolt, when frustration and the suspicion of treachery taught caution. From the expression 'nowadays' in the following, and its general form and tone, one is led to associate it with that period:

> Nowadays when anyone wishes to become a proselyte one says to him, 'Why do you wish to become a proselyte? Do you not know that nowadays Israel is miserable, oppressed, persecuted and in confusion?' If he replies, 'Yes, indeed, and I account myself unworthy [to be numbered amongst them]', he is accepted at once, and told some of the easy *mitzvot* and some of the more difficult ones.[46]

As we have seen, however, the Bar Kochba debacle was followed by an enhancement rather than an attenuation of Jewish missionary concern, and for the reasons suggested in section 9.3.3 it was at that time that the rules for conversion were formalised.

It was a much profounder and more tragic happening that forced Jews to avert their eyes, if not their ultimate hopes, from the outside world, to seek the inward world of the spirit, and to master the art of survival. For more than a millennium and a half in Christendom, and almost as long in the Islamic world, they were to be the 'despised religion', allowed to survive, allowed in principle if not always in practice to follow the religion of their fathers, but forbidden to raise their heads high and threatened with death or worse should they dare to offer to others what they believed to be the truth of God.

Constantine, called the Great (306–37), issued the following law on 18 October 315:

> We wish to make it known to the Jews and their elders and their patriarchs that if, after the enactment of this law, any one of them dares to attack . . . another who has fled their dangerous sect and attached himself to the worship of God [Christianity], he must speedily be given to the flames and burnt together with all his accomplices.
>
> Moreover, if any one of the population should join their abominable sect and attend their meetings, he will bear with them the deserved penalties.[47]

Thus a rule which might have made some sense in preserving a community (Christian or Jewish) under pressure from outside has now become a state law, and as such an instrument of repression.

There is irony in the criticisms occasionally voiced by Christians with regard to Jewish reservations on intermarriage. After all, it was the Christian Emperor Constantius who, in his law of 13 August 339, not only summarily dissolved all marriages between Jewish men and the (Christian) women who worked in the imperial weaving factory, but added,

> This prohibition [of intermarriage] is to be preserved for the future lest the Jews induce Christian women to share their shameful lives. If they do this they will submit themselves to a sentence of death. (The Jewish husbands are to be punished with death.)

Here are some points from novella III of Theodosius II's law of 31 January 439:

> No Jew shall obtain offices and dignities; to none shall the administration of city service be permitted . . . we forbid that any Synagogue shall arise as a new building. . . .

These laws were no dead letter but the foundation of the unequal Christian–Jewish relationship of the Middle Ages and beyond.

9.4.2   Under Islam

The birds came home to roost, so far as Christians were concerned, with the rise of Islam. 'The Pact of Omar is the body of limitations and privileges entered into by treaty between conquering Moslems and conquered non-Mohammedans';[48] even today there are Muslim countries where it is not a dead letter. True, it affords 'protected' (*dhimmi*) status to the 'People of the Book', and for that they have often enough expressed gratitude; things could have been worse.[49] But it is a far cry from the modern concept of civil rights and the equality of all men and women before the law; its model is the Christian standard for treatment of its own 'protected' group, the Jews.

The pact presumably grew from Omar's original Pact of about

637, and some scholars think it attained its present form only in the ninth century. In return for protection non-Muslims must agree, *inter alia*, to the following:

> We will not erect in our city . . . any new monastery, church, cell or hermitage . . . we will not repair any of such buildings that may fall into ruins . . . we will not refuse the Moslems entry into our churches by night or by day . . . we will not teach our children the Koran . . . we will not make a show of the Christian religion or invite any one to embrace it . . . we will not prevent any of our kinsmen from embracing Islam . . . we will honour the Moslems and rise up in our assemblies when they wish to take their seats . . . we will not imitate them in our dress . . . make use of their expressions . . . nor adopt their surnames . . . we will shave the front of our heads . . . we will not display the cross upon our churches . . . we will not recite our services in a loud voice when a Moslem is present.

These laws were not always strictly followed either in Christendom or in Islam. Sometimes a regime was liberal, but sometimes it was even harsher than the law demanded. Throughout the Middle Ages, however, the majority of Christians did not live under Muslim rule, nor did most Muslims live under Christian rule. Both Christians and Muslims could therefore develop their own faiths without much of an eye to what lay beyond. It was the fate of the Jews, and the Jews only, to be the 'despised religion' wherever they lived. Survival meant adaptation, and the adaptation was that of looking inwards, developing one's own traditions, meditating on the great classics of the past, creating in readiness for the days of the Messiah, dreaming the dreams of the ghetto, but leaving other people strictly alone. 'Mission' was to preserve the truth that God had entrusted to us, to preserve our faith in God and our heritage, not to meddle in the perilous affairs of the hostile, contemptuous world outside. Survival for the sake of this mission became the prime concern of the Jew.

The shadow of Constantine hovers yet. Even without the Holocaust looming over our recent history it would have been hard for Jews to regain the confidence to jettison the sense of being victims, of being everywhere the 'despised race', and to indulge in the luxury of addressing a message to the outside world.

9.4.3   Openness and demarcation

Throughout the Middle Ages Jewish teachers consistently upheld the non-exclusiveness principle – that is, the recognition that people of other faiths might know and please God. Indeed, this was arguably easier to maintain in a Christian or Muslim world than in the pagan one which had seen the formation of rabbinic Judaism. Mediaeval thinkers, unlike their forbears in late antiquity, were often aware of what Christians and Muslims actually taught and believed, and offered comment, whether by way of defence or instruction. Sometimes this is found in the context of 'disputation', which frequently elicited from Jews some of their best apologetic.[50] But there is also much thought about the other monotheistic religions in writing which is not primarily controversial. A critical attitude, as for instance that of Saadia (882–942),[51] to Christological doctrine (Islam, like Judaism abhorring the very idea of incarnation, presented a less serious doctrinal conflict) did not mean blindness to the moral and spiritual value of Christianity. Even Judah Halevi (*c.* 1075–1141), perhaps the most ethnocentric of our philosophers, recognises a role in God's plan for the other monotheistic religions, for 'they serve to introduce and pave the way for the expected Messiah, who is the fruition, and they will all become his fruit'.[52] We cited Maimonides' words on this theme in section 6.3.1.

The lines of boundary, of demarcation, were indeed strongly drawn in the Middle Ages. Nevertheless, as Jacob Katz has demonstrated,[53] the *halakhah* shows some relaxation of those laws which were designed specifically to separate Jews from pagans. The Provençal rabbi Menahem Hameiri (*d. c.* 1315), anxious to avoid identification of people of other religions in his own time with pagan idolaters, coined the phrase *umot ha-gedurot be-darkhei ha-datot* ('nations bound by the ways of religion'), and used this categorisation to justify what was probably already a customary relaxation of certain rabbinic laws.[54]

9.5   The Enlightenment

The Enlightenment stressed universal human values and reason rather than creeds, posing a challenge to the conventional Christian view. The new orientation was welcomed, however, by the small number of eighteenth-century Jews, mainly German, sufficiently emancipated to share in contemporary intellectual development. The Swiss deacon Johann Caspar Lavater[55] publicly challenged Moses Mendelssohn (1729–86) either to refute Christianity or to do what 'reason and integrity would otherwise lead him to do'. In his courageous reply Mendelssohn strongly affirms his faith in Judaism, and even claims superiority for that faith on the grounds that it is fundamentally more tolerant than Christianity. Here is part of his letter to Lavater:[56]

> According to the basic principles of my religion I am not to seek to convert anyone not born into our laws. . . . Our rabbis unanimously teach that the written and oral laws which comprise our revealed religion are obligatory upon our nation only. . . . We believe the other nations of the earth are directed by God to observe [only] the Law of Nature and the Religion of the Patriarchs. Those who conduct their lives in accordance with this religion of nature and reason are known as *hasidei umot ha-olam*, 'righteous gentiles', and are 'children of everlasting salvation'. So far are our rabbis from wishing to convert, that they instruct us to dissuade, by earnest remonstrance, any who come forward of their own accord. . . .
>
> If, amongst my contemporaries, there were a Confucius or a Solon, I could consistently with my religious principles, love and admire the great man; the ridiculous thought of converting Confucius or Solon would not enter my head. Convert him indeed! Why? He is not of the Congregation of Jacob, and therefore not subject to my religious laws; as concerns doctrine we should reach a common understanding. Do I think he would be 'saved'? I fancy that whosoever leads men to virtue in this life cannot be damned in the next – nor do I fear to be called to account for this opinion by any august college, as was honest Marmontel by the Sorbonne.

Mendelssohn was not unaware[57] that some of the early rabbis had taken a more outgoing attitude towards conversion, but he seems to have underestimated it or else to have played it down for apologetic reasons. His 'religion of nature and reason' is clearly an Enlightenment version of the Noahide commandments. As Katz writes, 'Mendelssohn based his predictions upon the assumption that there would come about a complete severance between

Church and State, i.e. between the institutions of religion and of government.'[58]

9.6   Modern Times

Jewish thinkers today, in working out their relationship with people of other faiths, share with others in facing the challenges which arise from the differences between our contemporary world and the world in which our faiths were first formulated. These challenges fall under the following headings.

1   Our concept of the world and its nature and 'purpose' have been radically changed by scientific discoveries from Copernicus onwards (see Chapter 6, especially section 6.4).
2   Philosophers have forced us to revise our notions of truth and its relationship to the way we use language (see Chapter 8).
3   Improved communications, in the understanding of language and literature as well as in pure physical mobility and through radio and electronics, rule out cultural/religious isolation as an option.
4   Greater firepower, and the historical demonstration that technological progress does not automatically reduce conflicts, make necessary a global approach, comprising all nations irrespective of their religions, to the achievement of peace.
5   Conservation of the planet and its resources demands global commitment and organisation. We share the planet with each other or else we all perish (see Chapter 2).

In view of the above and of Jewish tradition, what can be the Jewish attitude today to other people and other faiths? Let us examine it in terms of each of the three aspects we have been tracing.

9.6.1   Universality

The Jewish messianic hope focuses on the future, not on a specific past event. It therefore readily expresses the confidence that all humankind will be involved in any future 'redemption', whether gradual or sudden. In Chapter 6 we found that Enlightenment thinkers such as Moses Mendelssohn understood the messianic faith as a divine guarantee of the progress of mankind; whilst I rejected any notion of *inevitable* human progress, I accepted that such progress is possible, if reversible, and should in any case be held as an ideal. This ideal undoubtedly encompasses all humankind and, as we learned in Chapter 2, all creation.

Section 9.3.1 developed the idea of the *sheva mitzvot*, or Noahide commandments, as a framework that embraces the whole world within Torah, yet allows a distinctiveness to Israel. At first sight this might seem to compromise universality. However, I propose that Israel be seen within this system as a prototype for each and every nation, which will wish to maintain its distinctiveness under a broad universalist umbrella. Section 5.6 raised the question of 'local theologies', which are now recognised by most churches as a proper and legitimate expression of Christian faith, in no way contradicting its universal character. Provided that we do not tie ourselves to a narrow geopolitical definition of 'local', but instead understand 'local' in terms of cultural boundaries, it would be possible to develop a Jewish theology which would embrace other peoples and possibly other faiths, in slightly modified form, as 'local' Jewish theologies; it would be fascinating to work out the possible relationships.

The contemporary orthodox rabbi David Hartman,[59] if I understand him correctly, has proposed a variety of this approach. He finds in the Bible two covenants, that of Creation and that of Sinai. The Creation covenant (reflected in that of Noah) is with all mankind – universal and for all time. The Sinai covenant is with Israel, and does not preclude other, parallel covenants with other societies. This allows for a plurality of revelations, each God's way of speaking to a particular group of people. This is of course very different from the 'two-covenant' theology often (wrongly) attributed to Franz Rosenzweig, for it does not recognise a special covenant with Christianity, thereby excluding other faiths; in Hartman's view, Christianity would hold an equal place with numerous other 'covenant' societies.

The weakness of this type of approach, though, is that it attempts 'inclusiveness', as John Hick has called it; in effect it claims that others are 'implicit Jews', and thereby imposes itself on them.

It might be better, ultimately, to stop worrying about the theological status of other faiths or societies, and simply to concentrate on the business of living together harmoniously. Provided government remains secular, this is possible; but where, as in some Islamic states, law is determined on a religious basis, there is inevitably discrimination which favours the dominant faith community. Indeed, the whole future of the plural society depends strongly on the maintenance of secular government, as was clearly perceived by Mendelssohn (see the end of section 9.1.5).

9.6.2   *Openness*

Today, the traditional readiness of which we learned in sections 9.2.2 and 9.4.3 makes it natural for Jews to appreciate that others have a 'share in God'.

This need not create pressure towards relativism, for the recognition that others can know and be faithful to God has never been understood as implying that all that they do and believe is correct; as stressed in Chapter 1, there is no necessary connection between accurate knowledge about God's nature or revelation (correct belief) and the 'portion in the world to come'. We learned about one of the most politically significant consequences of this in section 5.5.2 (under 'How religious attitudes relate to traditional sources'), where we saw how the recognition by Ovadiah Yosef and Shilo Refael that Arab Muslims in Israel are not 'idolaters' but genuine worshippers of God enabled them to circumvent harsh biblical rules which might otherwise have applied, and in the name of Torah to demand, in effect, full civil equality for Arabs.

Perhaps a few constructive words on Judaism's relationship with Hinduism and Buddhism will not be out of place here. The historical and theological entanglements that blight the interrelationships of the three monotheistic faiths have no place here, and the main obstacle to a constructive relationship comes from the inherited monotheistic insistence that God is 'jealous' and that all who 'worship sticks and stones' are extremely wicked. The modern world view and situation must enable us to transcend this attitude, and it is good to remark that the few Jewish thinkers who have seriously addressed themselves to the 'Eastern' religions have revealed rich areas for exploration. Let me list some of the issues raised by the conservative rabbi Joseph P. Schultz.[60] Is a similar inner religious tension with regard to the primacy of intellectual perfection over ritual and ethics reflected by Sankara/Maimonides on the one hand and Ramanuja/Halevi on the other?[61] Whether or not there is some historical link, how does the Gita's idea of the world emanating from God, the source of good and evil, relate to, for instance, the Lurianic theory of creation/emanation?[62] On *karma* and the rabbinic theme of reciprocity (*middah ke-neged middah*), what is the range of approaches by Buddhist and Jewish thinkers to the effect of will on *karma* or *gezar din* (the decree of punishment)?[63] How does the mystical/spiritual progress described by Luzzatto in *Mesillat Yesharim* relate to the Eightfold Path?[64] Schultz does not explore the points of contact between the rabbinic laws of sacrifice and ritual and purity and those of Hindus, and for this we must turn to anthropologists; we should certainly not allow ourselves to be deflected by common Western prejudices against concerning ourselves in this area which is of such high significance in other societies.

9.6.3 Demarcation

Religions *do* make truth claims, such as that the Torah came from Heaven, that Jesus was the incarnation of God, born of a virgin, or that people are reborn in various forms until they attain *nirvana*, and many of these claims are contradictory. They also make practical claims, such as that one ought not to worship idols or that one ought to celebrate festivals or to marry or not to marry this one or that.

It would be wrong to gloss over any of this. The first task is to achieve a harmonious society, and in the light of all we have said this should be possible, under secular government, even with a plurality of religious faiths, communities and practices.

After that, there is a search for truth. Truth is delicate, too delicate for warring communities, but in a peaceful community there may be a common search for truth. The community must be very peaceful, though, with a positive peace, not just an absence of fighting. Truth can only emerge where those who search for it do not feel threatened, and are not browbeaten by those who think they already possess the truth, and who insist on 'sharing' it whether or not anyone wants to listen. So the society in which truth is to be sought will allow for distinctiveness, for commitments, for witness, but not for pressurising and aggressive proselytising.

9.7 Conclusion

I have aimed to portray Judaism as a religion with a commitment, a mission, to the world. This sense of responsibility has often been dimmed by the emphasis our leaders, in times of persecution, have had to put on the preservation of identity and distinctiveness so necessary for our survival in a hostile world, yet it has never been allowed to disappear. In bad times the sense of mission focuses on the messianic future; in enlightened times it is expressed in the Jewish desire to play a full part in the social and spiritual improvement of mankind. The 'covenant of Noah' offers a pattern for us to seek from others not necessarily conversion to Judaism, but rather that faithfulness to the highest principles of justice and morality which we perceive as the essence of revealed religion. The dialogue of faiths becomes in this way an imperative arising through our common mission with, rather than against, other faiths.

So we take joy in the bond that unites humankind, as descendants of the 'first created pair', Adam and Eve, and look forward to the restoration of that universal bond in time to come, when 'the earth shall be full of the knowledge of the Lord, as the waters cover the sea' (Isaiah 11:9).

Yet there *is* truth, there *is* a distinction between true and false, between right and wrong, *this* world is *not* beyond good and evil, and so there must be demarcation, and this is reflected both in our teaching and in our society. We cannot set the bounds of truth; we must listen and try to learn, grow in experience and forge language, remain open to the world around us with its myriad peoples and ways, and read and interpret the words of scripture and sage constantly, critically, in the context of our own age and society.

Tradition can only be captured for the present by a critical and creative process which does not shirk novel moral decisions. It is too tempting to evade responsibility for those decisions by deceiving oneself that there is some simple direct guiding line from ancient text to contemporary reality.

Appendix:
A Guide to the Main
Rabbinic Sources

Although, in an historical sense, the Hebrew scriptures are the foundation of Judaism, we have to turn elsewhere for the documents that have defined Judaism as a living religion in the two millennia since Bible times.

One of the main creative periods of post-biblical Judaism was that of the rabbis, or sages (*hakhamim*), of the six centuries preceding the closure of the Babylonian Talmud in about 600 CE. These rabbis (*tannaim* in the period of the Mishnah, followed by *amoraim* and then *seboraim*), laid the foundations of subsequent mainstream ('rabbinic') Judaism, and later in the first millennium that followers became known as 'rabbanites', to distinguish them from the Karaites, who rejected their tradition of interpretation in favour of a more 'literal' reading of the Bible.

In the notes that follow I offer the English reader some guidance to the extensive literature of the rabbis, noting also some of the modern critical editions of the Hebrew (and Aramaic) texts.

Following that, I indicate the main sources (few available in English) in which rabbinic thought was and is being developed. This should at least enable readers to get their bearings in relation to the rabbinic literature discussed and cited in this book.

Talmud

For general introductions to this literature see Gedaliah Allon, *The Jews in their Land in the Talmudic Age*, 2 vols (Jerusalem, 1980–4), and E. E. Urbach, *The Sages*, tr. I. Abrahams (Cambridge, Mass., and London: Harvard University Press, 1987), as well as the *Reference Guide* to Adin Steinsaltz's edition of the Babylonian Talmud (see below, under 'English Translations').

Hyam Maccoby's *Early Rabbinic Writings* (Cambridge: Cambridge University Press, 1988) is an excellent introduction, with selected texts, to rabbinic literature up to about 200 CE.

Professor Peter Schäfer, of Berlin, opened a recent debate on what he chose to call 'the *Status Quaestonis* of Research in Rabbinic Literature'; his controversy with I. Milikowsky can be read in the pages of the *Journal of Jewish Studies* (Oxford) from 1986 onwards. What seems to be at issue is the question of whether one can speak at all of 'definitive' texts (*Urtext*, original text) of the main rabbinic works, such as Mishnah, Tosefta and Genesis Rabbah. I incline to Shäfer's view of 'rabbinic literature as an open continuum in which the process of emergence is not to be separated or distinguished with further ado from that of transmission, and the process of transmission from that of redaction' – *JJS*, XL (1989) 89. Although 'critical texts' are referred to below, and approximate dates given for the composition of works, one has to be aware of the difference betwen the gradual consolidation and acceptance of particular recensions of, for example, the Mishnah, and the composition of a book (such as this one) at a definite time and place by a specific person or persons. It is, to the careful scholar, alarming that we have no Mishnah and Tosefta manuscripts, and few fragments, from within six or seven hundred years of the 'composition' of those works. What we are presented with is not the unmodified work of second-century Palestinian rabbis but a scene frozen at an arbitrary point in time within the dynamic transmission of a tradition, modified at least in the Babylonian academies and often enough in those of the mediaeval Rhineland as well. Halakhic texts, being regarded as authoritative for practical purposes, were more conscientiously preserved than aggadic midrashim, though on the other hand there was a temptation to bring them into line with whatever the 'transmitter' thought was the correct ruling. Wherever, in the next section, dates are given for 'compilation' or 'completion' of books, these terms are used for convenience only, and do not imply the existence at any time of some authoritative *Urtext*.

The main texts

The core of the Talmud is Mishnah, compiled under Judah the Patriarch in Galilee in the early third century CE. Mishnah is divided into six *sedarim* (volumes), subdivided into sixty or so *mesekhtot* (tractates), which subdivide further into chapters and paragraphs.

Tosefta is closely related to Mishnah, comprising supplementary material and commentary, and divided into the same orders and tractates. Though much of its material is contemporary with Mishnah, its formation continued somewhat later.

Mishnah, Tosefta and other tannaitic works were discussed in the schools of Palestine and Babylonia from the third century onwards. The debates, with much other material, are known as *gemara* (learning, completion). Written in the form of commentary on Mishnah, *gemara* together with Mishnah comprises the Talmud. The Palestinian, or Jerusalem, Talmud (in Hebrew *Yerushalmi*), reflects the discussions in the Holy Land; it was completed about 400. The Babylonian Talmud (*Bavli*) is much more comprehensive, except in agricultural law, and would have achieved much the form in which we know it by about 550. The Babylonian rather than the Jerusalem Talmud was formative for rabbinic Judaism throughout the Middle Ages, though recently, partly in view of its relevance to agriculture in the land of Israel, the status of the Jerusalem Talmud has been enhanced in orthodox circles.

How talmudic texts are referenced

Since Mishnah's division into tractates provides the framework for all these works, it is convenient to refer to texts by M (Mishnah), T (Tosefta), J or P (Jerusalem or Palestinian Talmud), or B (Babylonian Talmud), followed by the name of the tractate, in transliterated Hebrew, in *italic*. References to Mishnah (standard editions) and Tosefta (Zuckermandel's Hebrew edition) list tractate, chapter and paragraph; *Yerushalmi* (Jerusalem Talmud) is referred to by tractate, chapter and section; *Bavli* (Babylonian Talmud) references are to tractate and to the page in Bomberg's Venice edition of 1520–3: this has been followed by most subsequent editions, including the Vilna (1880–6) edition normally reproduced and used today.

Here are some examples.

M *Gittin* 7:4 means: Mishnah, tractate *Gittin*, chapter 7, mishnah (paragraph) 4.

T *Berakhot* 4:2 means: Tosefta, tractate *Berakhot*, chapter 4, paragraph 2.

B *Bava Qama* 42b means: Babylonian Talmud, tractate *Bava Qama*, second side (side 'b') of folio 42.

J *Shevi'it* 4:3 means: Jerusalem Talmud, tractate *Shevi'it*, chapter 4, halakha (law, section) 3. This could also appear as P *Shevi'it* 4:3, 'P' standing for 'Palestinian' (for the *Yerushalmi* was not indeed composed in Jerusalem, from which Jews had been banned). *Yerushalmi* references are sometimes made by page, but this causes confusion as unlike the *Bavli* it is not published in standard pagination.

Lists of the tractate names and their meanings will be found in any of the translations referred to below, or in appropriate encyclopaedia articles under 'Mishnah'. Of course, there are alternative transliterations of the Hebrew names.

English translations

MISHNAH
The following translations are available.

H. Danby (tr.), *The Mishnah* (London: Oxford University Press, 1933).
Mishnayot, Hebrew text of the Mishnah with translation and explanatory notes by Philip Blackman, 7 vols (New York: Judaica Press, 1951–6; 2nd edn 1963–4).

J. Neusner, *The Mishnah: A New Translation* (New Haven, Conn.: Yale University Press, 1987).

The Mishnah is subdivided into six *sedarim* ('orders'). Five of these are now available in translation and with form-critical analysis and historical assessment in the series published by Brill of Leiden and mainly written by or under the guidance of Jacob Neusner. There are forty-three volumes. Several volumes of the first order, *Zeraim* ('Seeds'), have appeared under different publishing arrangements. One can avoid tedious repetition by focusing on volume 22 of the sixth order, *Tohorot* ('Purities'), in which Neusner sums up his method and conclusions.

TOSEFTA

The Hebrew text was edited by M. S. Zuckermandel (Pasewalk, 1881; Jerusalem, 1937); an important critical commentary (incomplete), *Tosefta Kifshutah*, was added by S. Lieberman (New York: Jewish Theological Seminary of America, 1955–73). J. Neusner has published an English translation of the text: *The Tosefta*, 6 vols (New York: Ktav, 1977–86).

JERUSALEM TALMUD

J. Neusner, *The Talmud of the Land of Israel: A Preliminary Translation and Explanation*, 35 vols (Chicago: University of Chicago Press, 1982–7).

BABYLONIAN TALMUD

I. Epstein (ed.), *The Babylonian Talmud*, translation with notes, glossary and indexes, 18 vols (London: Soncino Press, 1935–48). There have been subsequent editions, including some individual tractates with Hebrew text.

Neusner has entered the field with his *The Talmud of Babylonia: An American Translation* (Atlanta, 1984–), but few volumes of this have as yet appeared.

A *Reference Guide* and the first volume of text with translation by Adin Steinsaltz have been published by Random House (New York, 1989).

Targum

The Aramaic translations (paraphrases) of scripture, known as targumim, have been used continuously by Jews since early rabbinic times, in both synagogue and study, and have recently received considerable scholarly attention. For an introduction see John Bowker, *The Targums and Rabbinic Literature* (Cambridge: Cambridge University Press, 1969); but lively debate on fundamental issues has taken place in the intervening twenty years. Among the published translations of the targumim is D. Rieder, *Pseudo-Jonathan: Targum Jonathan ben Uzziel on the Pentateuch* (Jerusalem, 1974).

Liturgy

Rabbi Gamaliel II, round about the year 100, presided over the institution of the forms of prayer which became normative for subsequent Judaism. However, there is no satisfactory account in English of the development of Jewish liturgy in the early centuries. especially since the revision of much earlier scholarship under the impact of Genizah studies. The works of Idelsohn, Heinemann and others remain valuable. See J. Heinemann and J. J. Petuchowski, *Literature of the Synagogue* (New York: Behrman House, 1975). Petuchowski edited a collection of some of the important papers from the late nineteenth century onwards in *Contributions to the Scientific Study of Jewish Liturgy* (New York: Ktav, 1970).

The standard orthodox prayer books, not least the Passover *Haggadah*, contain much early material, but editors and commentators rarely distinguish between rabbinic material and later accretions, being concerned with piety rather than scholarship.

Midrash

The term *midrash* means 'exposition', from the biblical root *darash*, 'to seek, interpret, inquire'. The process of interpretation, or *midrash*, starts within scripture itself: see for instance Deuteronomy 1:5; Nehemiah 8:8.

As a genre, the rabbinic midrash (preaching, interpretation, biblical exegesis) ranges very widely. One broad division, though not a sharp one, is into *midrash halakhah* (legal, concerned with deriving law from scripture) and *midrash aggadah* (more discursive, concerned with ethics, spirituality, history and legend).

For a general introduction, see J. Neusner, *Reading Scriptures: An Introduction to Rabbinic Midrash* (Chappaqua, NY, 1986).

Midrash Halakhah

The three tannaitic (that is, attributed to rabbis of the Mishnah period) works of scriptural exegesis in this mode date, in their earliest forms (no longer extant) from perhaps the late second century. Critical editions of the Hebrew text, and English translations, are as follows.

On Exodus: *Mekhilta*. J. Z. Lauterbach, *Mekhilta de-Rabbi Ishmael* (text and translation) 3 vols (Philadelphia: Jewish Publication Society of America, 1933–5). The *Mekhilta de-Rabbi Shimon ben Yohai* (ed. J. N. Epstein and E. Z. Melamed, Jerusalem, 1955) does not appear to have been translated.

On Leviticus: *Sifra*. Hebrew text edited by I. H. Weiss (Vienna, 1862). English translation by J. Neusner and R. Brooks: *Sifra: An American Translation* (Chicago: University of Chicago Press, 1985).

On Numbers and Deuteronomy: *Sifre*. Critical editions of the Hebrew texts are: on Numbers, the edition by H. S. Horovitz (Leipzig, 1917); on Deuteronomy, the edition by Louis Finkelstein (Berlin, 1939; New York: Ktav, 1969). I am not aware of an English translation.

All three exist in numerous recensions and versions.

Midrash Aggadah

Many English readers have had a pleasurable introduction to the world of midrash through Ginzberg's *The Legends of the Jews*, tr. Henrietta Szold, 7 vols (Philadephia: Jewish Publication Society of America, 1909).

The collection known as Midrash Rabbah (the 'Great Midrash') contains midrashim on the Pentateuch and the five Scrolls (Job, Song of Solomon, Ruth, Lamentations, Ecclesiastes). It has appeared in English as H. Freedman and M. Simon (eds), *The Midrash*, 10 vols (London: Soncino Press, 1939). However, Midrash Rabbah is not a unitary work, but a collection of arbitrarily selected recensions of independent midrashim on several books; its sources range over at least a thousand years.

A far better concept of what midrash is may be gained from W. G. Braude and I. J. Kapstein *Pesikta de-Rab Kahana* (Philadelphia: Jewish Publication Society of America 1975), a fine edition of text with translation of a 'homiletic' midrash, consisting of discourses on the Pentateuch portions of the three-yearly cycle, and perhaps redacted about the year 600. The best Hebrew text is B. Mandelbaum's (2 vols, New York: Jewish Theological Seminary, 1962).

Other midrashim cited in our main text include: *Derekh Eretz Rabbah*; *Midrash Tillim* (on Psalms – ed. S. Buber, Vilna, 1891); *Midrash Shohar Tov*; *Yalqut Shimoni*; *Tanna Debe Elijah*; *Pirqe de-Rabbi Eliezer* (tr. G. Friedlander, New York: Bloch; London: Kegan Paul, 1916).

Mystical works

Gershom Scholem and I. Tishby in particular revolutionised our understanding of the development of Jewish mysticism, and of its place within Jewish thought. Scholem's English works, including his *Major Trends in Jewish Mysticism*, 3rd edn (New York: Schocken, 1954) and *Jewish Gnosticism, Merkabah Mysticism and Talmudic Tradition* (New York, 1965) are the indispensable introduction to this field. We can be certain that mysticism has featured in Jewish sources at least since the first century; for an assessment of the involvement of mainstream rabbinic Judaism with mysticism see Ira Chernus, *Mysticism in Rabbinic Judaism* (Berlin and New York: Walter de Gruyter, 1982).

Few of the early mystical texts have been translated, and many of the translations which do exist are worthless. The translations of selected texts in D. R. Blumenthal's *Understanding Jewish Mysticism: A Source Reader* (New York, 1978) do not meet scholarly requirements, but are a helpful starting-point.

M. Sperling and M. Simon published the best English version of the thirteenth-century kabbalistic classic *The Zohar* (London: Soncino Press, 1949), though sections are missing. From *Zohar*, the mystical tradition continues through Isaac Luria (1534–72) to the Hasidic movement, and it is to the large corpus of Hasidic writings that the English reader should turn for some insight into the most recent phase. One of the most accessible Hasidic mystical texts in English is *Dobh Baer of Lubavitch: Tract on Ecstasy*, tr. with introduction and notes by L. Jacobs (London: Vallentine, Mitchell, 1963).

Codes

The literature of the talmudim and midrashim is vast and unwieldy; furthermore, social and economic changes occur constantly. It therefore became necessary, as rabbinic sources were studied in later centuries, to produce systematic codes of law which were easy to access and up-to-date. The Gaonic period (Gaon was the title of the leaders of the Babylonian academies until at least the eleventh century) saw several attempts at codification, but the following eventually emerged as the authoritative codes, to which other rabbis often added notes and commentaries.

Moses Maimonides (1135–1204), *Mishneh Torah*

See I. Twersky, *Introduction to the Code of Maimonides* (New Haven, Conn., and London: Yale University Press, 1980). *The Code of Maimonides* (New Haven, Conn., and London: Yale University Press, 1951 onwards) is a complete translation, in fourteen volumes, by various authors (including three different Kleins). P. Birnbaum's single-volume English abridgement *Mishneh Torah* (New York: Hebrew Publishing Company, 1944) offers a 'taster'.

Jacob ben Asher (Spain, *c.*1270–1343), *Arba'a Turim*

This has not been translated. Its four main divisions, as well as its chapter divisions, are the model for Karo's code. The four divisions are as follows.

Orach Hayyim ('Path of Life'): liturgy and festivals.
Yore De'ah ('Teacher of Knowledge'): dietary laws, interest, mourning, respect for parents, and sundry religious matters.
Even ha-Ezer ('Stone of the Helper'): on marriage and divorce.
Hoshen Mishpat ('Breastplate of Judgement'): on civil and criminal law.

Joseph Karo (1488–1575), *Shulchan Arukh*

Karo's Code, composed in Safed, Israel, in the mid sixteenth century, corresponds to Sephardic usage, and was complemented by the notes of Moses Isserles, an Ashkenazi of Cracow. The combined work was quickly accepted as am authoritative code, and became the basis for later commentary and development. C. N. Denberg's *Code of Hebrew Law* (Montreal, 1954–5) is a bilingual edition of parts of *Yore De'ah* and *Hoshen Mishpat*. S. I. Levin and Edward A. Boyden's *The Kosher Code* (1940; New York: Hermon Press, 1969) has a translation of those parts of the *Yore De'ah* concerned with injuries to animals which would render them unacceptable under Jewish dietary law, and is remarkable for its combination of anatomy and Jewish law. J. L. Kaddushin's *Jewish Code of Jurisprudence* (2 vols, New Rochelle, NY, 1923) is a translation of *Hoshen Mishpat*. Translations of *Orach Hayyim* manifesting piety rather than scholarship have appeared recently.

Responsa

Since Gaonic times (seventh century onwards) *she'elot u-teshuvot* ('questions and answers' – responsa) have been a major medium for recording the application of Jewish law and teaching in changing times and societies; most of the leading rabbis right up to the present day have published volumes of such responsa. Though the conclusions generally find their way in the course of time into codes and commentaries, one must turn to the responsa themselves to appreciate the full reasoning and the social and historical context of the arguments.

None of the major collections of responsa has been fully translated, though there is no serious work on Jewish history or law which does not cite them copiously. Solomon B. Freehof's *The Responsa Literature* (Philadelphia: Jewish Publication Society of America, 1955) is an enjoyable introduction to the genre, with full examples. J. David Bleich's *Contemporary Halakhic Problems* (New York: Ktav, Yeshivah University Press, 1977–89) gives an insight into current developments in *halakhah*, drawing heavily on contemporary responsa. Three volumes have so far appeared.

Poetry, Philosophy and other Genres

No attempt will be made here to review the vast corpus of liturgical poetry, religious philosophy and Bible commentary of the Middle Ages and later, as references to such works in the main body of the book should be self-explanatory and bibliographies are readily available elsewhere.

Notes

Chapter 1   What I Want to Prove

1. David Hume, *A Treatise of Human Nature* (London and New York: J. M. Dent 1911) II, 177 (III.i.1).
2. M *Avot* 5:25. In *Avot de-Rabbi Nathan* 12 the saying is ascribed to Hillel, who was probably Ben Bag Bag's teacher. Both men lived early in the first century.
3. Luther's table-talk as recorded by Lauterbach (3 June 1539), in Martin Luther, *Collected Works*, vol. 4, ed. and tr. Theodore G. Tappert (Philadelphia: Fortress Press, 1967) pp. 358–9. Though Copernicus's *de Revolutionibus Orbis* was not printed until 1543, he had already been teaching at Wittenberg.

Chapter 2   Conservation

1. The first version of this chapter appeared as 'Judaism and Conservation' in *Christian Jewish Relations*, XXII (Summer 1989).
2. The Talmud consists of (a) the Mishnah, a comprehensive compendium of Jewish law compiled *c*. 200, and (b) the Gemara, a broad commentary on the preceding, incorporating much other material. The Babylonian Talmud was completed *c*. 550. For an overview of the main Jewish sources see Appendix.
3. Most Bible translations in this volume follow the New English Bible (NEB), though I have substituted my own translation where necessary.
4. See Psalms 8, 104, 148. I do not know enough about other religions to corroborate Gerhard von Rad's claim in *Wisdom in Israel* (Nashville: Abingdon Press, 1974) p. 175: 'The idea of a testimony emanating from creation is attested to only in Israel.'
5. I have in mind Matthew Fox. See the refutation of his viewpoint by Margaret F. Brearley, in 'Matthew Fox: Creation Spirituality for the Aquarian Age', *Christian Jewish Relations*, XXII (Summer 1989).
6. I cannot ascertain in the exact date of the conference, and the only paper which was published was Lichtenstein's excellent one; it appeared (in Hebrew) in *Haggut*, V (Jerusalem, 5740/1980: Religious Education Department of the Israel Ministry of Education) 101–8.
7. See Samuel Cooper's anthropological study of the 'laws of mixture' in Harvey E. Goldberg (ed.), *Judaism: Viewed from Within and from Without* (Albany NY: State University of New York Press, 1987) ch. 1. Our approaches are radically different but not mutually exclusive.
8. See the special World Ships issue of the *Journal of the British Interplanetary Society*, XXXVII (June 1984), for some detailed engineering observations. Alexander G. Smith's article 'Worlds in Miniature – Life in the

Starship' explores the ecological aspects of such Arks.

9. To the third-century Palestinian Rabbi Abbahu the midrash *Bereshit Rabbah* 3:9 attributes the statement that God 'created and destroyed worlds before he made these': which is presumably his final design.

10. Malachi Beit-Arieh prepared a critical edition of the work as a PhD thesis (Jerusalem, 1966), but recently informed me that it has not been published. I have based my remarks on the texts in the large *Siddurim* (Prayer Books), particularly those of Jacob Emden and Seligmann Baer.

11. Seligmann Baer (1825–1907), in his introduction to *Pereq Shira* on p. 547 of his masterly 1868 edition of the Prayer Book *Seder Avodat Israel*, correctly denies the authenticity of these introductory dicta, and omits them from his edition.

12. See David Ehrenfeld and Philip J. Bentley, 'Judaism and the Practice of Stewardship', *Judaism*, XXXIV (1985) 310–11.

13. Abraham Isaac Kook (1865–1935) was born in Latvia and emigrated to Palestine in 1904, becoming Chief Rabbi of the Ashkenazi communities of Palestine when the office was instituted in 1921. A man of great piety and erudition, his numerous works are imbued with mysticism, and he emphasised the role of holiness in establishing the Jewish presence in the Holy Land. A selection of his writings translated into English is published under the title *Abraham Isaac Kook* in the series Classics of Western Spirituality (New York: Paulist Press, 1978).

14. This is a traditional Jewish understanding of the text. Versions such as 'For ever is mercy built' (translation of the Jewish Publication Society of America, consonant with several English versions) are grammatically sounder.

   I have taken the quotation from the texts on 'Protection of Animals' published (in Hebrew) by the Israel Ministry of Justice in February 1976, but have been unable to check the original source. This publication of the Ministry of Justice together with its volume on 'Protection of the Environment' (July 1972) is an excellent resource for traditional texts on these subjects, having been compiled to assist those responsible for drafting legislation for the Knesset. The volumes were compiled by Professor Nahum Rakover, in his capacity as Adviser on Jewish Law to the Ministry of Justice.

15. In view of the ending of the verse this is a more appropriate translation of Hebrew *adam*, a generic term for humankind, than the sexist 'man'.

16. Joseph Albo, *Sefer ha-Iqqarim*, III. C 1.

17. B *Eruvin* 100b. We respect Yohanan's reverence for nature, not his skill in scientific observation.

18. Heb. *mazzal* – literally 'constellation', but understood also as 'guardian angel'.

19. A reminiscence by Aryeh Levine in *Lahai Roi* (Jerusalem, 5721/1961) pp. 15, 16.

20. The 'seven laws of the children of Noah' attempt to define the religious obligations of humankind in general, for all people are descended from Noah. The laws, unknown in this form in sources earlier

than the third century, are: do not blaspheme; do not worship idols; do not murder; do not commit adultery; do not steal; establish courts of justice; do not eat 'a limb torn from a living animal'. The last of these covers cruelty to animals; it is well explained in David Novak, *The Image of the Non-Jew in Judaism*, Toronto Studies in Theology, no. 14 (New York and Toronto: Edwin Mellen Press, 1983), ch. 8. We shall discuss the 'seven laws' (*sheva mitzvot*) more fully in Chapter 8.

21. B *Bava Metzia* 85a and *Bereshit Rabbah* 33.
22. Moses E. Gaster (ed.), *Maaseh Book*, I (Philadelphia: Jewish Publication Society of America, 1934).
23. In B *Shabbat* 128b it is suggested that this principle is of biblical status (*d-oraita*).
24. B *Berakhot* 40a. See *Shulchan Arukh*: *Orach Hayyim* 167:6.
25. See Elijah Judah Shochet, *Animal Life in Jewish Tradition: Attitudes and Relationships* (New York, 1984). On halakha and animal experimentation see J. David Bleich, *Contemporary Halakhic Problems*, vol. 3 (New York: Ktav, 1989) pp. 194–236.
26. Albo, *Sefer ha-Iqqarim*, III.15.
27. Isaac Abravanel, commentary on Isaiah 11:6 ('The wolf shall lie down with the lamb').
28. Isaac Abravanel, commentary on Genesis 2.
29. See Richard Schwarz, *Judaism and Vegetarianism* (Smithtown, NY: Exposition Press, 1982) and J. David Bleich, *Contemporary Halakhic Problems*, vol. 3, pp. 237–50.
30. In his commentary *Baer Heitev* on *Shulchan Arukh*: *Orach Hayyim*, 134:3.
31. Known as the 'Ponevezher Rav', from the Lithuanian town where he established his reputation as a yeshiva lecturer, Kahaneman survived the Shoah and spent his latter years in Israel, where he built up a network of *yeshivot*, orphanages and other institutions. My information on his diet was received in conversation with his disciples.
32. Israel Ministry of Justice publication on 'Protection of Animals' (see above, n. 14), p. 7ff. Rakover gives a wide range of references to the responsa, many of which come from Renaissance Italy, which provided most of the very few instances of Jews in pre-modern times engaging in hunting.
33. Since the prey, even if a kosher animal, will not have been slaughtered lawfully.
34. Time should be devoted to study and good deeds.
35. The inference is that participating in hunting takes one out of the company of Torah scholars and into that of those who mock at religious values.
36. 'Thou shalt not walk in their statutes' sounds more 'biblical' but is less felicitous than the NEB translation. The point is that hunting is contrary to the Jewish ethos.
37. For an interesting account of tension within the Islamic world between religious teaching and social norms on the subject of hunting see John R. Willis, 'Hunting, Hawking and Learning: "Manly" Attainments and the Pursuit of Knowledge in Early Islam', *Maghreb Review*, XIII (1988).

38. Literally, 'not to destroy', In B *Makkot* 22a, Ravina (fourth century) stresses the positive aspect of the commandment, 'but you *shall* eat [the fruit of the trees]'.
39. *Sefer ha-Hinnukh* Mitzvah 529.
40. M *Bava Qama* 7:7.
41. See for instance Gedalian Allon, *Toldot ha-Yehudim be-Eretz Israel bi-Tequfat ha-Mishnah ve-ha-Talmud* (Tel Aviv: Ha-Kibbutz ha-Meuchad, 1953–5) I 173–8 and 359.
42. Some caution is needed here. The rabbis of the Talmud did not envisage vegetarianism, and did not ban the raising of large cattle in the land of Israel. They assumed that meat would be eaten but tried to ensure that its production would not interfere with agriculture.
43. A frequent expression – see for instance Deuteronomy 16:11.
44. B *Bava Qama* 82b.
45. These matters are dealt with in the Talmud in *Bava Batra* 2. They are codified, with subsequent developments, in *Shulchan Arukh*: *Hoshen Mishpat* 145. Maimonides, in his philosophical work *Guide for the Perplexed* III.45, argues that the purpose of the incense in the Temple was to counteract the smell of the processing of the animal offerings.
46. M *Bava Batra* 2.
47. T *Bava Batra* 1:7.
48. S. Assaf (ed.), *Teshuvot ha-Gaonim* (Jerusalem: Darom, 5689/1929) p. 32. The Gaonim were the heads of the Babylonian academies after the completion of the Talmud; they occupy a major place in the development and transmission of rabbinic law.
49. Meir Sichel, 'Air Pollution – Smoke and Odour Damage', *Jewish Law Annual*, V (Boston, Mass.: Boston University; and Leiden: E. J. Brill, 1985) pp. 25–43. I have used Sichel's translation of the Israeli legislation referred to.
50. T *Bava Metzia* 11:31 (ed. Zuckermandel).
51. Cited in *Shulchan Arukh*: *Hoshen Mishpat* 155:21.
52. Rashi on B *Bava Batra* 21a. Nahmanides, in his commentary on the passage, hazards a guess that the permissible noise limit would be exceeded by a school of more than fifty pupils.
53. *Shulchan Arukh*: *Hoshen Mishpat* 156:3.
54. On B *Sota* 22b.
55. See Maimonides, *Mishneh Torah*: *Shekhenim* 10.
56. In the name of Judah bar Ezekiel (third-century Palestinian) in B *Berakhot* 43b. A whole chapter of *Shulchan Arukh* (*Orach Hayyim* 226) is devoted to it.
57. For a full treatment of these issues see David M. Feldman, *Marital Relations, Birth Control and Abortion in Jewish Law* (New York: Schocken Books, 1974).
58. Ibid., p. 302.
59. B *Taanit* 11a.
60. *Shulchan Arukh*: *Orach Hayyim* 240:12 and 574:4.
61. Feldman, *Marital Relations*, p. 304.
62. B *Yevamot* 62a.
63. In this section I am indebted to the summary provided by Robert

M. White in 'The Great Climate Debate', *Scientific American*, July 1990.

64. E. Rubinstein, 'Stages of Evolution and their Messengers', *Scientific American*, June 1989, p. 104.

65. The ancients thought this had come from the gods, but Genesis 4:20–2 polemically credits humans with technological innovation.

66. See (in addition to Feldman, *Marital Relations*) Immanuel Jakobovits, *Jewish Medical Ethics* (New York: Bloch, 1967). Huge numbers of responsa appear in halakhic journals, and there are specialist periodicals on Jewish medical ethics in Hebrew and English. The Federation of Jewish Philanthropies of New York issues frequent updates (for instance, 6th edn 1984) of its *Compendium on Medical Ethics*, which reflects a broad consensus of views across the Jewish denominations.

67. See Abravanel's commentary on Genesis 2. He taught that in the Messiah's time, as in Eden, we would wear no clothes, build no houses, abandon technology and have no government; in this he is more indebted to Seneca's Epistle XC than to Jewish sources.

Chapter 3 Ethics of Commerce

1. David Hume, *A Treatise on Human Nature* (London and New York: J. M. Dent, 1911) II, 88 (III.ii.6, *original emphasis*).

2. M *Bava Metzia* 4:1.

3. Meir Tamari, *With All Your Possessions* (London: Macmillan; and New York: Free Press, 1987) p. 160. Sir Thomas Gresham (1519–79) was the founder of the Royal Exchange, London, rather less than 1500 years after the completion of the Mishnah.

4. B *Nedarim* 28a; *Gittin* 10b; *Bava Qama* 113a/b; *Bava Batra* 44b/45a.

5. There is a fine study of this rule and its ramifications in Shmuel Shilo, *Dina de-Malkhuta Dina* (Jerusalem: Academic Press, 1974).

6. Salo W. Baron, *A Social and Religious History of the Jews*, 2nd edn (New York, 1952–67) V 324 n. 93.

7. The Mishnah (*Peah* 6:1) presupposes this principle, but it is explicit only in Gemara, for instance B *Gittin* 36b. Sometimes it is referred to as a power of confiscation, but I have avoided this term as it seems to suggest that the court takes possession of the *hefqer* object, whereas in fact it merely dispossesses the original owner, and the object would not enter new ownership without the further legal procedure of *qinyan*.

8. B *Shabbat* 31a.

9. Hillel's statement is recorded in B *Shabbat* 31a and that of Rabbi Akiva in J *Nedarim* 9:4. The accuracy of the attributions, and the fact that Hillel expresses the rule in its 'negative' and Akiva in its positive, biblical, form, are immaterial here; the reports reflect at the very least the broad concern amongst the rabbis that interpersonal relationships be founded on the 'golden rule'.

10. Moshe Hayyim Luzzatto, *The Path of the Just*, tr. Shraga Silverstein, 2nd edn (New York: Feldheim, 1987) ch. 11.

11. That is, do not deny that something belonging to another is in your possession.

12. This verse is developed in rabbinic law to cover all cases of infringement of proprietary rights, including 'intellectual' rights such as copyright.

13. Luzzatto here alludes to the reluctance with which any form of advertising was permitted by the sages. It is only allowed subject to a strict requirement of fair competition. See Aaron Levine, *Free Enterprise and Jewish Law* (New York: Yeshiva University Press, 1981) 26–7; and Tamari, *With All Your Possessions*, pp. 46–7.

14. As is well known, the early versions of the 'pound of flesh' story, such as that in the tale of the fourth wise master of the 'Seven Wise Masters of Rome' in the Sindbad series, have no Jewish reference.

15. B *Bava Metzia* 30b. There is an excellent chapter on *lifnim mishurat ha-din* in S. Federbush, *Ha-Musar ve-ha-Mishpat bIsrael* (Jerusalem: Mosad Harav Kook, 5708/1947) ch. 11.

16. M *Bava Metzia* 4:2.

17. Menachem Elon, *Ha-Mishpat ha-Ivri* (Jerusalem: Magnes Press, 1978) p. 176. See the discussion in Louis E. Newman's article 'Law, Virtue and Supererogation in the Halakha', *Journal of Jewish Studies*, XL (1989) 61–88. Newman (following Elon) cites several instances where later authorities have made legally enforceable something which the Talmud referred to as *lifnim mishurat ha-din*.

18. Isadore Twersky, 'Some Aspects of the Jewish Attitude toward the Welfare State', *Studies in Jewish Law and Philosophy* (New York: Ktav, 1982) p. 137ff.

19. B *Bava Batra* 10a (Twersky's translation).

20. Twersky here draws attention to Bahya ben Pakudah's section on *bitahon* in his *Duties of the Heart*.

21. B *Sota* 14a. See Maimonides, *Mishneh Torah: Hilkhot Deot* 1:6, for a reconstruction of this passage.

22. T *Yoma* 1 and *Shevi'it* 1, cited in B *Yoma* 23a.

23. B *Bava Metzia* 75b.

24. *Shulchan Arukh: Hoshen Mishpat* 76:2.

25. Israel Zangwill, *The King of the Schnorrers* (various London editions from 1897 onwards). The exchange between Grobstock and Manasseh near the beginning of the book, for all its wit, is a treasury of rabbinic and biblical and rabbinic texts on benevolence.

26. B *Shabbat* 151b, attributed to the school of Rabbi Ishmael. See also *Tur: Yoreh Deah* 247.

27. B *Ketubot* 50a. It is clear from the codes (for instance *Shulchan Arukh: Yoreh Deah* 249) that this limit does not apply where the need is great or where one is making a will.

28. Maimonides, *Mishneh Torah: Arakhin Vaharamin* 8:13. It is not without significance that Maimonides codified this rule in the section of his work dealing with temple gifts rather than in the section on charity.

29. See the elaboration of this concept in Bachya ben Asher's *Kad Hakemach*, section on wealth. This work has been translated and annotated by Charles B. Chavel as *Encyclopedia of Torah Thoughts* (New York: Shilo, 1980), 484ff.

30. B *Berakhot* 35b.
31. Tamari, *With All Your Possessions*, p. 87.
32. Luzzatto, *The Path of the Just*, ch. 13, pp. 181–3.
33. For an evolution of Jewish attitudes to asceticism see Ephraim E. Urbach, 'Ascesis and Suffering in Talmudic and Midrashic Sources', *Baer Jubilee Volume* (Jerusalem: Historical Society of Israel, 1960) p. 48ff.
34. I have cited this passage in Francis McHugh's translation, in his article in *Business and Society* (London: Institute of Business Ethics, 1988).
35. M *Avot* 4:1.
36. M *Qiddushin* 4 (end).
37. See particularly Max Weber, *The Protestant Ethic and the Spirit of Capitalism* (New York: Scribner, 1938); and R. H. Tawney, *Religion and the Rise of Capitalism* (New York: Mentor Books, 1954).
38. 'Torah with the way of the land'. The phrase derives from Gamaliel III's statement in M *Avot* 2:2, understood by Hirsch as 'Torah together with a worldly occupation is an excellent thing.' The chapter on Hirsch in Zvi Kurzweil, *The Modern Impulse of Traditional Judaism* (Hoboken, NJ: Ktav, 1985), is a useful, if uncritical, introduction. An interesting collection of essays on the growth and influence of the movement is Mordechai Breuer (ed.), *Torah im Derekh Eretz* (Ramat Gan, Israel: Bar Ilan University, 1987).
39. The Archbishop's report was published as *Faith in the City* (London: Church House, 1985). The Chief Rabbi's views may be read in Immanuel Jakobovits, *From Doom to Hope* (London: Office of the Chief Rabbi, 1986). Jakobovits acknowledges his great debt to Hirsch in *Samson Raphael Hirsch* (London: Office of the Chief Rabbi, 1971).
40. *Faith in the City*, ch. 3 ('Theological Priorities').
41. Ibid., pp. 47–8.
42. See the reference to this debate in section 2.5.6.
43. Adam Smith, *An Inquiry into the Nature and Causes of the Wealth of Nations* (1776) IV.9.
44. Ibid., IV.2.
45. John Rawls, *A Theory of Justice* (London: Oxford University Press, 1972).
46. 'Put no stumbling-block before the blind' (Leviticus 19:14) – 'before one who is blind in respect of that matter' (*Sifra* ad loc.).
47. In his fine study of Jewish contract law in Economic theory (*Free Enterprise and Jewish Law*, ch. 4), Aaron Levine acknowledges his debt to Dr Shillem Warhaftig's two Hebrew volumes *Dine-Avodah ba-Mishpat ha-Ivri*.
48. See the excellent account of rabbinic law on 'ruinous competition' in Levine, *Free Enterprise and Jewish Law*, ch. 3. Louis I. Rabinowitz's *Herem ha-Yishuv* (London: Goldston, 1945) was the pioneering English text on the *Herem ha-yishuv*, and there is a short but perceptive account in Tamari, *With All Your Possessions*, pp. 113–17.
49. M *Taanit* 2:9.
50. The declaration constituting the 'Community Charter of the Fundamental Social Rights of Workers' was adopted by the heads of state or government of the eleven member states of the European Community at Strasbourg on 9 December 1989. The full texts of the declaration and

the charter may be consulted in *Social Europe*, 90/1 (Luxembourg: Office for Official Publications of the European Communities, 1990) pp. 45–50.

51. There is for instance the precedent of the seating in the Synagogue of Alexandria, which was apparently arranged to help newcomers meet persons who could offer employment in their own trade. See B *Sukkah* 51b.

52. B *Qiddushin* 30b.

53. M *Bava Metzia* 7:1.

54. For the material in this paragraph see Levine, *Free Enterprise and Jewish Law*, pp. 18–19, and the references there to primary sources.

55. Edward Zipperstein, *Business Ethics in Jewish Law* (New York: Ktav, 1983).

56. For the English reader, an interesting responsum of Joseph Colon on this topic is available in Solomon B. Freehof, *The Responsa Literature* (Philadelphia: Jewish Publication Society of America, 1959) pp. 121–4.

57. There is a translation of the Hebrew text of the Oath of Asaph the Physician in *Annals of Internal Medicine* LXIII (1963) 317–20. See also S. Muntner, *Mavo le-Sefer Asaph ha-Rofe* (Jerusalem: Geniza, 1957), and his article on Asaph in the *Encyclopedia Judaica*.

58. A second edition of the code was published in 1983.

59. See Peter Bohm, *Social Efficiency: A Concise Introduction to Welfare Economics*, 2nd edn (London: Macmillan, 1987) ch. 2.

60. See for instance J. K. Galbraith, *The Nature of Mass Poverty* (Cambridge, Mass.: Harvard University Press, 1979; Harmondsworth, Middx: Penguin, 1980).

61. In a large number of works, of which perhaps the most popular is M. and R. Friedman, *Free to Choose* (1979; London: Pan, 1990).

62. For instance, ibid., p. 53.

Chapter 4   Economic Topics

1. Dan Cohn-Sherbok, *On Earth as it is in Heaven: Jews, Christians and Liberation Theology* (Maryknoll, NY: Orbis, 1987).

2. Marc H. Ellis, *Toward a Jewish Theology of Liberation* (Maryknoll, NY: Orbis, 1987).

3. *Christian Jewish Relations*, XXI (Spring 1988).

4. From the summary of the consultation published under the joint auspices of the two bodies as item SE/85 in *Study Encounter* (Geneva: World Council of Churches), XI, no. 4 (1975), under the title 'The Concept of Power in Jewish and Christian Traditions'.

5. Gustavo Gutiérrez, Introduction to *Théologie de la libération*, tr. François Malley OP (Brussels: Editions Lumen Vitae, 1974).

6. Gregory Baum, 'Option for the Powerless', *Ecumenist*, XXVI (Nov–Dec 1987).

7. Bachya's *Kad Hakemach* has been translated and annotated by Charles B. Chavel as *Encyclopedia of Torah Thoughts* (New York: Shilo, 1980), which is the version cited here (from p. 496).

8. *Sifre* ad loc.

9. B *Taanit* 21a.

10. L. Boff and V. Elizondo (eds), *Concilium Option for the Poor: Challenge to the Rich Countries* (Edinburgh: T. & T. Clark, 1986) p. ix.
11. B. *Yoma* 35b. Hillel was one of the great teachers at the beginning of the first century CE; he was a poor Babylonian immigrant.
12. John-Paul II, *Laborem Exercens* (1981), esp. no. 8.
13. John-Paul II, *Sollicitudo Rei Socialis* (1988) no. 39.
14. Yohanan bar Nappaha, who died in 279, was a leading Palestinian rabbi. This discourse is found in the B *Megilla* 31a; the translation is that of the slightly different version in the Prayers for the Conclusion of the Sabbath, as they appear in J. H. Hertz (ed.), *Authorised Daily Prayer Book* (London, 1941, and subsequent eds).
15. See his article in the spring 1988 issue of *Christian Jewish Relations*.
16. See in particular his commentary on Genesis 2. For a summary in English of Abravanel's messianic teaching see B. Netanyahu, *Abravanel* (Philadelphia: Jewish Publication Society of America, 1953) pp. 195–257.
17. J. P. Miranda, *Marx and the Bible: A Critique of the Philosophy of Oppression* (Maryknoll, NY: Orbis, 1974).
18. Julio de Santa Ana, 'How the Rich Nations Came to be Rich', in Boff and Elizondo, *Concilium Option for the Poor*.
19. J. K. Galbraith, *The Nature of Mass Poverty* (Cambridge, Mass.: Harvard University Press; Harmondsworth, Middx: Penguin, 1980) ch. 1.
20. See P. Freire, *Education for Critical Consciousness* (New York: Seabury Press, 1973) and *Pedagogy of the Oppressed* (New York: Herder and Herder, 1970).
21. Franz J. Hinkelammert, *Las Armas Ideológicas de la Muerte* (San José, Costa Rica: Departmento Ecuménico de Investigationes, 1977; 2nd edn 1981); tr. Phillip Berryman as *The Ideological Weapons of Death* (Maryknoll, NY: Orbis, 1986).
22. Hinkelammert, *The Ideological Weapons of Death*, p. xxi.
23. I expect Christian preachers do this. Jewish ones, of whom I have far more experience, never cease.
24. See Hinkelammert, *The Ideological Weapons of Death*, p. 268.
25. Ibid., p. 178.
26. Ibid., p. 92.
27. Ibid., p. 77.
28. Friedrich A. Hayek, *Individualism and Economic Order* (Chicago: University of Chicago Press, 1948) p. 31; cited in Hinkelammert, *The Ideological Weapons of Death*, p. 50.
29. Hinkelammert, *The Ideological Weapons of Death*, p. 173.
30. Ibid., p. 272.
31. Joseph Ratzinger, *Instructions on Certain Aspects of the Theology of Liberation* (Vatican City, Aug 1984).
32. M *Shevi'it* 7.
33. Exodus 22:24; Leviticus 25:36; Deuteronomy 23:20. The New Testament has nothing to say on the subject unless, as is suggested by the Vulgate and was assumed in the Church, Luke 6:34, 35 is a prohibition of usury.
34. *Decretum Gratiani*, distinctions 46 and 47 and cause 14.
35. Thomas Aquinas, *Summa Theologica*, II.ii.78.

36. For an overview of economic affairs in the late Middle Ages see M. M. Postan and E. E. Rich (eds), *The Cambridge Economic History of Europe*, III: *Economic Organization and Policies in the Middle Ages* (Cambridge: Cambridge University Press, 1963); pp. 564–70 contain a useful summary of theological attitudes to usury. See also B. N. Nelson, *The Idea of Usury* (Princeton, NJ: Princeton University Press, 1949); and J. T. Noonan, *The Scholastic Aspects of Usury* (Cambridge, Mass: Harvard University Press, 1957).

37. I have treated this subject more fully in Norman Solomon, 'The Codification of Law', *Maghreb Review*, 13 (1988) 109–15.

38. There is an English translation by Aisha Abdarahman al-Tarjumana and Ya'qub Johnson: Imam Malik, *Al-Muwatta* (Norwich: Diwan Press, 1982).

39. See Appendix for bibliographical details and translations.

40. Much research has been published on the topic of Maimonides as codifier. A short bibliography to 1971 appears in David Yellin and Israel Abrahams, *Maimonides: His Life and Works*, rev. Jacob J. Dienstag (New York: Hermon Press, 1972) p. 130 n. 31; and there are several papers on the theme in the *Jewish Law Annual*, I (Leiden: E. J. Brill, 1978).

41. The *Sefer ha-Mitzvot*. The Arabic text was published by Bloch (Paris, 1888). The work is usually studied in one of the numerous editions of the ibn Tibbon's Hebrew version.

42. References are to *The Guide of the Perplexed by Moses Maimonides*, tr. Shlomo Pines with an introduction by Leo Strauss, 2 vols (Chicago: University of Chicago Press, 1963). A revision of S. Munk's edition of the original Arabic text was produced by Dr Judah Jonowitz in Jerusalem, 5691 (1931). Maimonides' division of the commandments into fourteen groups is set out in book III of the *Guide*, commencing with chapter 35, which has a summary.

43. Maimonides, *Guide*, p. 536.

44. Ibid., p. 550 (III.39).

45. Postan and Rich *Cambridge Economic History of Europe*, III, 566 n. 1.

46. Various expressions of this view may be gleaned from the commentaries in Karo's *Shulchan Arukh*: *Yoreh Deah* 159.

47. B *Makkot* 24a. See *Gilyon Hashass* ad loc.

Chapter 5 Religion, Community and State

1. Karl Marx, *The Holy Family*, tr. R. Dixon (London: Lawrence and Wishart, 1975) p. 151.

2. Daniel J. Elazar and Stuart A. Cohen, *The Jewish Polity* (Bloomington: Indiana University Press, 1985).

3. Ibid., p. 10.

4. Ibid., p. 8.

5. They acknowledge their debt to Louis Guttman's paper 'An Additive Metric from All the Principal Components of a Perfect Scale', *British Journal of Psychology*, VIII, pt 1 (1955) 233–78.

6. Elazar and Cohen, *The Jewish Polity*, p. 11.
7. Ibid., p. 260.
8. Elie Kedourie, *Nationalism*, 3rd edn (London: Hutchinson, 1966) p. 9.
9. Ibid., p. 74.
10. The Cardinal Bea Memorial Lecture, given at Westminster Catheral on 20 March 1988 jointly with John Pawlikowski. The papers were published in *The Month*, March 1989.
11. Arthur Hertzberg, *The Zionist Idea* (New York: Athencum, 1969) p. 15. Jacob Katz has a fuller analysis in *Jewish Emancipation and Self-Emancipation* (Philadelphia: Jewish Publication of Society of America, 1986) p. 89ff. Katz acknowledges a debt to B. Halpern, *The Idea of the Jewish State* (Cambridge, Mass.: Harvard University Press, 1961).
12. By Nathan Birnbaum. See Alex Bein, 'Von der Zionsehnsucht', in *Robert Weltsch zum Geburtstag* (Tel Aviv: Irgun Olej Merkas Europa, 1961) p. 33.
13. See Cecil Roth's works *The House of Nasi: Dona Gracia* (Philadelphia: Jewish Publication Society of America, 1947) and *The Duke of Naxos* (Philadelphia: Jewish Publication Society of America, 1948).
14. Alain Finkielkraut, *La Défaite de la Pensée*, tr. Dennis O'Keeffe as *The Undoing of Thought* (London and Lexington: Claridge Press, 1988) p. 15.
15. See his 1772 essay on German architecture.
16. Hence the title of Hess's main work, *Rome and Jerusalem*, in which Rome is not ancient imperial Rome but the Italian republican movement. See Isaiah Berlin, 'The Life and Opinions of Moses Hess', *Against the Current* (New York: 1980); and Edmund Silberner, *Moses Hess. Die Geschichte seines Lebens* (Leiden: E. J. Brill, 1966).
17. In section 6.3.4. I write about a group of rabbis at the very beginning of the nineteenth century whose practical attitude to the resettlement of the land of Israel deserves to be better known.
18. Heinrich Graetz, *Geschichte der Juden von den ältesten Zeiten bis auf die Gegenwart* (Leipzig, 1853–76). There have been several English versions with various degrees of updating, commencing with *History of the Jews* (London: Myers, 1904 and later edns).
19. Heinrich Graetz, *Die Konstruktion der Jüdischen Geschichte* (1846; Berlin, 1936). See Lionel Kochan, *The Jew and his History* (New York: Schocken Books, 1977) ch. 8.
20. See Hermann Cohen, 'Religion und Zionismus', (1916), in *Jüdische Schriften*, ed. F. Rosenzwerg (Berlin, 1924) II, 319.
21. Cohen, 'Deutschtum und Judentum, ibid., II, 237ff.
22. A. Roy Eckardt, *Jews and Christians: The Contemporary Meeting* (Bloomington: Indiana University Press, 1986) p. 9.
23. Avineri, *The Making of Modern Zionism*, p. 63, lists 'six reasons', citing Hertzberg, *The Zionist Idea*, pp. 152–3. Avineri, who is clearly dependent here as elsewhere in his book on Hertzberg, has a text which is even further from the original than Hertzberg's, though he follows Hertzberg in arbitrarily reducing Smolenskin's seven reasons to six. In the interest of accuracy I have retranslated the text of Smolenskin's essay 'Nachpesa Derakhenu' from P. Smolenskin, *Maamarim* (Jerusalem: Qeren Smolenskin, 1925–6) III 119–20.

24. Leo Pinsker, *Autoemancipation*, tr. D. S. Blondheim, ed. A. S. Super (London, 1932) p. 22; cited in Avineri, *The Making of Modern Zionism*, p. 81. Pinsker's work was originally published in German in Berlin in 1882.
25. Avineri, *The Making of Modern Zionism*, p. 89.
26. Max Nordau, letter dated 17 July 1903 to Herzl, in Michael Heymann (ed.), *The Minutes of the Zionist General Council: The Uganda Controversy* (Jerusalem: Zionist General Council, 1977) p. 122. Cf. Avineri, *The Making of Modern Zionism*, p. 110.
27. This comes across most clearly in Herzl's vision of the New Society in his novel *Altneuland*. The first English translation of this was by Jacob de Haas, and appeared in *The Maccabean* (New York, 1902–3).
28. See Daniel B. Sinclair, 'The Fundamentals of Law Bill, 5738–1978', *Jewish Law Annual* III (Leiden: E. J. Brill, 1980) 165–7; Nahum Rakover, 'The Foundations of Law Act, 1980, and its Implementation', 'Jewish Law Annual, V (Leiden: E. J. Brill; and Boston, Mass.: Boston University, 1985) 80–4; Y. Meron, 'Practical Applications of the Foundations of Law Act', *Jewish Law Annual*, VIII (Chur, London, Paris, New York and Melbourne: Harwood Academic Publishers, 1989).
29. Paul Eidelberg, in *Judaism*, Fall 1987, p. 392.
30. Immanuel Jakobovits, *Territory for Peace?* (London: Office of the Chief Rabbi, 1990).
31. *Christians and Jews: Notes for Preaching and Teaching* (Vatican City: Pontifical Commission for Religious Relations with the Jews, June 1985).
32. The classical expression of this debate is the dispute between Maimonides and Nahmanides as to whether the traditional number of 613 *mitzvot* includes one to dwell in the land of Israel.
33. In this context, 'early authorities' means the post-talmudic rabbis preceding Joseph Karo (1488–1575); 'late authorities' means Karo and his successors.
34. Literally, 'do not show them kindness'. By a play on words this was taken to mean 'not to give them dwelling [*haniyya*] in the land'.
35. See Sol Roth, *Halakhah and Politics: The Jewish Idea of a State* (New York: Ktav, 1988). On the 'just war' see J. David Bleich, *Contemporary Halakhic Problems*, vol. 3 (New York: Ktav, 1989) pp. 268–305.

Chapter 6 Messiah

1. I should perhaps remind readers that 'Bible' and 'scripture' are throughout to be understood as referring to the Hebrew scriptures ('Old Testament') only.
2. The work in question, *Kaf ha-Qetoret*, remains unpublished. It is described by Gershom Scholem in *Major Trends in Jewish Mysticism* (Jerusalem: Schocken Books, 1941) p. 244.
3. I am using this expression loosely. It is of course not biblical or talmudic, but classical. See Hesiod's *Works and Days* and Virgil's 4th *Eclogue*.
4. See for example 2 Samuel 7:9 and Ezekiel 37:21 (son of David); Joel 3:14

and Amos 5:18 (the day of the Lord); Isaiah 27:13 (in gathering of the exiles); Zechariah 14:9 (the unity of all peoples); Isaiah 11 (the golden age). In scripture itself, the closest to a unified description is Zechariah 9:9–10.

5. B. *Makkot* 24a. The verses cited are Leviticus 26:38 and Isaiah 27:13.
6. Though both Messiahs occur, it is not certain that any one author believes in both. See D. S. Russell, *The Method and Message of Jewish Apocalyptic* (London: SCM, 1964) pp. 312. 322. The rabbinic idea of a Messiah of the House of David and another of the House of Joseph (see B *Sukkah* 52a), clearly symbolising the reunification of Israel and Judah, is not found in pre-rabbinic sources.
7. M *Sanhedrin* 10:1. For an account of the systematic formulation of Jewish belief in later times see Menachem Kellner, *Dogma in Mediaeval Jewish Thought* (Oxford: Oxford University Press, 1989).
8. B *Sanhedrin* 99a. See Ephraim E. Urbach, *Chazal* (Jerusalem: Hebrew University, 1975) p. 609ff; tr. Israel Abrahams as *The Sages* (Cambridge, Mass., and London: Harvard University Press, 1987).
9. B *Sanhedrin* 98b. See Urbach, *Chazal*, p. 611.
10. Urbach, *Chazal* p. 605ff.
11. Two points seem to me unclear.

 1. Urbach maintains that Eleazar ha-Mudai opposed Akiva's support for Bar Kochba on the grounds that, unlike Akiva, he expected a supernatural messianic event. But how strong is the evidence that Akiva did not expect Bar Kochba's victories to lead to supernatural events?
 2. The evidence that Akiva regarded Bar Kochba as the real Messiah, son of David, and not merely as a 'normal' saviour or deliverer from oppression seems to be very flimsy indeed.

12. Eliezer died in about 117, shortly after the 'diaspora rising' quelled by Trajan. On the date and nature of this uprising see T. D. Barnes, 'Trajan and the Jews', *Journal of Jewish Studies*, XL (1989) 145–62. Books such as 2 Baruch, 4 Ezra and 5 Sybillines would have been newly in circulation.
13. B *Sanhedrin* 97b. J has a different reading.
14. Urbach, *Chazal*, p. 601ff. As against his view we find that Eliezer, in opposition to Akiva, maintains that the Ten Tribes are to return: cf M. *Sanhedrin* 10:3.
15. B *Sanhedrin* 97b.
16. B *Sanhedrin* 97a and *Avodah Zarah* 9a. see Urbach, *Chazal*, p. 609 n. 93.
17. The 'Creation' reckoning in early rabbinic literature does not tally with that in use amongst Jews now. There is a two-year discrepancy between the systems, as shown by E. Frank, *Talmudic and Rabbinic Chronology* (New York: Feldheim, 1956). The correct equivalent for the date in Rabbi Joseph's scroll is not 471 CE, as is sometimes claimed, but 473.
18. D. Sperber argues strongly *In Roman Palestine 200–400: Money and Prices* (Ramat Gan, Israel: Bar Ilan University, 1978) that the third

century was a time of high inflation. Later scholars have cast doubt on this, and as inflation is known to have occurred in several periods it can scarcely be taken as a firm indication of date of composition.

19. B *Sanhedrin* 97a.

20. See Gershom Scholem, *Sabbatai Sevi: The Mystical Messiah* (Princeton, NJ: Princeton University Press; and London: Kegan Paul, 1973).

21. Though in B *Sanhedrin* 97b the statement is attributed to Jonathan, in *Derekh Eretz Rabbah* a similar statement is attributed to José ben Halafta. Urbach (*Chazal*, p. 612 n. 9) prefers the latter attribution; I prefer the former.

22. B *Sanhedrin* 98b, 99a. See M. M. Kasher *Ha-Tequfah ha-Gedolah* (Jerusalem: Torah) Shelemah Institute, 1968) p. 130ff.

23. Rashi, commenting on the words *ein lahem* in B. *Sanhedrin* 99a.

24. *Midrash Tillim* 31:2. See Urbach, *Chazal*, p. 622 n. 52.

25. There is no contemporary account of Hillel's decision to fix the calendar. Isaac Israeli, in the fourteenth century, seems to have thought that the calendar was not fixed until 500, long after the death of Hillel. The earliest known claim that Hillel fixed the calendar in 358 is that of Abraham bar Hiyya, in his *Sefer ha-Ibbur*, composed in the early twelfth century.

26. Hillel's activity spanned the years of the abortive Jewish revolt against Gallus, crushed in 351–2 with the destruction of Sepphoris, Tiberias and Lydda.

27. Epiphanius, *Haereses*, I.ii.4,16.

28. L. Ginsberg, 'Die Haggada bei den Kirchenvaetern', in A. S. Freidus, *Studies in Jewish Bibliography* (New York: A. Kohut Memorial Foundation, 1929) p. 4ff, argues that the pre-existence of 'names' rather than of the Messiah himself was an anti-Christian polemic, intended to convey the idea that whereas the name (= idea) of the Messiah was pre-existent, the Messiah himself was not, but was to be a mortal man like any other. Urbach rightly rejects this suggestion.

29. B *Sukkah* 52a.

30. *Midrash Shohar Tov* on Psalm 107.

31. *Midrash Shohar Tov* on Psalm 21.

32. *Bereshit Rabbah* 98:14. Compare this with the version near the beginning of J *Avodah Zarah* 2.

33. The text of the midrash is uncertain. I have read it as suggested by I. B. Katz in his commentary *Matnot Kehuna*, on the basis of J.

34. J *Avodah Zarah* 2:1. Cf. B *Avodah Zarah* 2b and 3a.

35. B *Eruvin* 43b.

36. T *Sanhedrin* 13:1.

37. *Yalqut Shimoni* Exodus 212 from *Tanna Debe Elijah*.

38. M. D. Gross, *Otsar ha-Aggada*, I.161, cites this from *Pirqe de-Rabbi Eliezer* 34.

39. This translation is from the *Authorised Daily Prayer Book* (London, 1941, and subsequent edns) pp. 327–8. See K. Kohler's comments on the wording of the blessing in *Hebrew Union College Annual*, I (1924) 415–18. We cannot recover the original, probably third-century, text.

40. J *Berakhot* 1:1.

41. Urbach, *Chazal*, p. 609.
42. A collection of such statements is preserved in B *Sanhedrin* 98b. Note that two fourth-century Babylonians – Rav Joseph and Abaye – reject this attitude.
43. B *Sanhedrin* 97b. Both Rav and Yohanan had been disciples of Judah, and members of Hiyya's circle.
44. B *Hagiga* 14a. See Urbach, *Chazal*, p. 605 n. 75. This is the usual interpretation. I suggest that Eleazar ben Azariah's statement *lekh etzel aggadah* is a rebuke not of any lack of expertise on Akiva's part, but of Akiva's eagerness to find proof texts to justify his radical political approach.
45. This is apparently Akiva's view, according to M *Sanhedrin* 10:3. Did Rabbi Akiva believe that the exiles, at least, would return?
46. Moses Maimonides, *Mishneh Torah: Melakhim* 12.
47. Nevertheless, in his *Iggeret Teman* (Epistle to the Jews of Yemen) he defends Saadia's calculation as an attempt to raise the morale of the people at a particular time of difficulty.
48. Moses Maimonides, *Guide of the Perplexed*, III. 54.
49. The fullest treatment in English is B. Netanyahu, *Isaac Abravanel* (Philadelphia: Jewish Publication Society of America, 1953).
50. See Abravanel on Joshua 10 and 1 Samuel 3:7.
51. This is evident in his first mature work, *Ateret Zegenim*.
52. This was at its height during and shortly after Charles VIII's invasion of Italy in 1494 – an invasion which directly affected Abravanel.
53. Netanyahu, *Abravanel*, p. 242ff.
54. He includes passages such as Isaiah 11 which not all Jewish commentators apply to Messiah.
55. See *Ma'ayne Yeshua* (his commentary on Daniel) 8.10. See also Netanyahu, *Abravanel*, p. 216ff.
56. Seneca, *Epistulae Morales*, XC. Cf J. F. Baer's article 'Don Yischag Abravanel', *Tarbitz*, VIII (1937) 248–53. Netanyahu (*Abravanel*, p. 304) suggests the direct influence of Plato, *Laws*, III.679.
57. Augustine, *City of God*, XIX.15. A similar doctrine is found in Kabbala at least as early as the Zohar (late thirteenth century). This raises the interesting question of the extent of Abravanel's knowledge of and susceptibility to kabbalistic teaching; he rarely acknowledges such a debt, but this may be because he regards Kabbala as esoteric.
58. Abravanel, commentaries on Deuteronomy 17 and 1 Samuel 8.
59. Gershom Scholem, *The Messianic Idea in Judaism* (New York: Schoken Books, 1971) p. 43.
60. This concept is found in several early rabbinic passages which speak of God as being in exile with Israel, for instance B *Megilla* 29a, *Mekhilta Beshallach*.
61. A. J. Heschel, *The Prophets* (New York, Evanston and London: Harper and Row, 1969) II, ch. 4 ('Anthropopathy') expresses this 'pathos' powerfully. In his diatribe against Marcion in ch. 6 Heschel does less than justice to Jewish traditions rejecting anthropomorphism and to the acceptance by Jewish philosophers of the doctrine of the impassivity of God.

62. See Scholem, *Major Trends in Jewish Mysticism*, lecture 7.
63. Kasher, *Ha-Tequfah ha-Gedolah*. Kasher's Introduction to *Qol ha-Tor* is on pp. 412–60. In sections commencing on pp. 412 and 455 he discusses the provenance and history of the manuscript and the previous attempts at publication; *Qol ha-Tor* itself appears on pp. 461–539. The sixth and seventh (final) chapters are missing, as is probably the end of the fifth. Moreover, the whole manuscript is referred to as *tamtzit* (a précis).
64. For instance, the dates – though 5500 (1740) appears on p. 465 as the date at which the Gaon, then aged twenty, was first moved to 'reveal the secrets' relating to the 'first Messiah'; and his attempt to journey to the land of Israel is described as taking place at the end of the first 'day' (i.e. 42 years and 8 months) of this messianic dawn. In 93 on p. 471 (the notes are attributed on p. 461 to Rabbi I. Z. Rivlin) we are told that in chapter 5 it is explained that 'the last generation' refers to the period 5600–5750. But there is no such passage in the printed edition – unless he really means chapter 4, the end of which indeed relates to this subject, but does not give precise year numbers (see p. 521). Far from predicting the Holocaust, the Gaon thought that the birth pangs of the Messiah would be 'spread out' bit by bit so as to avoid too much suffering at any one time (see p. 475 and the bottom of p. 521).
65. Kasher, *Ha-Tequfah ha-Gedolah*, p. 516.
66. Ibid., pp. 468, 469, 520.
67. *Hatznea lekhet*: to walk humbly, quietly, modestly (cf. Micah 6:8). See Kasher, *Ha-Tequfah ha-Gedolah*, p. 474. The Gaon meant that the commencement of redemption should not be publicised to all and sundry, and that its advancement should be entrusted to pious and learned initiates. Perhaps he feared the corruption of ideals which might affect a mass movement.
68. Kasher, *Ha-Tequfah ha-Gedolah*, pp. 471–6.
69. Ibid. on pp. 476–7 he insists on the fulfilment of 'in righteousness shalt though be established' (Isaiah 54:14) in the two senses of righteousness (social justice and charity). See below, ch. 3, on commercial ethics.
70. Kasher, *Ha-Tequfah ha-Gedolah*, p. 472. See also B *Sanhedrin* 98a and B *Megilla* 17b.
71. Kasher, *Ha-Tequfah ha-Gedolah*, pp. 535–6.
72. Ibid., p. 472.
73. Ibid., p. 477.
74. Ibid., p. 502.
75. Ibid., p. 520.
76. Ibid., p. 519.
77. Ibid., pp. 503, 519.
78. This is debatable. Whilst the era of Messiah ben Joseph is 'within history', it appears in *Sifra ditzni'uta* – a tract by Elijah of Vilna on hidden things – that the same is not true of Messiah ben David's era.
79. Hermann Cohen, *Die Religion der Vernunft aus den Quellen des Judentums*, first published posthumously in 1919 (3rd edn Darmstadt,

1966). It was translated into English by S. Kaplan as *Religion of Reason out the Sources of Judaism* (New York, 1972).

80. Hermann Cohen, *Jüdische Schriften*, ed. F. Rosenzweig (Berlin, 1924) I, 105ff.
81. Ibid., p. 106.
82. Ibid., p. 124.
83. Slogan on car sticker promoted by the Lubavitch Hasidim.
84. See section 6.1, on the 'nothing changes' philosophy of the 'wisdom' books.
85. B *Sukkah* 52a.
86. The title of Karl Popper's well-known book.
87. Milovan Djilas, *The Unperfect Society*, trs. Dorian Cooke (London: Methuen, 1969; and New York: Harcourt, Brace and World, 1969) p. 2.
88. Karl Marx, *Economic and Philosophical Manuscripts*. This translation is from Karl Marx, *Selected Writings in Sociology and Social Philosophy*, ed. T. B. Bottomore and M. Rubel (Harmondsworth, Middx: Penguin, 1963) p. 250.
89. Karl R. Popper, *The Poverty of Historicism* (London: Routledge and Kegan Paul, 1961) p. 105ff. See also Isaiah Berlin's lecture 'Historical Inevitability', *Auguste Comte Memorial Trust Lectures* (London: Oxford University Press, 1954).
90. Reinhold Niebuhr, Preface to *Faith and History* (London: Nisbet, 1949).
91. Max Horkheimer and Theodor W. Adorno, Preface to *The Dialectic of Enlightenment*, 2nd edn (London: Verso, 1979) p. 9.
92. Alain Finkielkraut, *La Défaite de la Pensée*, tr. Dennis O'Keeffe as *The Undoing of Thought* (London and Lexington: Claridge Press, 1988).
93. Norman Cohn, *In Pursuit of the Millennium*, 3rd edn (London: Granada, 1970).
94. Moses Maimonides, *Mishneh Torah – Teshuvah* 9:2 and *Melakhim* 12. Apparently he holds that the office of Messiah is hereditary.
95. Gonzales, in William Shakespeare, *The Tempest*, I.ii. The scene is a spoof on Arcadian idylls.
96. Plato, *Phaedo* 114c.

Chapter 7   Shoah and Theology of Suffering

1. Other versions of this chapter have appeared as *Jewish Responses to the Holocaust*, Studies in Jewish-Christian Relations no. 4 (Birmingham: Centre for the Study of Judaism and Jewish–Christian Relations, 1987), and 'Does the Shoah Require a Radically New Theology?', *Holocaust and Genocide Studies* (Oxford: Pergamon), VI (1991).
2. Theodor W. Adorno, *Negative Dialektik* (Frankfurt am Main: Suhrkamp, 1966) p. 336.
3. *Shoah* is the biblical Hebrew for 'destruction'; Zephaniah 1:15 speaks of *yom shoah*, the 'day of destruction'. It seems to have been first applied to the Holocaust by Raphael Lemkin, in *Axis Rule in Occupied Europe* (Washington, DC, 1944) pp. 79–95, and is preferred to 'Holocaust' because it does not carry theological overtones.

4. Julie Heifetz, *Oral History and the Holocaust* (Oxford: Pergamon, 1985).
5. The allusion is to Job 42:5, a verse I must hold constantly before me as I write.
6. See for instance, Ilkka Niililuoto, *Truthlikeness* (Dordrecht: D. Reidel, 1987), ch. 6.
7. The word 'genocide' was coined only in the 1940s, with specific reference to the Holocaust. But it is a general term, and cannot be withheld from any other event it fits.
8. Vahakn N. Dadrian, 'Towards a Theory of Genocide Incorporating the Instance of Holocaust', *Holocaust and Genocide Studies*, V (1990) 129–43.

   Others have produced analyses of the relationship of the Holocaust to other persecutions and genocides. Amongst papers read at the 1988 Oxford Conference on Holocaust and Genocide and appearing in *Holocaust and Genocide Studies* are Henry Huttenbach, 'Locating the Holocaust on the Genocide Spectrum' (III, 1988); Steven Katz, 'Quantity and Interpretation – Issues in the Comparative Historical Analysis of the Holocaust' (IV, 1989); and Frank Chalk, 'Revolutionary Genocide' (IV). See also the Bauer article cited in the next note; and Steven Katz, *Post-Holocaust Dialogues* (New York and London: New York University Press, 1985) p. 287, on the '"unique" intentionality of the Holocaust'.
9. Yehuda Bauer, 'Is the Holocaust Explicable?', *Holocaust and Genocide Studies*, V (1990) 145–55.
10. Emil L. Fackenheim, *To Mend the World: Foundations of Future Jewish Thought* (New York: Schocken Books, 1982) p. 12.
11. See ibid., esp. p. 206ff.
12. Ibid., p. 29.
13. See Gill Seidel, *The Holocaust Denial* (Leeds: Beyond the Pale Collective, 1986), for an analysis of the phenomenon of right-wing Holocaust denial.
14. Moses Maimonides, *Mishneh Torah*: *Hilkhot Yesodey ha-Torah*, 5.
15. From B *Sanhedrin* 74 it appears that formal codification originated at the rabbinical council in Lud (Lydda) in the second century. B *Pesachim* 53b refers to Hananiah, Mishael and Azariah in Daniel 3 as prototypes for *qiddush ha-Shem* and of course the examples of Eleazar and of Hannah and her seven sons (2 Maccabees 6 and 7) were well known to the rabbis. 4 Maccabees develops the concept even further.
16. On the other hand, the very negative account given by Elie Wiesel in *Night* must not be generalised; it is, after all, the later reconstruction by a gifted author of his experiences as an impressionable fifteen-year-old. There are several English versions of Wiesel's *Night*, including the translation by Stella Rodway in Elie Wiesel, *Night, Dawn, The Accident* (London: Robson Books, 1974). The original French was published by Les Editions de Minuit in 1958.
17. Robert Kirschner, *Rabbinic Responsa of the Holocaust Era* (New York: Schocken, 1985) p. 11.
18. Ephraim Oshry, *Responsa from the Holocaust*, Y. Leiman (New York: Judaica Press, 1983) p. ix. The Hebrew volumes (vol. V appeared in 1978), under the title *Min ha-Ma'amaqim*, are published by the Brothers Gross, New York.

19. Oshry, *Responsa*, p. 85.
20. Dan Cohn-Sherbok misleadingly asserts, 'All Jews are obliged to accept the divine origin of the Law, but this is not so with regard to theological concepts . . .' – *Holocaust Theology* (London: Lamp Press, 1989) p. 127. Orthodox teachers from the Mishnah onwards have consistently regarded the rejection of belief in life after death as heresy (cf. M *Sanhedrin* 10:1), though they have not all insisted on any particular interpretation of it; today, it is normal amongst the orthodox to invoke the afterlife in reconciling the Shoah. Cohn-Sherbok is unusual amongst contemporary Reform Jews in taking the concept of life after death seriously enough to let it qualify as an 'explanation' for the Shoah, though indeed the Pittsburgh Platform of 1885 clearly commits Reform to the doctrine that 'the soul of man is immortal', and the 1937 Columbus Platform reaffirms that 'his spirit is immortal'. One of the best accounts of Jewish doctrines on life after death (but not of reincarnation) is Louis Jacobs' *Principles of the Jewish Faith* (London: Vallentine, Mitchell, 1964) ch. 14.
21. The Gaon Saadia (882–942) in his *Book of Beliefs and Opinions* 6:8 strongly attacked the doctrine of *gilgul* (transmigration of souls) held, in his time, by 'people who call themselves Jews'. On the other hand, Abraham bar Hiyya (early twelfth century) in *Hegyon ha-Nefesh* (Leipzig, 1860), tr G. Wigoder as *The Meditation of the Sad Soul* (London: Routledge and Kegan Paul, 1969), cites the concept approvingly (Hebrew text, p. 5). Undoubtedly, the spread of kabbalistic ideas through Hasidism contributed to the widespread acceptance of the doctrine among the orthodox.
22. Maimonides' views on Providence are worked out in his *Guide of the Perplexed*, III. 8–24. He has often been misunderstood by scholars attempting to read 'hidden meanings' into his words, and it is good to see the straightforward account of his ideas on Providence and the afterlife in Oliver Leaman's *Moses Maimonides* (London: Routledge, 1990) ch. 8.
23. Wasserman was a disciple of Israel Meir Hacohen (1838–1933), the 'Chafetz Chayim'. The best biography of Wasserman is A. Sorsky, *Or Elchanan*, 2 vols (1978).
24. Notwithstanding the Aramaic title, *Iqvata di-Meshicha* was originally written in Yiddish. It has been reissued many times in Hebrew and other languages. An earlier, Hebrew sketch was appended to the second (Baranovichi, ?1936) edition of the first volume of Wasserman's halakhic work *Qovetz he-Arot*, originally published in Pietrkow in 1922. The development of this small but significant work (i.e. Iqvata) is explained in Sorsky, *Or Elchanan*, ch. 23. It has been translated by David Cooper as *The Epoch of the Messiah* (London: Hachinuch, 1964).
25. Gershon Greenberg, 'Orthodox Theological Responses to the Holocaust', *Holocaust and Genocide Studies*, III (1988) 439.
26. See for instance Benjamin Maza, *With God's Fury Poured Out* (New York: Ktav, 1984); and David Krantzler, *Thy Brother's Blood* (New York: Artscroll, 1987).
27. Kirschner, *Rabbinic Responsa*, pp. 98–9, from M. Eliav, *Ani Maamin* (Jerusalem, 1965) pp. 30–1.

28. The declaration of faith as formulated by Maimonides.
29. Deuteronomy 6:4–9, declaring God's unity and the duty to love him and obey his commandments. It is read daily at the morning and evening services and forms part of the death-bed confession.
30. M *Sotah* 9:15. It would be out of place here to refer to the several other versions, to the parallels in Christian (e.g. Mark 13:12) and other literature, or to the textual obscurities and problems of translation.
31. See Ben Zion Bokser, *Abraham Isaac Kook* (New York: Paulist Press, 1978), for an English translation of some of Kook's smaller works. See also the discussion of 'commencement of redemption' in section 6.3.4 above.
32. S. Zuker and G. Hirschler, *The Unconquerable Spirit* (New York: Mesorah, 1980) p. 27ff.
33. He is not boasting, but expressing gratification at the divine compliment of having been selected for a sacred task.
34. The place where the Jews of Slobodka (Kovno) were murdered.
35. This phrase occurs in the liturgy for 9Ab and is reminiscent of Lamentations 4:11.
36. See note 24 on editions of the pamphlet. I have translated the Yiddish version, which appears in the introduction to the 1952 New York edn of the first volume of Wasserman's major halakhic work, *Kovetz he-Arot*. Greenberg ('Orthodox Theological Responses to the Holocaust', *Holocaust and Genocide Studies*, III) chose to translate the same passage, but refers to the version in Oshry's *Churbn Litta* (New York, 1951) pp. 48–50.
37. B *Sukkah* 45b. Note that the carefully chosen term attributed to Simon is *liftor* (exempt) not *ligol* (redeem).
38. As the literature on this is vast, suffice it to mention Shalom Spiegel's *The Last Trial* (New York: Behrman House, 1979), and Ephraim of Bonn's poem *Et Avotay Ani Mazkir*, conveniently available with translation in the *Penguin Book of Hebrew Verse* (Harmondsworth Middx: Penguin, 1981) p. 379. Chapter 7 of Jacob Katz's *Exclusiveness and Tolerance* (1959; Oxford: Oxford University Press, 1981) is also a useful starting point. Glenda Abramson's article 'The Reinterpretation of the Akedah in Modern Hebrew Poetry', *Journal of Jewish Studies*, XLI (1990), gives an interesting sidelight on the working-out of the theme in modern secular terms.
39. Ignaz Maybaum, *The Face of God after Auschwitz* (Amsterdam: Polak and van Gennep, 1965) p. 35.
40. Psalm 44 is more explicit, more agonised, on the subject of hiddenness.
41. Martin Buber, 'Dialogue between Heaven and Earth', in *At the Turning: Three Addresses on Judaism* (New York: Farrar, Straus and Young, 1952) pp. 47–62.
42. E. Berkovitz, *Faith after the Holocaust* (New York: Ktav, 1973).
43. *Guide of the Perplexed*, III.10–12. The idea of evil as the *privatio boni* is generally traced back to Pseudo-Dionysius, and is represented in Christian tradition from Augustine onwards.
44. Hannah Arendt, *Eichmann in Jerusalem: A Report on the Banality of Evil*

(New York: Viking, 1963). See Berel Lang's article 'Hannah Arendt and the Politics of Evil', *Judaism*, XXXVII (Summer 1988).

45. Barry Clarke, 'Beyond the Banality of Evil', *British Journal of Political Science*, X (1980) 417–39.

46. W. V. O. Quine, 'Two Dogmas of Empiricism', *From a Logical Point of View*, 3rd edn (Cambridge, Mass.: Harvard University Press, 1980) p. 42.

47. Fackenheim, *To Mend the World*, p. 19.

48. Ibid., p. 191. See also p. 278. Kierkegaard's remark appears in *Either/Or* tr. Walter Lowrie (New York: Anchor Press, 1959) p. 344.

49. Lionel Kochan, 'Towards a Rabbinic Theory of Idolatry', *Jewish Law Annual*, VIII (Leiden: E. J. Brill, 1990) 112.

50. Gershom Scholem, *The Messianic Idea in Judaism* (New York: Schocken Books, 1971) pp. 35–6.

51. Irving Greenberg, 'Cloud of Smoke, Pillar of Fire', in E. Fleischner (ed.), *Auschwitz: Beginning of a New Era?* (New York: Ktav, 1977).

52. Richard L. Rubenstein, *After Auschwitz: Radical Theology and Contemporary Judaism* (Indianapolis: Bobbs-Merrill, 1966).

53. Harold S. Kushner, *When Bad Things Happen to Good People* (London: Pan, 1981).

54. Walter J. Hollenweger has written 'A narrative exegesis does not divorce the theological element from its cultural and social base, but has to argue its theology in its involvement, in its function, in these other fields of conflict' – *Conflict in Corinth* (New York: Paulist Press, 1982) p. 66.

55. I have in mind Elie Wiesel's story *The Gates of the Forest* (New York: Avon, 1967) pp. 9–12. The same thought is explored in a work by a Christian, Franklin H. Littell's *The Crucifixion of the Jews* (New York: Harper and Row, 1975). See also Ziva Amishai-Maisels' paper 'Christological Symbolism of the Holocaust', *Holocaust and Genocide Studies*, III (1988) 457ff.

56. Marcia Sachs Littell (ed.), *Liturgies on the Holocaust: An Interfaith Anthology* (New York: Edwin Mellen Press, 1986).

57. Fackenheim, *To Mend the World*, p. 310ff. challenges this view. But Chief Rabbi Jakobovits, in his booklet *Religious Responses to the Holocaust* (London: Office of the Chief Rabbi, 1987) argues strongly against the introduction of new fast days.

58. Viktor E. Frankl, *Man's Search for Meaning* (New York: Simon and Schuster, 1959). The work was first published in Austria under the title *Ein Psycholog erlebt das Konzentrations lager*.

59. In Shaul Esh, 'The Dignity of the Destroyed', in Y. Gutman and L. Rotkirchen, *The Catastrophe of European Jewry* (Jerusalem: Yad Vashem, 1976) p. 355.

60. Likewise, in the Warsaw ghetto, an orchestra gave concerts under the baton of Szymon Pullmann (Simon Pulver).

61. Josef Bor, *The Terezin Requiem* (New York: Alfred A. Knopf, 1963).

62. Joza Karas, *Music in Terezin: 1941–1945* (New York: Beaufort Books, 1985) p. 197. Much of the information in this paragraph comes from Karas's book.

63. Fackenheim *To Mend the World*, pp. 201–77.
64. *Tikkun* (*tiqqun*) means mending or restoration and is an important term for Fackenheim, whose use of it owes something to the Lurianic Kabbala. I expect he wishes to avoid anything that sounds like 'salvation'.
65. Fackenheim, *To Mend the World*, p. 266.
66. *Judaism*, XVI (Summer 1967). On the 613 commandments see p. 227 and p. 277.
67. Fackenheim's book *Tikkun* has just been announced (1990).
68. B. *Shabbat* 88a.
69. His statement is cited without a specific reference in a letter dated 6 November 1987 from Dr Pierre Duprey to Dr Eugene Fisher and Bishop Keeler in the aftermath of the 'Ratzinger affair' (see below, section 7.2.8B).
70. Dow Marmur, *Beyond Survival* (London: Darton, Longman and Todd, 1982).
71. Robert Gordis, *Judaic Ethics for a Lawless World* (New York: Jewish Theological Seminary of America, 1986).
72. Irving Greenberg, 'On the Third Era in Jewish History: Power and Politics', *Perspectives* (New York), 1980. See also his 1981 article in the same journal.
73. Dan Cohn-Sherbok's article 'Jews, Christians and Liberation Theology' appeared in *Christian Jewish Relations*, XVII (Mar 1984). His book *On Earh as it is in Heaven* (Maryknoll, NY: Orbis, 1987) appeared shortly before Ellis's work cited in the next note.
74. Marc H. Ellis, *Toward a Jewish Liberation Theology* (Maryknoll, NY: Orbis, 1987). See his contribution and the discussion in the dedicated issue of *Christian Jewish Relations* on the Jewish–Christian dialogue and liberation theology (XXI, Spring 1988).
75. For a detailed appreciation see Pinchas Lapide's *Three Popes and the Jews* (New York: Hawthorn Books, 1967) ch. 5.
76. Ibid., p. 113. Evidently, however, the Pope's words became known; they are cited by J. H. Hertz, then Chief Rabbi of the British Empire, in the *Book of Jewish Thoughts* issued from 1940 onwards to Jewish members of His Majesty's forces.
77. Polish partisans did not always welcome Jewish co-operation. How different might things have been had Christians and Jews in Poland worked together against Nazi oppression.
78. Sorsky, *Or Elchanan*, II, 277.
79. Adolf Hitler, *Mein Kampf*, end of ch. 2.
80. English Christians, I am ashamed to say. Although Josephus, in *Contra Apionem*, rebuts a similar accusation, the first recorded use of this base fabrication by Christians was at Norwich in 1144.
81. See Jean Halpérin and Arne Sovik (eds), *Luther, Lutheranism and the Jews* (Geneva: Lutheran World Federation, 1984). This is a report of the second consultation between representatives of the International Jewish Committee for Interreligious Consultations and the Lutheran World Federation; the consultation took place in 1983, the 500th anniversary of Luther's birth. The Lutheran participants made the

courageous statement, 'We Lutherans take our name and much of our understanding of Christianity from Martin Luther. But we cannot accept or condone the violent verbal attacks that the Reformer made against the Jews . . . we believe that a christological reading of the Scriptures does not lead to anti-Judaism, let alone antisemitism' (ibid., p. 9).

82. Robert Michael, 'Theological Myth, German Antisemitism and the Holocaust: The Case of Martin Niemoeller', *Holocaust and Genocide Studies*, II (1987) 105.

83. Christian works calling for a radical revision of Christology on this basis include R. R. Ruether, *Faith and Fratricide: The Theological Roots of Anti-Semitism* (New York: Seabury Press, 1974). This was subjected to searching criticism in Alan T. Davies (ed.), *Antisemitism and the Foundations of Christianity* (New York: Paulist Press, 1979).

84. Fackenheim, *To Mend the World*, p. 279.

85. Ibid., p. 282.

86. A. Roy Eckardt, *Jews and Christians: The Contemporary Meeting* (Bloomington: Indiana University Press, 1986) p. 16.

87. Ibid., ch. 8: 'Along the Road of Good Intentions'. The models are those of (1) Joseph E. Monti, (2) Ronald Goetz, (3) Paul van Buren, (4) J.-B. Metz and John Pawlikowski, and (5) Eckardt himself! In ch. 8 he offers tentatively 'another road'. Notwithstanding Eckardt's strictures, the works of Monti and the others offer a foundation for the reconstruction of Christian thought after the Holocaust.

88. Interview in *Il Sabato*, 24 October 1987. Ratzinger subsequently said that the Italian text was misleading, and clarified his meaning in a letter to Cardinal Willebrands, who forwarded it to Christian and Jewish leaders in the United States who had requested the clarification.

89. Greenberg, in Fleischner, *Auschwitz: Beginning of a New Era?*, p. 22.

90. John Milton, *Paradise Lost*, 1.6–7. Leibniz's *Theodicy* addresses an age-old problem.

91. Fackenheim, *To Mend the World*.

92. Arthur A. Cohen, *The Tremendum: A Theological Interpretation of the Holocaust* (New York: Crossroad, 1981).

93. M *Avot* (Ethics of the Fathers) 4:19.

Chapter 8   Language and Dialogue

1. The first version of this chapter appeared as 'The Language of Dialogue in World Religions' in *World Faiths Insight* (London), 1987.

2. In C. K. Ogden and I. A. Richards, *The Meaning of Meaning*, 7th edn (London: Kegan Paul, Trench, Trubner, 1945) supplement I.

3. William Downes, *Language and Society* (London: Fontana, 1984) p. 337; see the whole of ch. 11. The philosophical concept of 'speech acts' was elaborated by John R. Searle in his seminal paper 'What is a Speech Act?' in Max Black (ed.), *Philosophy in America* (Ithaca, NY: Cornell

University Press, 1965) pp. 221–39. Searle's main concern, however, is with the intentionality of verbal speech acts.

4. D. Hymes, in J. Gumpertz and D. Hymes, *Directions in Sociolinguistics* (New York: Holt, Rinehart and Winston, 1972); cited in Downes *Language and Society*, p. 257.

5. G. E. M. Anscombe, *Intention* (Oxford: Basil Blackwell, 1957).

6. See J. L. Austin, *How to Do Things with Words*, William James Lectures (Oxford: Clarendon Press, 1955).

7. W. V. O. Quine, *From a Logical Point of View* (Cambridge, Mass.: Harvard University Press, 1953) p. 43. Of course, before Quine was born Ferdinand de Saussure had already made clear that language units can only be defined in relation to other units within the system; but neither he nor his structuralist followers made the correct philosophical inferences.

8. Hubert L. Dreyfus, *What Computers Can't Do* (New York: Harper and Row, 1972).

9. John R. Searle, *Minds, Brains and Science*, Reith Lectures (Cambridge, Mass.: Harvard University Press, 1984); Paul M. Churchland, *A Neurocomputational Perspective: The Nature of Mind and the Structure of Science* (Cambridge, Mass.: MIT Press, 1990).

10. L. Klenicki and G. Wigoder (eds), *A Dictionary of the Jewish–Christian Dialogue* (Ramsay, NJ: Stimulus Foundation, Paulist Press, 1984).

11. Compare Paul F. Knitter, *No Other Name?* (London: SCM Press, 1985) p. 101.

12. Moses Maimonides, *The Guide of the Perplexed*, Shlomo Pines, 2 vols (Chicago: University of Chicago Press, 1963).

13. Ibid., p. 145, (I.60).

14. Knitter, *No Other Name?*, p. 98.

15. Ibid., p. 102.

16. Ibid., p. 39.

17. Ibid., p. 45.

18. António Barbosa da Silva, *Can Religions Be Compared?* (Uppsala: Theological Faculty, Uppsala University, 1986) p. 28ff. See also the same author's 'The Phenomenology of Religion as a Philosophical Problem', a doctoral thesis of the University of Uppsala, 1982. Da Silva considers the 'semantic argument' against phenomenology. This has two forms: (1) the *unrestricted* – this alleges that the whole content of the mystic's concepts, beliefs, cult and background experience determine his experience; (2) the *restricted* – the experience is only partly so determined.

19. K. M. Colby, *Artificial Paranoia* (New York: Pergamon Press, 1975).

20. Jerry A. Fodor, *The Modularity of Mind* (Cambridge, Mass.: MIT Press, 1983). On input and language systems see esp. p. 47ff. On central systems see p. 101ff.

21. Quine, *From a Logical Point of View*, p. 42.

22. S. Stich, 'Beliefs and Subdoxastic States', *Philosophy of Science*, XLV (1973) 499–518. See Fodor, *The Modularity of Mind*, p. 84.

Chapter 9   The Plurality of Faiths

1. The first version of this chapter, under the title 'Judaism and World Religions', was the 1985 Sir Francis Younghusband Memorial Lecture for the World Congress of Faiths, published in *World Faiths Insight* (London), 1985, and reprinted as Studies in Jewish–Christian Relations, no. 3 (Birmingham: Centre for the Study of Judaism and Jewish–Christian Relations, Selly Oak Colleges, 1985).
2. See John Hick, *God and the Universe of Faiths* (London: Collins, 1977), *God Has Many Names* (London: Macmillan, 1980; Philadelphia: Westminster Press, 1982), and *An Interpretation of Religion* (London: Macmillan, 1989). There has been much discussion of Hick's pluralist views; see for instance Gavin D'Costa, *Theology and Religious Pluralism* (Oxford: Basil Blackwell, 1986).
3. Keith Ward, 'Truth and the Diversity of Religions', *Religious Studies*, XXVI (1990) 1–18.
4. Not NEB, which is wild at this point, translating *hesed* as 'loyalty' and *hatznea* as 'wisely'.
5. There is a voluminous literature. One of the classics in the field is Gershom Scholem, *Jewish Gnosticism, Merkabah Myticism and Talmudic Tradition*, 2nd edn (Philadelphia: Jewish Publication Society of America, 1965).
6. Ibid., p. 19.
7. Yehezkel Kaufmann, *Toldot ha-Emunah ha-Israelit*, 4 vols (Tel Aviv: 1948–). The work was translated into English and abridged by M. Greenberg under the title *The Religion of Israel* (Chicago: University of Chicago Press, 1960).
8. Philo of Alexandria, *De Specialibus Legibus*, I.53 (Loeb edn, VII. 128). Both he and Josephus have in mind Exodus 22:27(28) and Leviticus 24:15.
9. In *Antiquities*, IV.viii.10 (Loeb edn, IV, 207), Josephus informs the reader that Moses instructed the people 'Let no one blaspheme those gods which other cities esteem such; nor may one steal what belongs to strange temples; nor take away the gifts that are dedicated to any god.' The apologetic intent is clear. See also *Against Apion*, II.144.
10. J. H. Hertz, *The Pentateuch and Haftorahs*, 2nd edn (London: Soncino Press, 1960) p. 759, commenting on Deuteronomy 4:19, suggests that the words 'which he apportioned to them' indicate a biblical recognition that it is acceptable for the nations to worship their own gods. This is disingenuous.
11. See for instance B *Hullin* 13b and J *Berakhot* 9:2. Of course, this does not imply that the rabbis did not expect that eventually idolatry would be uprooted from the whole world; cf T *Berakhot* 6:2.
12. B *Makkot* 23b. See also Mekhilta Bachodesh 5 and Sifré Deuteronomy 76.
13. The best-known attempts at enumeration are those of Simeon Kayyara and Maimonides. Significantly, Nahmanides, in his notes on Maimonides' *Sefer ha-Mitzvot*, expresses reservations as to how seriously the number 613 should be taken.

14. T *Avodah Zarah* 9:4. Some scholars have claimed to discover a hint of the *sheva mitzvot* in Acts 15:29; this is far-fetched and anachronistic.
15. David Novak, *The Image of the Non-Jew in Judaism*, Toronto Studies in Theology, no. 14 (New York and Toronto: Edward Mellen Press, 1983) ch. 1. Novak has returned to the theme in his *Jewish–Christian Dialogue* (Oxford: Oxford University Press, 1989), the first chapter of which contains an excellent summary.
16. See the references in Novak, *The Image of the Non-Jew*, pp. 7 and 38. Biberfeld published his articles in the 1920s and strongly reflects the views of Rabbi Samson Raphael Hirsch (*d.* 1888). The substance of the articles appeared in book form in Germany in 1937 under the title *Das Noachidische Urrecht*, and Biberfeld took up the theme again after the war.
17. Chaim Tchernowitz, *Toldot ha-Halakhah* (New York, 1934; 2nd edn, New York: Jubilee Committee, 1945) I, 62ff. and 335ff.
18. Louis Finkelstein, *Pharisaism in the Making* (New York: Ktav, 1972) p. 226.
19. B *Avodah Zarah* 64b. See S. Lieberman, *Greek in Jewish Palestine* (New York: Jewish Theological Seminary, 1942) pp. 81–2.
20. Michael Guttman, *Das Judenthum und seiner Umwelt* (Berlin: Philo Verlag, 1927).
21. Novak cites Jacob Agus's *The Evolution of Jewish Thought* (New York and London: Abelard Schuman, 1959) and *Jewish Identity in an Age of Ideologies* (New York: Frederick Unger, 1978). Agus's most searching examination of the relationships between Judaism an other faiths is perhaps his *Dialogue and Tradition* (London, New York and Toronto: Abelard-Schuman, 1971) – though he offers no comment on the relations between Judaism and Hindu and Buddhist religion.
22. Greek and Hebrew terms for 'those who fear the Lord' (Psalm 115:11).
23. See for instance Novak's interesting discussion (*The Image of the Non-Jew*, p. 231ff) of Samuel Atlas's suggestion that the distinction between the Noahide law of robbery and the Jewish law of robbery was the rabbi's way of making a conceptual distinction between natural and covenantal law. Nahum Rakover, 'The "Law" and the Noahides', *Jewish Law Association Studies*, IV (Atlanta: Scholars Press, 1990) 169–80, explores the differences between Noahide and Jewish law, and finds it helpful to understand Noahide law as 'a sort of natural human law' (p. 172).
24. Finkelstein, *Pharisaism in the Making*, p. 34.
25. B *Megilla* 13a.
26. Novak, *Image of the Non-Jew*, p. 108, referring to B *Sanhedrin* 56b.
27. Moses Maimonides, *Mishneh Torah: Hilkhot Melakhim* 8:11. For a full discussion see Novak, *Image of the Non-Jew*, ch. 10.
28. Moses Mendelssohn, *Gesammelte Schriften* (Berlin: Akademie Verlag, 1929; facsimile repr. Stuttgart: Frommann Verlag, 1971–) XVI, 178–80. I have used Novak's translation in *Image of the Non-Jew*, p. 370, to which reference should be made.
29. E. Benamozegh, *Morale Juive et Morale Chrétienne* (Paris, 1867). Benamozegh's *magnum opus* first appeared in Paris in 1914 under the title

Israel et l'Humanité, and a new and revised edition has been published by Albin Michel (Paris, 1961). Marco Morselli's Italian translation *Israele e l'Umanità* was published by Casa Editrice Marietti, Genva, in 1990. Pallière's main work is *Le Sanctuaire Inconnu* (Paris, 1927); the most recent English version is *The Unknown Sanctuary*, tr. L. W. Wise (New York, 1985).

30. This information is taken from Aaron Lichtenstein's 'Who cares about the Seven Laws of Noah? A Status Report', *Jewish Law Association Studies*, IV (Atlanta: Scholars Press, 1990) 181–90. See also Lichtenstein's book *The Seven Laws of Noah*, 2nd edn (New York: Rabbi Jacob Joseph School Press, 1986).

31. It would be useful to have a bibliography of Lubavitch writings on the Noahide laws. There are numerous pamphlets and addresses, and even a 'moral video' directed to non-Jews. An 'Abbreviated Code of Jewish Law for Non-Jews' is also said to be in preparation. In fact, compilations of this sort already exist – for instance, Joel Schwartz's *Or Leamim* (Jerusalem: Devar Yerushalayim, 1984).

32. T *Sanhedrin* 13.

33. Augustine, *De Bapt.*, IV.C.xcii.24. Cf. Cyprian's earlier *habere non potest Deum patrem qui ecclesiam non habet matrem* ('no one can have God as father who does not have the Church as mother'), in *De Cath. Eccl. Unitate*, VI.

34. Diogenes Laertius, I.33. See Martin Hengel, *Jews, Greeks and Barbarians* (London: SCM, 1980) p. 78 and ch. 7, for an exploration of the idea of racial superiority in the Hellenistic world.

35. The version I have translated is that in *Yalkut Shimoni* on Judges 5. See also T *Berakhot* 7:18; J *Berakhot* 9:2; B *Menahot* 43b.

36. See P. Joyce, *Divine Initiative and Human Response in Ezekiel*, Journal for the Study of the Old Testament, Supplement 51 (Sheffield: JSOT Press, 1989).

37. The topic is large and well researched. A good starting place is Alexander Guttman's discussion of the 'eighteen measures' in his *Rabbinic Judaism in the Making* (Detroit: Wayne State University Press, 1970) pp. 102–16.

38. See William Schoedel 'Theological Norms and Social Perspectives in Ignatius of Antioch', in E. P. Sanders (ed.), *Jewish and Christian Self-Definition* (London: SCM, 1980) I, 31f, where Schoedel refers to *inter alia* the Christian observance of Sunday rather than Saturday as part of the Church's deliberate policy of 'separation' from Jews and Judaism.

39. See Ernst Simon, 'The Neighbour We Shall Love', in M. Fox (ed.), *Modern Jewish Ethics* (Columbus: Ohio State University Press, 1975) pp. 29–56, for an attempt to define the application of the 'golden rule' within Judaism. Simon has not clearly grasped the fact that the rabbis used general ethical principles rather than specific scriptural 'rules' to regulate behaviour towards those 'outside the covenant'.

  Tiqqun olam is, strictly speaking, an 'extra-legal' measure introduced within the community to prevent impossible situations from arising; cf. B *Gittin* 34b, 36a. The *locus classicus* for *darkhei shalom* is M *Gittin* 5:8–9. *Qiddush ha-Shem* often bears the meaning of 'martyrdom': for its use in setting standards of moral behaviour in dealings with non-Jews see B *Yevamot* 79a, *Bava Qama* 113a.

40. Josephus, *Antiquities*, XX.2. See also book XIII on John Hyrcanus's forcible conversion of the Idumaeans, and the amusing story in XVIII.3 of Fulva and the fraudulent missionaries – though Suetonius puts the latter in a different light. See also Matthew 23:15.

41. S. J. Bamberger, *Proselytism in the Talmudic Period* (1939), 2nd edn (New York: Ktav, 1968); W. G. Braude, *Jewish Proselytising in the First Five Centuries of the Common Era*, Brown University Studies no. 6 (Providence, RI, 1940).

42. See Norman Solomon, 'The Political Implications of a Belief in Revelation', *Heythrop Journal*, XXV (1984) 134ff.

43. M *Yadayim* 4:4. See also B *Keritot* 9a and *Rosh hashanah* 31b.

44. Martin Goodman, 'Proselytising in Rabbinic Judaism', *Journal of Jewish Studies*, XL (1989) 175–85. See also his article 'Jewish Proselytizing in the First Century AD', in T. Rajak, J. North and J. Lieu (eds), *The Jews in the Religious Life of the Roman World* (London: Methuen, forthcoming).

45. See David Kessler, *The Falashas*, 2nd edn (New York: Schocken Books, 1985); and Tudor Parfitt, *Operation Moses* (London: Weidenfeld and Nicolson, 1985). Others, notably Edward Ullendorff, deny that the Falashas were 'original' Jews; Ullendorff's view is most elegantly expressed in his *The Two Zions: Reminiscences of Jerusalem and Ethiopia* (Oxford and New York: Oxford University Press, 1988).

46. B *Yevamot* 47a.

47. The texts are from Jacob R. Marcus, *The Jew in the Mediaeval World* (Philadelphia: Jewish Publication Society of America, 1961). See also the list at the end of James Parkes, *The Conflict of Church and Synagogue* (New York: Atheneum, 1969).

48. Marcus, *The Jew in the Mediaeval World*, ch. 3.

49. See Bat Ye'or, *The Dhimmi: Jews and Christians under Islam* (London and Toronto: Associated University Presses, 1985), for a passionate but well-documented account of the *dhimmi* peoples and the realities of their life under Muslim rule. The book first appeared in French as *Le Dhimmi: Profile de l'Opprimé en Orient et en Afrique du Nord depuis le Conquête Arabe* (Paris: Editions Anthropos, 1980).

50. See H. Maccoby, *Judaism on Trial: Jewish Christian Disputations in the Middle Ages* (London and Toronto: Associated University Presses, 1982).

51. Saadia ben Joseph, *Kitab fi al-Amanat wa-al-Itaqadat*, II.5. Samuel Rosenblatt's translation has been republished as *The Book of Beliefs and Opinions* (New Haven, Conn., and London: Yale University Press, 1989).

52. Judah Halevi, *The Kuzari*, tr. H. Hirschfeld, 2nd edn (New York: Schocken Books, 1964) V.23.

53. Jacob Katz, *Exclusiveness and Tolerance* (London: Oxford University Press, 1961).

54. Ibid., ch. 10.

55. See Alexander Altmann, *Moses Mendelssohn* (London: Routledge and Kegan Paul, 1973) ch. 3. Altmann thinks (p. 203) that Lavater was 'put up to the job' by Spalding.
56. Translated from *Schreiben an den Herrn Diaconus Lavater zu Zurich.*
57. See for instance his remarks on a pamphlet by J. Koelbele.
58. Katz, *Exclusiveness and Tolerance*, p. 179, with reference to Mendelssohn's predictions in *Jerusalem*.
59. David Hartman, 'On the Possibilities of Religious Pluralism from a Jewish Point of View', *Immanuel* (Jerusalem, 1983). Hartman again argues the Jewish theological case for religious pluralism in *Conflicting Visions* (New York: Schocken Books, 1990) pp. 246–53.
60. Joseph P. Schultz, *Judaism and the Gentiles* (London and Toronto: Associated University Presses, 1981), esp. chs 2 and 3.
61. Ibid., p. 80.
62. Ibid., p. 91.
63. Ibid., p. 108.
64. Ibid., p. 123.

Index

This Index should be used in conjunction with the detailed table of contents on pp. v–xv and with the Appendix on pp. 245–52. Duplication is avoided other than where it is needed to save confusion.

References to citations are to the page on which the source is specified, whether this is in the body of the text (most biblical quotations) or in the notes (most other quotations).

Abbreviations: numbers followed by 'c' indicate centuries, for instance '3c' means third century; all centuries are CE (AD). With reference mainly to the rabbinic sages, 'P' means 'Palestinian' and 'B' 'Babylonian'.